TURNAROUND

TURNAROUND

Leading Stressed Colleges and
Universities to Excellence

James Martin, James E. Samels & Associates

The Johns Hopkins University Press
Baltimore

The Johns Hopkins University Press
2715 North Charles Street
Baltimore, Maryland 21218-4363
www.press.jhu.edu

Library of Congress Cataloging-in-Publication Data

Turnaround : leading stressed colleges and universities to excellence /
James Martin, James E. Samels & Associates.
    p. cm.
    Includes bibliographical references and index.
    ISBN-13: 978-0-8018-9068-0 (hardcover : alk. paper)
    ISBN-10: 0-8018-9068-3 (hardcover : alk. paper)
    1. Universities and colleges—United States.   2. Educational change—United
States.   I. Martin, James, 1948 Jan. 14–   II. Samels, James E.
LA227.4.T86 2008
378.1'070973—dc22   2008013943

A catalog record for this book is available from the British Library.

*Special discounts are available for bulk purchases of this book. For more
information, please contact Special Sales at 410-516-6936 or specialsales@
press.jhu.edu.*

The Johns Hopkins University Press uses environmentally friendly book
materials, including recycled text paper that is composed of at least 30 percent
post-consumer waste, whenever possible. All of our book papers are acid-free,
and our jackets and covers are printed on paper with recycled content.

Contents

Preface

Turnaround: Leading Stressed Colleges and Universities to Excellence is a comprehensive handbook for higher education practitioners with diverse needs and points of view. Focusing principally on the needs of presidents, trustees, provosts, senior faculty leaders, and chief financial, advancement, and student affairs officers, the following chapters define fragility in higher education; identify key types of institutions that are vulnerable and why; and offer multiple routes for mitigating risks in the future. In the process, the authors, with sixteen contributors, present twenty characteristics of stressed status and provide a broad set of successful strategies that have worked in leading these colleges and universities back to stability.

Although the authors are not aware of any published estimates, it is their view after serving for twenty years as higher education consultants that perhaps one thousand of the nation's more than four thousand colleges and universities can be described as stressed. Realizing that fragility and decline can take many forms, the chapters demonstrate that there are multiple methods and approaches to lead these institutions effectively and that no single leadership approach should be adopted on all campuses. Different levels and kinds of risk require different responses, and an examination of these varied approaches forms the core of the book's sixteen chapters. Nevertheless, after analyzing the risk factors on several hundred campuses over the past two decades and after assessing the abilities and the *wills* of those institutions to succeed, the authors have identified five core strategies necessary to accomplish a turnaround. These strategies are highlighted in the conclusion along with ten leadership lessons offered by presidents and other decision makers who have facilitated a turnaround process.

Contributors include current and former college and university presidents who have managed institutions back from the brink of closure, as well as current or former national education and accreditation association presidents and officers, and scholars who have published widely on trustee effectiveness, presidential leadership, new forms of student engagement, and fund-raising and public relations in fragile circumstances. They offer the following insights, among others:

—Twenty characteristics of a stressed college or university.

—A set of best practices for chief student affairs officers to develop effective forms of student leadership at stressed institutions.

—The key legal strategies and resources for protecting the leaders of at-risk universities and colleges during periods of extended vulnerability.

—Candid advice from a regional accreditation association president regarding how to disclose and discuss fragile status in a pending institutional self-study.

—Best practices in designing a capital campaign for an institution perceived by alumni and the general public as vulnerable.

The book is divided into five sections: defining institutional fragility, analyzing long-term risk via the leadership team, addressing the financial factors in a turnaround, identifying best practices and strategies that work for the key areas of institutional operations, and synthesizing the core strategies in a successful turnaround. The parts of the book are punctuated by quotations from presidents and other institutional leaders who achieved, or failed to achieve, a campus turnaround.

Part I, "Defining Risk: The Nature of Stressed Institutions," begins with a chapter by James Martin and James E. Samels that identifies twenty characteristics shared by stressed universities and colleges and places those institutions in the broader context of current trends in higher education leadership and management. Martin and Samels focus on methods for board chairs, presidents, and provosts to assess the degree to which their institution is at risk and then, through a coordinated set of steps, to address this status. Because Martin and Samels are aware that the leaders of vulnerable institutions, in particular, often lack the time for outside reading, the chapter's leadership lessons seek to integrate and synthesize best practices and successful turnaround models.

In chapter 2, D. Bruce Johnstone, director of the Center for Comparative and Global Studies in Education at the University of Buffalo, offers two framing perspectives that explain how many colleges and universities have slid into their current condition and why a good number may not survive their decline in their present identities: causes of vulnerability in entire systems of higher education and an international perspective on what constitutes fragility among institutions in other parts of the world. Johnstone, author of more than one hundred books and articles on higher education leadership and management, is candid on why even major systems worldwide are struggling and how these struggles directly influence the stability of individual colleges and universities in a precarious marketplace.

Daniel J. Levin, former vice president for publications for the Association of Governing Boards of Universities and Colleges, offers a view from Washington in chapter 3. Drawing on the 2006 report of the AGB Task Force on the State of the Presidency in American Higher Education and focusing on an insider's view of the dominant legislative, financial, and leadership trends that now influence the plans and decision making of presidents, provosts, and student consumers, Levin acknowledges that there is no apparent single "view from Washington" regarding effectiveness in higher education leadership, and that this is where to begin a serious conversation.[1]

Part II, "Analyzing Risk via the Leadership Team: New Approaches, New Results," opens with a discussion of leadership at stressed institutions by Charles R. Middleton, president of Roosevelt University in Chicago, one of the most entrepreneurial major universities in the Midwest. Middleton offers pointed commentary on the major strengths and weaknesses of current presidential management styles and on the challenges of leading the cabinet of a vulnerable institution.

In chapter 5, William Weary, president of Fieldstone Consulting and a senior advisor on board relations to the Association of Governing Boards of Universities and Colleges, focuses on effective trusteeship at fragile institutions and presents the five most important guidelines trustees should follow when developing policies within at-risk environments. A number of national reports from associations such as the AGB and the American Council on Education over the past two decades have agreed that there are two core responsibilities for trustees: effective financial stewardship and hiring and supervising the president. This chapter highlights both of these responsibilities in the context of fragile campus leadership structures.

Provosts, vice presidents for academic affairs, and deans are still most often charged with the major responsibility to address and eliminate weaknesses at fragile institutions, aside from those that are purely financial. Whatever the institution's actual circumstances, its

chief academic officer quickly comes to realize that this process requires a courageous but humble "manager-scholar" to lead faculty colleagues forward when morale and instructional resources are in decline
and prospects for the year ahead are bleak. Patricia Cormier, president
of Longwood University since 1996, served as a chief academic officer
at several stages of her career, and she offers in chapter 6, "Preserving
and Extending the Academic Mission of Vulnerable Institutions: Best
Practices for Chief Academic Officers," a set of academic strategies to
manage vulnerable institutions successfully when challenges seem to
outnumber opportunities.

Completing the section on the campus leadership team, three
administrators originally at the University of Missouri–Kansas City
(UMKC) focus on a new approach to student services for stressed colleges. Lori Reesor, now associate provost for student success at the
University of Kansas, Steven LaNasa, associate dean and assistant professor at UMKC, and Patricia Long, now president of Baker University,
explain in chapter 7 how students have been traditionally viewed during an institutional crisis either as the enemy—consumers whining for
expensive services—or as distant from the real centers of campus
power. In their view, students in partnership with their senior student
affairs officers (SSAOs) can make critical differences in a variety of key
areas to help a university or college overcome at-risk status. Reesor,
LaNasa, and Long contend in "The Challenge for Student Affairs in
Stressed Institutions" that by including the SSAO and student leaders
at key points in decision-making situations, presidents, provosts, and
the board can build an institutional network of more trusting, effective
relationships.

Part III, "Who Is at Risk and Why: The Financial Factors," offers
chapters by Michael Townsley, professor of business at Becker College
and author of one of the most influential publications in recent years
on effective campus financial management, the 2002 NACUBO book
The Small College Guide to Financial Health: Beating the Odds, and
W. Stephen Jeffrey, Vice President for Development and External Relations at the American University of Beirut. In chapter 8, Townsley updates his landmark research and defines risk from the key perspective
of financial resources while providing a tested plan to turn around a
stressed institution no matter what its size is. He concludes with exclusive advice on an emerging area of concern for many institutional leaders: the profitable management of online degree programs.

In chapter 9, Jeffrey answers two persistent questions: how is a capital campaign even conceptualized at an at-risk institution, and should
it be? As a university sinks deeper into enrollment shortfalls, endow-

ment shrinkage, and a weakened reputation, how can significant funds be raised? Jeffrey explains the major challenges—along with methods to overcome them—for advancement officers at vulnerable institutions from his current role as chief fund-raiser for an institution much closer to major conflict and open warfare than any on American soil.

Part IV, "Strategies That Work: New Solutions for Key Operations," offers detailed recommendations from national association heads, campus leaders, and higher education researchers in six operational areas critical to the survival of a vulnerable organization. Sandra Elman, president of the Northwest Commission on Colleges and Universities, one of the nation's six regional accrediting associations, offers in chapter 10 an accrediting officer's candid advice for the leaders of fragile colleges who are preparing to tell their stories in institutional self-studies. In fact, the institution's regional accreditation commission is often the group that knows most of its bad news and may be the only outside agency that knows the full story. Nevertheless, board members, presidents, and academic deans often resist telling that story in a simple, straightforward manner. Elman responds to this negative tradition with helpful, practical recommendations for leaders in this position along with specific suggestions on how to manage the accreditation process that drives the document.

Robert C. Andringa served for many years as president of the Council for Christian Colleges and Universities, one of the nation's leading organizations for faith-based, religiously affiliated institutions. Now a higher education consultant and writer, Andringa contributes chapter 11, in which he addresses directly the stereotype that all at-risk institutions are small, private, residential, and church related. Andringa offers an informed, pragmatic look into the structures and missions of faith-based institutions, as well as action steps to make these colleges and universities more competitive by distinguishing rather than extinguishing their missions.

In chapter 12, Michael Hoyle, former director of finance for the Massachusetts campuses of the University of Phoenix and former president of McIntosh College, a for-profit institution in New Hampshire, writes from the inside about how for-profit competitors have become a significant factor across the national higher education landscape, particularly for midrange, traditional colleges. Following the sometimes-controversial victories earned by for-profit learning organizations like the University of Phoenix and Apollo Group, Career Education Corporation, and Corinthian Management over the past twenty years, an increasing number of traditional campus leaders now concede that for-profit higher education, once anathema, is not only here to stay but also perhaps to prevail in many geographic markets. Hoyle comments on how timid not-for-profit institutions must respond to these new challenges not simply by competing but also by collaborating through strategic alliances.

Fragile universities and colleges can also face some of the most severe legal dilemmas of any higher education enterprise, ranging from lawsuits by student consumers to the loss of federal financial aid, and resource-challenged schools often need significant, ongoing legal resources at times when they literally have no money to pay. In chapter 13, James E. Samels, a higher education attorney for almost thirty-five years, and James Martin, a former provost, offer ten guidelines for stressed institutions to overcome some of the most persistent and complex legal hurdles to their survival.

Kevin W. Sayers, vice president for planning and strategy and assistant to the president at Capital University, and John F. Ryan, assistant provost with similar responsibilities at Ohio State University, argue in chapter 14 that offices of institutional research (IR) are too often viewed as an afterthought during a campus crisis, or as the one office that should have been contacted earlier, before the institution's situation deteriorated precipitously. Sayers and Ryan present a new model to involve the IR office through the development of a "decision-support network" before the onset of major difficulties by linking the four areas of planning, assessment, data gathering, and budget management into a new, more transparent and integrated set of management relationships.

In the final chapter of Part IV, John Ross, a veteran higher education public relations officer and principal of RossWrites Education Communications, explains how perhaps no category of higher education institutions needs positive public relations more than those perceived as fragile or at-risk, and how no institutions are more tempted to push a public relations point beyond accepted norms. In a manner consistent with themes and approaches in earlier chapters, Ross outlines the potential for institutional resurrection via a new, more candid and transparent public relations model.

This book concludes with a synthesis by James Martin and James E. Samels of the necessary strategies to achieve a successful turnaround. Drawing on their own research and observations as higher education consultants along with those of the sixteen contributors, they close with the five necessary steps and ten complementary leadership lessons gathered during the course of this project. *Turnaround: Leading Stressed Colleges and Universities to Excellence* closes with a bibliography of fresh and classic readings on institutional vulnerability and effective leadership.

The authors would like to thank the many individuals who made this book possible. First, we would like to thank the group of more than four hundred presidents, provosts, and board chairs with whom we held conversations on these issues over the past decade, and who produced many of the ideas behind this study, as well as reasons to complete it. We would also like to thank, for the fourth time, our editor at the Johns Hopkins University Press, Jacqueline Wehmueller, for her continuing faith in two writers who are looking for new ways to frame issues about higher education. We would like to thank, for the first time, Ashleigh McKown for her welcome advice and insight into the purposes of this book. In particular, we would like to single out James Jacobson, Esq., of Samels Associates, Attorneys at Law, for his key contributions to chapter 13 on the legal challenges for at-risk institutions and, once again, Cat Jacquet for her good cheer in copy editing the entire manuscript.

In closing, we dedicate this volume to all the presidents with whom we spoke over the past decade and who are now facing the conclusion of their years of leadership on campus. In our view, no matter how fragile some institutions may become in the future, this generation of American leaders succeeded with less training and fewer resources than almost any of the presidents now moving through a more competitive, less collegial professional pipeline. More than one in this group told us over the years, "I trusted the money would be there, I trusted the students would stay, and I trusted myself to do the job," thus providing a fitting opening and closing to this study of their contributions to American higher education.

J. M.
J. E. S.

I

Defining Risk:
The Nature of Stressed Institutions

We lacked a strong and clear marketing plan to identify who
our students were, who our donors were, and how to get
more state support. In the end, the financials just did not
work. Even though we improved educational programs, got
alumni involved, and raised endowment, we could not
attract enough students. Financial aid discounting hurt
us the most.

> —Joseph Short, former president of Bradford College,
> Massachusetts, in a telephone interview
> with James Martin, 27 April 2007

We began to be viewed as a second- or third-rate institution,
a "parking place."

> —Alan Balboni, former professor of political science at
> Boston State College, Massachusetts, in a telephone
> interview with James Martin, 22 April 2007

CHAPTER ONE

Defining Stressed Institutions and Leading Them Effectively

James Martin and James E. Samels

Financial difficulties are the foremost reason colleges and universities become stressed, according to George Keller, author of *Academic Strategy: The Management Revolution in American Higher Education* (1983).[1] In a 2005 interview with the authors, Keller observed that "the number one reason institutions are stressed is for financial causes, many different kinds of financial causes. Too many colleges don't understand what's happening to them. They invest poorly with too much endowment in property, or they build too large a sports program, or they fail to understand key demographic changes."[2] Keller offers a contrary perspective to the stereotype that only small, tuition-dependent, religiously affiliated colleges are at risk: "It's amazing how even fairly affluent universities can run deficits and slide into vulnerability. They construct too many buildings and get into debt way beyond what they can afford. Too many schools are really only concerned with next year's budget. For those institutions, an external appraisal of what's coming over the horizon could save or kill them."[3]

What has befallen many of these institutions? Why have so many slipped from earlier positions of strength and even prestige? For the purposes of this book, a stressed college or university is defined as an institution that is dependent on tuition or state appropriations, smaller than it should be and needs to be, and lacking in name-brand recognition. The school's enrollment, endowment, gifts, and grants have been flat, at best, for several years, and most, if not all, long-range planning efforts address subsistence rather than sustained growth. With this definition in mind, the following section offers an analysis of five basic reasons why so many institutions are now vulnerable, moving beyond the dated stereotype of a college that is smaller than one thousand students, private, religiously affiliated, residential, and fully dependent on tuition. Subsequent sections of this chapter provide the reader with an original checklist of twenty indicators to assess the degree of any institution's fragility, as well as, in closing, the ten skills presidents, provosts, and board chairs now need to demonstrate in turning around these institutions.

The following five drivers are among the most powerful in producing a campus under stress:

1. *"Churning" presidents.* The American Council on Education has continued to report in its *American College President* series over the past twenty years or more that presidents are remaining in their positions for increasingly shorter time spans than did leaders of two or three decades ago. Although the general figure for presidential tenures has plateaued over the past two studies, the average length of service for presidents today is barely six years. If one factors in the aging of the traditional American white male chief executive and rising retirement rates, it is clear that higher education institutions face a crisis simply in finding presidents, let alone in keeping them. George Boggs, president and CEO of the American Association of Community Colleges, noted in a conversation with the authors in 2004 that approximately 45 percent of community college presidents planned to retire by 2007, according to his data, and 79 percent of the same group planned to retire by 2012.[4] This trend has given rise to widely read articles in *Community College Week* with titles like "The Leadership Gap: Crisis or Opportunity?" and "The Changing of the Guard,"[5] as well as related pieces in the *Chronicle of Higher Education* and the *Wall Street Journal* on the need to find presidents and CEOs from outside the academy.[6]

Presidents are older in office and are staying for shorter terms than at any previous time in American higher education. This leads to what we have labeled "churning," that is, the stirring up of the campus for a two-year transition when one president leaves and another arrives. The focus is often more on the transition than on strategic decisions to lead the institution forward and increase its quality. Repeated churning of presidents begins to cause institutional deterioration and neglect as one leader after another invests briefly in this or that major or pet project, only to be overtaken by a career decision to leave or the need to spend time and resources on another pressure point on campus. Over time, systems do not receive the resources they need to thrive, and key financial questions go unanswered for too long a period, but prospective students and their parents do not notice this. Although consumers may not be aware of many of the internal triggers that mark an institution's weakening condition, they will notice the rise of a competitor institution via the *U.S. News & World Report* annual rankings, a dynamic new residence hall, or a smartly revised website and literature package.

2. *Declining state appropriations for higher education.* One only needs to review the titles of national reports on declining funding for higher education since 2002 to grasp their trend: *Losing Ground* (2002), "Financing Higher Education: A Crisis in State Funding" (2003), "The Long-Term Economic Effects of Declining State Support for Higher Education: Are States Shooting Themselves in the Foot?" (2003), and, most recently, "State Shortfalls Projected to Continue despite Economic Gains: Long-Term Prospects for Higher Education No Brighter" (2006).[7] With the release of U.S. Education Secretary Margaret Spellings's Commission on the Future of Higher Education's report in the summer of 2006, the somber tone continued to dampen any hopes for a return to funding levels of prior decades when nationwide state funding to public institutions of higher education was significantly higher.

In their issue paper "Setting the Context," written to inform the work of the Spellings Commission, Charles Miller and Cheryl Oldham explain, "States play a critical role in funding higher education, yet most states face long-term budget shortfalls and structural deficits, and higher education has received a diminishing proportion of state appropriations in the past few years. . . . At both federal and state levels, financial support for higher education programs is seen—and will likely continue to be seen—as less important or urgent than other budget priorities."[8]

In a related issue paper Dennis Jones, president of the National Center for Higher Education Management Systems (NCHEMS), observes even more pointedly about the 2005–2013 period that "all states face potential budget deficits that will serve to limit the funding of higher education." Although the report had originally taken shape during a brief period of "brightened" economic prospects, by the time of its release, the economic outlook for higher education had become troubling. Jones confirms, "The study also finds, in 46 states, growth in demand for other services (such as K–12 education, social services, corrections, and Medicaid) will be greater than growth in demand for higher education. . . . For the nation as a whole, the projections indicate that state revenues will be 5.7% lower than the level required to maintain current services."[9]

As churning presidents weaken individual institutions, declining state support weakens whole categories of institutions—not just publicly funded ones—and, in an interesting reverse noted by Philip

Trostel, a Maine public policy economist, it weakens the states themselves: "The economic consequences of the relative decline in state support for higher education are not going to be falling incomes, or rising unemployment, welfare, and crime. . . . The long-term economic effects of declining state support for higher education are the lost opportunities. Moreover, the lost opportunities are not just for the individuals who could have gone to college. The states are losing out too [because] the production of college graduates has the potential to be a very cost-effective economic development tool."[10]

The issue of declining support is not simply an American phenomenon. The journal *International Higher Education* reported in its winter 2006 issue that this has become a worldwide trend: "The decline in public expenditure on higher education has been a global crisis and the most important trend. Compelled by economic reform policies or convinced of the rationale for the reduced role of the state in funding higher education, most countries have inflicted serious cuts in public budgets for higher education. . . . The decline is not confined to developing countries, though it is more prevalent in developing than developed countries."[11]

3. The menace of rising technology budgets. From less than 1 percent of the total institutional budget only a generation ago to 15 or even 18 percent today, the burgeoning campus technology budget is draining financial support from other, critical aspects of teaching and learning on vulnerable campuses that clearly cannot afford it, but whose leaders persist in believing that they must afford it to attract the sophisticated student consumers profiled later in this chapter. In fact, not only students but also parents, aunts, and uncles are demanding the newest, most expensive technology resources. As students arrive each fall immersed in personal technologies, it is natural for them to expect that higher education should challenge them in this area with more and better resources than they have previously experienced. Thus although many midrange schools may have spent prodigiously to increase their technological competitiveness over the past decade or more, overall they have arguably become weaker institutions as the budget lines for faculty, staff, curriculum, and physical plant have been funded at continually smaller percentages.

In response, fragile institutions can take several steps, many of which focus on controlling costs and on gathering far more accurate information on how much their technologies actually cost on a monthly basis. Olin L. Adams III and David M. Shannon advocate, "If student learning is the goal of instruction, the faculty should accept the fundamental change in students, whose learning, future employment, and indeed lives, are connected to technology as never before. The learning communities of the future are likely to be in cyberspace. . . . The physical campus is an ideal, but an extensive physical campus might be an expensive reality for some institutions in the future."[12] With an aggressive cost-containment commitment and more comprehensive systems to monitor technology costs, some universities and colleges will be able to control some portion of the massive technology growth and its cost within their campus communities, virtual and otherwise.

4. *Demanding student and alumni consumers.* Whether the pressure is coming from the hovering, "helicopter" parents of current undergraduates or anxious young alumni lacking full-time employment and the security of a trusted academic advisor and a career mentor, the "consumer services" aspects of college life are also squeezing out the resources that traditionally were spent on faculty salaries, research support, and the broadest range of athletic programs possible. Personal counseling, professional networking and introductions, blogs and facebooks, financial planning, travel advice, and even mentored spiritual exploration are all part of the college package for today's students. One learning consultant describes the Net generation: "They expect results immediately. They carry an arsenal of electronic devices—the more portable the better—and they are able to juggle several conversations on Instant Messenger, surf the Web, and listen to music on their iPod while reading *Othello* for homework."[13] If students today read any newspaper, it is most likely *USA Today,* which estimated that 35 billion e-mails were sent each day in 2005.[14] Cumulatively, these lifestyle trends and needs shape a first-year student's expectations of college life, which are more complex and varied than traditional teaching and learning agreements and which place enormous demands on the faculty, staff, and infrastructure of colleges and universities already at risk.

Even the leaders of vulnerable colleges realize that they need the help of student-market watchers and consultants, and these consultants are increasingly stressing the need for higher education institutions to promise more than they have in the past and to pay for it with future tuition revenues. Robert Sevier, author of *Building a Brand That Matters,* writes in *University Business,* "There are two important nuggets here. First, the idea of lifetime customer relationships. It is not about a one-time sale or buy, but a lifetime of sales and buys. It is not about recruiting freshmen, but freshmen who want to be seniors. It is not about recruiting one-time donors, but lifetime donors."[15] Student consumers, then, need not only to be housed, fed, and taught but also to be "managed" in ways not apparent to many of the college and university leaders of former generations.

5. *The commodification of American higher education.* In this area as well, the titles of several recent articles indicate the concerns shared by many observers that the *process* and *values* that have contributed to the strength of the nation's higher education systems have eroded as "higher" education has been reduced principally to the production of degrees, called "tickets," which then can be bought and sold on international "markets": "Crisis of Confidence" (2006), "Mud on the Ivory Towers: Colleges Turn to 'Crisis Consultants' for Image Repair" (2005), and "Knowledge and Education as International Commodities: The Collapse of the Common Good" (2002).[16] Increasingly influenced by public relations consultants, brand developers, and trustees who come from the world of for-profit decision making, many midrange, medium-quality colleges and universities have become more vulnerable in part by spending their few discretionary dollars on marketing and competitive positioning packages instead of faculty and curriculum development resources.

To demonstrate how easily colleges, particularly small ones, can lose their bearings in an intensely competitive market, Brian Foster, provost of the University of Missouri at Columbia, speaking at the 2006 annual meeting of the American Council on Education, shared the broader concern that "colleges have embraced with gusto the idea that they are engines of economic development, but they have pretended that everything fits neatly together between colleges' traditional roles and their new ones related to the economy. Colleges need to abandon their 'romantic fantasies' about how 'you get a $1 billion business out of a freshman learning community.'"[17]

Even more to the point of how commodification is creating a new category of stressed colleges and universities, Philip G. Altbach describes how "open markets, at least in higher education, reinforce the inequalities that already exist. If education borders are completely open, the strongest and wealthiest education providers will have unrestricted access. Countries and institutions that cannot compete will find it difficult to flourish."[18] As explained earlier, sometimes the most decisive mark of an institution's decline is the acknowledgment by the external community of the rise of one or two of its primary competitors in annual ranking surveys.

These are among the most influential forces that keep perhaps one thousand midrange universities and colleges at risk no matter what strategy a new president or academic leadership team chooses to implement. In the following section the authors provide an original model to assess institutional stress via a checklist of twenty indicators.

At-Risk Indicators: A New Checklist

The following indicators are all components, in differing combinations, of a stressed institutional environment. A fragile college or university may not demonstrate all twenty, nor does the presence of three or four guarantee vulnerability. However, a preponderance of these twenty indicators clearly means that an institution has slipped, possibly far, from its founding vision and strength, and that some form of surgery will most likely be required to bring it back to health. In their book *Wise Moves in Hard Times: Creating and Managing Resilient Colleges and Universities*, David W. Leslie and E. K. Fretwell note, "When an institution is overextended—much as a lifeboat or a medical staff gets overburdened—hard decisions about how to use scarce resources have to be made."[19] They continue, "Resilient institutions need not be wealthy as measured in traditional economic terms, but they succeed because their faculty, staff, students, and friends are committed to them."[20]

With this in mind, we interviewed Dennis P. Jones, president of NCHEMS, twenty-one years after he had created an influential report for the National Center for Education Statistics in 1985 titled "Indicators of the Condition of Higher Education."[21] Our questions focused on what new indicators of institutional fragility Jones might have discovered since that early study and what had happened to the national conversation about "indicators" of institutional health. Jones began, "I guess the overall lesson learned would be that we are no closer now, in 2006, to having a set of indicators people pay attention to than we were 20 years ago. However, among these indicators of stress to consider now, I would pay most attention to those that speak to the extent to which an institution is depreciating its assets, such as deferred maintenance or the technology budget. Pay attention to buildings and technology."[22]

In accordance with the earlier cautions of George Keller and Dennis Jones, the following checklist begins with an initial group of ten indicators that focus comprehensively on institutional budget and resource challenges:

1. *Tuition discounting more than 35 percent.* This indicator is presented first both because it is the institutional condition those with little inside knowledge of higher education accept as the key characteristic of a stressed college and because it is also true that vulnerable schools

consistently discount a dangerously high percentage of their tuitions. The key question, then, is what is *too* high. Brian Bissell, vice president for business affairs at Colorado Christian College, believes that discounting tuition to the level of 35 percent or more is "right on target" as perhaps the most important proof of an institution at risk. Bissell explains, "It is all about the value proposition. For the chief finance officer, there are two primary questions: do parents believe that they are receiving value for the net price, and is the institution earning enough revenue to address the needs of the provost and the faculty? CFOs need to 'feed the beast'—the ongoing resource needs of the faculty—but that's a good thing. The trick is in learning how economies of scale dictate what can be accomplished and in managing that factor."[23]

Gordon Winston, director of the Williams College Project on the Economics of Higher Education, sharpens the demographic and socioeconomic implications of this indicator: "Old style competition was stable (indeed, rigid); the new style is fluid, and none of us really knows where it's going to wind up. There's growing consensus, though, that schools'(limited) ability to cut price is increasingly being used to bid for peer quality of wealthy students at the expense of more costly poor students of equal quality who have to be given additional need-based price discounts (financial aid)."[24]

2. Tuition dependency more than 85 percent. Regarding dependence on tuition income, Bissell sets 85 percent as the cut line for at-risk status. He believes that "above this, it is difficult to maintain adequate funds for policy and development at the institution and, importantly, strong relations with the provost and the faculty. Schools need to be mission centered and market-smart because this whole rubric has nothing to do with actual dollars; it is the previously discussed value proposition that most importantly helps grow our brand. At some smaller schools, a few percentage points one way or the other in this area means another million dollars a year to work with."[25]

At multiple points in our research, one or more presidents shared the simple observation that when an administration has to "beat the bushes" to balance the budget every spring and at least four of every five budget dollars is based on tuition, it is time to face the fact that the institution is at risk.[26]

3. Student default rate above 5 percent. According to the U.S. Department of Education, student default rates for 2003 (issued in September 2005, the most recent data available) were at their lowest level since 1987. The average institutional student default rate was 4.5 percent in 2003, down from 5.2 percent in 2002, yet more than one-third of institutions in the study maintained default rates above 5 percent.[27] Setting a specific percentage point for this indicator is challenging, but it remains one of the key determinants of institutional stress.

One chief finance officer observed, "Default rates may not be the best indicator for this issue. By this, I mean, when someone defaults on a Stafford loan today, not much happens. A better measure would be the percentage of bad debt write-off. An accounts receivable percentage of debt greater than 10 percent with a bad debt write-off of 5 percent, for me, is a closer indicator of fragility."[28]

4. *Debt service more than 10 percent of annual operating budget.* Jeffrey J. Williams relates the level of debt service to the broader issue of debt across the whole of American higher education in his 2006 study "Debt Education: Bad for the Young, Bad for America": "Debt is not just a mode of financing but a mode of pedagogy. We tend to think of it as a necessary evil attached to higher education but extraneous to [the] aims of higher education."[29] Standard and Poor's credit-rating service assessed the 2005 fiscal year for private higher education with the following comment: "In fiscal 2005, U.S. private colleges and universities uniformly exhibited high debt volumes associated with the repair of aging plants, technology upgrades, and changing consumer preferences for housing and athletics facilities, as well as a steady stream of refunding transactions." On the specific issue of debt service, its July 2006 report continued, "One way to measure a university's debt burden is to compare maximum annual debt service (MADS) to annual operating expenses. A ratio greater than 10% generally indicates an excessive debt burden."[30] Several CFOs additionally noted that two of the most critical markers within the 10 percent indicator are whether the institution's auxiliary and student-housing debts are self-funded.

5. *Less than one-to-three ratio between endowment and operating budget.* For many years the benchmark has been a one-to-one ratio between annual operating budget and endowment. Charles R. Middleton, president of Roosevelt University and author of the chapter in this book on presidential leadership, agrees: "For financial indicators, the one I am working on the most is raising the endowment to the level of the annual operating budget, one-to-one, as a signal of institutional strength. This means forgoing expenditures of money that comes in unencumbered by estates and redirecting it from current expenditures, where it can do some real good, to endowment and then using the

payouts from it to start funding those things annually. I now intercept all such funds when they reach $25,000 or more."[31]

6. *Average tuition increase greater than 8 percent for five years.* Between 1995 and 2005 tuition and fees at public four-year colleges rose at an average rate of 6.9 percent (4.4 percent after inflation), according to the College Board. Public four-year college tuition, fees, and room and board charges had the dubious distinction of rising more rapidly between 2000 and 2006 than in any five-year period since 1975. For private four-year colleges, tuition and fees rose 5.7 percent between 1995 and 2005 (3.2 percent after inflation).[32]

Although numbers slightly more than twice the rate of general inflation may seem manageable to some consumers' untrained eyes, *FinAid: The Smart Student Guide to Financial Aid*, via its website www.finaid.org, provides an insider's look at the impact of rising tuition while discussing this indicator of institutional fragility: "A good rule of thumb is that tuition rates will increase at about twice the general inflation rate. . . . On average, tuition tends to increase about 8% per year. An 8% college inflation rate means that the cost of college doubles every nine years."[33] In our view, tuition can rise less than 8 percent each year and still confirm fragility, in part because desperate institutions continue to lock themselves into raising tuition levels as the principal, and sometimes only, way to accumulate new revenues.

7. *Deferred maintenance at least 40 percent unfunded.* Marjorie Simmons and Anthony Duce explain in "Maintenance Crunch," "A deferred maintenance backlog almost always exists. The key questions to ask: How large is the backlog? How long will it take to reduce the backlog given various levels of expenditure?"[34] In our view, a backlog that approaches 50 percent unfunded is one of the most powerful indicators of institutional fragility. As Dennis P. Jones explained earlier in this chapter, although many of the indicators higher education leaders had high hopes for over the past two decades have faded in influence, the two that he still stands by are deferred maintenance and the size of the technology budget because they "speak to the extent to which an institution is depreciating its assets."[35]

E. K. Fretwell, in a 2006 interview with the authors, linked deferred maintenance to institutional risk status in simple, blunt terms: "Stop deferred maintenance problems with simple solutions. First, avoid getting into difficult situations by not purchasing the attractive 'bells and whistles' during new construction. It is extremely difficult to do, but presidents need to do it, especially in construction projects involving new technologies. Hold back the appetite of your institution and don't go further than is necessary. Don't pay for 'frills.'"[36] It is not lost on many fragile university campuses that Standard and Poor's tracks the ages of college and university physical plants "because campus facilities and attractiveness are important drivers in the higher education market," and that their current assessment is that "the average age of plant slightly increased for 2005 when compared to fiscal 2004 in all rating categories."[37] Even more succinctly, Debra Townsley, president of Nichols College, adds, "Don't borrow now what your successor cannot afford to pay back."[38]

8. *Short-term bridge financing required in the final quarter of each fiscal year.* Although a search of "bridge financing" in almost any higher education index will produce multiple options for students to cover the gap between their personal resources and those offered by their university or college, the CEOs and CFOs of schools at risk are equally familiar with the kind of "bridge financing" defined by Dartmouth's Center for Private Equity and Entrepreneurship as "temporary funding that will eventually be replaced by permanent capital."[39] In these instances presidents typically seek short-term funds during the final quarter, sometimes the final week or two, of their fiscal years to meet payroll and keep their buildings open.

Weymouth Spence, president of Columbia Union College, has secured this type of bridge financing on more than one occasion and comments, "Short-term financing such as this is a reality for many at-risk institutions today. They should not look away from it; rather, senior officers need to make sure that all short-term financing decisions relate directly to long-range planning objectives as a way to ensure accountability within the process and to move the institution to the point at which such 'bridges' are no longer needed."[40]

9. *Less than 10 percent of operating budget dedicated to technology.* In the course of our research, presidents and provosts complained frequently about the painful increases technology caused in their financial planning each spring, with the technology portion of some budgets running as high as 15 or even 18 percent. An annual budgetary allocation of 10 percent is seen as too low by many presidents, although barely a generation ago technology plans might have claimed 1 percent, at most, of yearly resources.

In its 2006 publication "Trends in Higher Education," the Society for College and University Planning commented on technology and budgets: "Facts: The cost of maintaining and developing IT infrastructure and services continues to grow. . . . Students arrive with greater expectations for the level of connectivity and access to resources, tools, and support. Our thoughts: The cost of IT to institutions, in absolute and relative terms (to budgets), is unlikely to peak and begin decreasing any time soon. Cost and funding will remain the top issue to watch."[41]

10. Average alumni gift is less than $75, and fewer than 20 percent of alumni give annually. Annual gifting levels vary considerably across higher education institutions, but there are still understandings of what constitutes an appropriate level of giving to one's baccalaureate alma mater. A random selection of suggested minimum giving levels taken from the websites of several public and private institutions of differing histories and geographic locales produced the following figures:

—University of Washington, College of Arts and Sciences: $500+

—Claremont McKenna College: $150–$299

—Saint Joseph's College of Maine: $100–$249

—North Central College (Illinois): $100

—Wells College: $50–$149

—Palmer College of Chiropractic: Up to $99

W. Stephen Jeffrey, author of this book's chapter on development at fragile institutions, who has spent his career at an international university, an elite women's college, and a major private university, sets an individual level of $75 and 20 percent of alumni contributing annually as the baseline indicators of a stressed environment.[42]

11. Institutional enrollment of one thousand students or fewer. As the saying now goes among many baby boomers still not ready to retire, "60 is the new 45." Our view is that 2,500 is the new 1,000 students. In other words, smaller colleges and universities can no longer afford to stay small when small is fewer than 1,000 students. By changing their thinking about student recruitment to that of cohort-sized multiples rather than individual student "retail" growth patterns, these schools can begin to achieve new economies of scale and efficiencies of operation. As globalization shapes many aspects of American higher education over the next two decades, it is likely that groups of colleges and smaller universities with fewer than 1,000 students will begin to arrange themselves—or be arranged—into new consortial and strategic models, thus raising their collective size by a factor of three or four. By

2025 "small college" in America may be viewed by increments of a thousand rather than a hundred student.

12. Conversion yield is 20 percent behind that of primary competitors. Conversion-yield success constitutes one of the key elements of the intensely debated *U.S. News & World Report* annual rankings in its "Student Selectivity" category. Many vulnerable colleges and universities are not selective to any extent because they lack what Charles Goldman calls reputation and prestige. Goldman contends, "Reputation can be built through word of mouth based on information from people who've used an institution's services or experienced them in some way. It's also updated frequently. Prestige, which is always either zero or positive, is more intangible; it applies to an institution as a whole."[43]

For most, if not all, vulnerable colleges, prestige is only a distant dream, and building a reputation is the strongest opportunity to move beyond fragility. Goldman thinks that reputation-based institutions "typically focus on meeting student needs for economic advancement and personal growth and pursue research programs that are tied to the local economy. The best strategic decision for many campuses may be to focus on enhancing customer satisfaction rather than pursing prestige."[44] Quite a few fragile institutions appear to understand that their best hope of building a sustainable reputation lies in quality customer service and directly supporting their present students as well as or better than any similarly situated school in their state or region can; the challenge for these institutions is rather to actualize the plans to accomplish this dependably and with very limited resources and staff support. Failure to accomplish this is a core factor in causing an ineffective conversion yield that can lag 10, 15, or even 20 percentage points behind that of local and regional rivals.

13. Student retention is 10 percent behind that of primary competitors. Like student yield, the student retention percentage provides an annual statistical snapshot that cannot be reformulated into another, higher number no matter how aggressively the institution's marketing director provides a fuller context for why his or her college's numbers trail those of competitors by 10 percent. To develop effective retention strategies, not-for-profit admissions officers and chief student affairs officers are increasingly hiring consultants who specialize in this one product line and studying the success of the corporate university model in which retention is more directly and closely tied to the company's bottom-line revenues. A writer in *Chief Learning Officer* magazine notes,

"For several years, the corporate university focused on fast cycle time with a value proposition of operational excellence in support of the need for speed." Although this description reflects a vocabulary somewhat trapped in for-profit jargon, the author's subsequent point, that successful retention depends on strong relationships between individual students and college or university employees, whether faculty or staff members, is a solid one supported by dozens, if not hundreds, of the conversations we have held with campus leaders over the past six to eight years. Even for-profit language does not obscure its simple truth: "The corporate university requires relationship management and disciplined processes."[45]

14. *The institution is on probation, warning, or financial watch with a regional accreditor or a specialty degree licensor.* The internal technical reasons that produce accreditation probation, whether significant or relatively transitory, are not as pivotal as the fact that "probation" has been attached to the university's name in the media, perhaps most problematically "for financial reasons." These descriptors are extremely difficult to remove from public perception, and they cannot be removed quickly. The path to a renovated reputation requires major, multiyear contributions of time and talent from the administration, the faculty, and the board of trustees. Accreditation probation requires transparent solutions and brings public scrutiny. The systems of Louisiana and Oregon are random examples. The Louisiana Board of Regents requires that "an institution must report all disciplinary actions, such as warning, probation, or withdrawal of accredited status, and a brief explanation of the conditions and/or deficiencies that resulted in the action to the Board of Regents."[46]

In Oregon the model is similar, as described in the Oregon State University *Accreditation Handbook*'s section on probation: "1. . . . While on Probation, the institution may be subject to special monitoring by the Commission, which may include a requirement to submit periodic prescribed reports and to receive special visits by representatives of the Commission."[47] Although the causes of probation typically pose a debilitating set of challenges to institutions already under significant stress, the public scrutiny mentioned earlier can last considerably longer and prove even more challenging to eradicate.

15. *The majority of faculty do not hold terminal degrees.* Although the authors are unaware of any national institutional average of full-time faculty who hold terminal degrees, there is a clear trend, on the basis of our research, for institutions to achieve a level of at least 70 percent ter-

minally degreed faculty, with a level of 80 percent recommended. Not to achieve a level of 50 percent terminally degreed faculty members indicates an inability to recruit, support, and retain a body of professorial talent necessary to overcome legitimate questions of fragility. Monitoring this indicator at five disparate institutions confirms a common zone of percentages of faculty with terminal degrees:

—Malone College: 71 percent[48]

—Indiana University, South Bend: 81 percent[49]

—College of Charleston: 85 percent[50]

—Whittier College: 96 percent[51]

—University of Colorado at Boulder: 98 percent (tenured faculty only)[52]

16. Average age of full-time faculty is fifty-eight or higher. The average age of the American professoriate has been rising steadily for two decades or more as the bulging baby-boom generation moves toward retirement. The *Chronicle of Higher Education* reported in 1999 that nearly a third of the nation's full-time faculty were fifty-five or older, contrasted with about a quarter in that age group in 1989.[53] Thus it appears safe to assume that over the most recent decade the average age of faculty members nationally has climbed at least one to two more years. As a rough comparison, over relatively the same time period as that in the *Chronicle*'s report, the average age of higher education presidents rose from fifty-two in 1986 to fifty-eight in 2001, and female presidents averaged almost a year older than men in 2001.[54]

A survey of more than thirty thousand faculty members conducted by the Higher Education Research Institute revealed several points of interest regarding the effects of aging among faculty members. One example addressed the impact of technology on professors now at the start and now at the conclusion of their careers: "Fewer than half of the professors who were under 35 found technology to be stressful, compared with more than two-thirds of faculty members 45 or older. . . . Age also affected how professors use computers. More than 90 per cent of those under 45 communicated via e-mail at least twice a week, compared with 67 per cent of those 65 or older."[55]

Because senior professors are traditionally granted lighter teaching loads and have less direct contact with students, particularly those taking first-year seminars, Introduction to Psychology, English 101, and other service courses, a collective portrait emerges at many resource-poor, middle-tier institutions of a professoriate that is becoming increasingly disconnected from the lifestyles and learning styles of current students.

17. The leadership team averages more than twelve years or fewer than three years of service at the institution. For the four final indicators we examine campus culture rather than national data banks and indexes. As noted earlier, aging faculty members may almost imperceptibly begin to drift away from the learning styles and vocabularies of their students, and it is students who note this first in their end-of-semester evaluations and elective course choices from that point forward.

Cabinets and senior leadership teams that average well over a decade of service together put themselves in danger of becoming too familiar with "the ways things have always been handled" when a new president or chief academic officer proposes a change. Similarly, leadership groups that hold fewer than three years of service as a team may be poised as agents of change but lack the necessary span of academic and fiscal years together to learn each others' strengths and weaknesses in order to avoid major pitfalls when there is no time to develop a plan B.

18. No complete online program has been developed. Many middle-tier institutions advertise that they offer online programs. However, there is a serious difference between several or even many online *courses* and a full online *program*. Many of these colleges and universities would struggle to mount a complete online program but still want the marketing advantages of "online education" in their viewbooks and, more important, on their websites. William Rezak, former president of the State University of New York College of Technology at Alfred, has commented, "Successful colleges and universities of the 21st century will offer the kinds of coursework that students want and need at times of the day or night and the days of the week that students find convenient. . . . Distance education, asynchronous learning, evening and weekend programs for nontraditional students . . . will be the norm. Colleges that prove themselves flexible and adaptable to these market demands will meet with success."[56]

In fact, the reasons for failure in full online programming, even among stronger, more prominent institutions, are many: "In some cases, immature technology is to blame for the online woes. Yet far more often, distance learning initiatives fail because of internal cultural issues across multiple departments—academic, financial, marketing, and so forth."[57] One thing should be clear for schools that are contemplating this major step: programs should be driven by workforce needs and quality instruction, not simply by a new technology. Mark Fenton-O'Creevy, director of programs and curriculum at the Open University Business School, agrees: "The e-learning products that have crashed and burned . . . are those that have based their product on technology, rather than on teaching and learning."[58] Fragile colleges that keep their focus on the competitiveness of their teaching rather than on the bells and whistles of expensive new technologies can raise their chances for success significantly.

19. No new degree or certificate program has been developed for at least two years. If the institution's chief academic officer, deans, and department chairs have not implemented a new degree or certificate program for at least two years, and if there is not at least one in the pipeline moving toward approval, a critical pathway out of vulnerability status has been overlooked.

Eventually, depending on the anxiety or aggressiveness of the president or board chair, the chief academic officer may receive a memorandum asking why the university has dropped out of or failed to enter a competitive program market.[59] When this happens, the CAO should first be aware that a quick consensus among faculty members about what new programs to consider may be difficult to accomplish if no preparatory work has been undertaken. Second, all the trust building she or he may have engaged in will now be necessary to mobilize a sluggish or nonexistent curriculum development process. Whatever their genesis, questions like this will come and should serve as a wake-up call for provosts who have spent too much of their time on institutional sidelines as their schools have declined in reputation and resources.

20. Academic governance and curriculum development systems require more than one year to approve a new degree program. The tradition for a century or more in higher education has been that curriculum is the province of the faculty and that the faculty will bring forth a new degree proposal only after it has been carefully designed, critiqued, and voted on by department, college, and all-university curriculum committees. Driven in part by the speed—some have said the unwise speed—with which the University of Phoenix and other for-profit learning organizations identify, develop, and bring to market new degree options, almost within weeks, this model is changing on traditional campuses. To remain competitive, vulnerable institutions must become more adroit and bold in moving proposals through appropriate committees within one semester and then through administrative, budget, and even board committees within the next semester.

Reflecting these expectations, William Rezak declares in his previously mentioned article on good business practices, "To the extent that faculty governance engages in development of dynamic, attractive, and effective new academic programming that meets the needs of students and employers, it is effective and appropriate. . . . Too often faculty governance becomes an excuse to suggest that faculty 'know best' with respect to allocation of resources and the agenda for the future."[60] Experienced academic vice presidents learn how to develop pilot degree and certificate programs that do not require the full curriculum development apparatus to be engaged and that can provide the institution with a valuable one-year trial run to test the scope and timeliness of the curriculum against a real student market.

As noted earlier, not all of these indicators need to appear for an institution to be defined as at risk. However, the presence of a group of these indicators spells trouble for any middle- or lower-tier institution and signals the approach of at-risk status. In response, some board chairs, presidents, and cabinets are realizing that they need better skills in many of these areas, coupled with a fresh way of looking at things. The following section identifies ten new ways to address these issues in the context of skills necessary to complete a campus turnaround.

Ten New Skills for Leaders of Stressed Colleges and Universities

Leading a stressed college or university is crisis management every day. With little money to support the meager planning that may occur, the chief executive officer needs "a broad and deep understanding of [the] organization and its people so that you can deploy staff according to their talents and secure necessary things quickly."[61] The highly anticipated report from U.S. Education Secretary Spellings's Commission on the Future of Higher Education, titled *A National Dialogue* and published in the summer of 2006, also spoke to the need for innovation among campus managers, even those challenged by limited resources: "Too many of our colleges and universities have not embraced opportunities to be entrepreneurial, from testing new methods of teaching and content delivery to meeting the increased demand for lifelong learning. For their part, state and federal policymakers have also failed to make supporting innovation a priority. . . . We recommend that America's colleges and universities embrace a culture of continuous innovation and quality improvement."[62]

However, innovations across a campus, especially significant ones, require more than simple courage and imagination; they require time, personnel, and teamwork. For the presidents and chief academic officers of vulnerable institutions, it can be agonizing to sense what could and should be done and then not be able to accomplish it, particularly over a period of years. The following ten skills ask presidents and provosts to take hard looks at the quality of their faculty and staffs, the timeliness of their mission and programs, and their continuing abilities to survive among those competitors:

1. *Focus on mission before admissions.* Many presidents of fragile colleges expect weekly, if not daily, admissions deposit reports, and they spend great amounts of time from May to September huddled with the vice president for enrollment and the dean of admissions actively wondering if last year's numbers can be matched and then exceeded. Their focus is often exclusively on increasing enrollments to stabilize the institution. We suggest that conditions of risk can be more successfully overcome by asking the cabinet and members of key college committees to pause and seriously reconsider the mission of the institution before annual admissions anxieties drive new program development, new faculty hires, late resource purchases, and expanded marketing campaigns. Rather than blindly continuing to assume that increasing the institution's size is the best, or only, solution, it may be wiser to increase selectivity, counterintuitive as this may seem, as part of a plan intentionally to resize the institution downward.

E. K. Fretwell defends this approach: "To draw students of higher quality, refocus your mission. Start by bringing the community together to sharpen and even significantly change institutional mission as the first step toward raising recruitment expectations."[63] Roy Austensen, longtime provost at Valparaiso University, has experienced a number of course corrections in this area over his career, and he cautions a fragile institution that is considering this option to "avoid becoming something it is not. Be careful and do not try to accomplish this overnight. 'Buying' students who will not be loyal to the institution won't help, and, in the process, it may offend some of those students in the school's former market. Bring along previous student stakeholders, and do not forget to secure Board support for the refocused mission as a part of the process."[64]

At the same time, simply telling a team of young and worried admissions recruiters that the institution plans to become more selective will not work. The community, led by the president and chief academic officer, needs to focus on "mission before admissions" and work collaboratively to define what a new, modestly more selective environment would look like. One experienced chief finance officer recommends focusing on what has come to be called the institution's "value proposition" as a simple way to begin this transition: "Work with admissions officers to clarify that the point is not simply filling seats, but also preserving and extending the value proposition of the entire institution. In this sense, admissions officers become revenue partners. There is no simpler way to put it."[65]

Old skill: Tell the community to manage lean and live with less.
New skill: Rethink mission and resize the institution.

2. Only spend what mission allows. The second skill links the budget development process at these institutions to their mission and vision statements much more closely. Rather than rethinking mission in isolation, the goal is to design and manage the budget-building and mission review processes simultaneously. The goal, traditionally described as impossible in higher education environments, is to raise quality and student market share while cutting costs. Nevertheless, there is evidence that some believe that this is the future for many vulnerable universities and colleges. James L. Fisher and Scott D. Miller explain in *College Planning and Management*:

> In the aftermath of 9/11, with institutional endowments still weakened and philanthropic giving impacted by shrunken portfolios, universities are finally being forced to pay serious attention to reducing costs. College presidents and CFOs nationwide now need to know more than just "when" but rather "where" and "how" to do it. We contend that virtually any institution can cut costs while actually *improving* quality. And, contrary to the conventional wisdom, operating expenses may be reduced without jeopardizing the delivery of academic and student services.[66]

In line with this thinking, Debra Townsley, president of Nichols College, is one of the few chief executive officers to lead an institution back from a junk-bond rating to that of BBB–. As even some informed colleague presidents said that it could not be done, Townsley continued to press forward while successfully challenging her cabinet and faculty to spend only what their mission allowed. Townsley offers one key to Nichols's success:

> Put plainly, your institution simply must have a distinctive, desired mission. There *must* be a purpose to your school beyond effectively teaching your students good values for their lives ahead. As one example of how we accomplished our goals, we denied some legitimate requests for additional staff growth and support in 2005 and dedicated those same funds to an area of operations that had not made requests for additional staff or resources. We did this because that latter area was core to the College's

evolving mission. Presidents should make very sure that they have board support for strong decisions like these, and, finally, when it comes to institutional bond-rating agencies, make sure that you follow through in every single area in question and do what you told them you would do.[67]

Old skill: Poll cabinet for givebacks unrelated to mission.
New skill: Only spend what the new or revised mission allows.

3. *Learn the new language of money.* The new language of money is based on two principles: diversify institutional revenue streams and reduce tuition dependence by increasing gifts, grants, and contracts. James C. Hearn observes, "The central question is therefore how institutions can become more adaptable while remaining true to their essential traditions of self management and intellectual achievement. . . . The offering of degrees online, for example, involves the 'brand' of the institution in a very fundamental way. In those circumstances, institutional leaders should ask: 'Is this effort truly core to who we are and who we want to be?' "[68] He continues this thought in a related article: "Any new revenue-seeking initiative should meet criteria relating to mission, cultural, and strategic fit, substantive quality, short- and long-term financial prospects . . . [and] organizational sustainability."[69]

In this context as well, rethinking mission emerges as a key tool to address stressed conditions. Whether it is a summer-camp forensics lab for children in a residence hall or a more complex option such as franchising and licensing arrangements with third parties that carry implications for faculty compensation levels, presidents and CFOs are exploring new business models that differ considerably from those of their predecessors. In turn, institutional advancement offices are also coming under new pressures from presidents and board members. Dennis Berkey, in his third year as president of Worcester Polytechnic Institute, described this changing dynamic:

> Presidents of fragile institutions need to acknowledge that advancement has become a "contact sport" in which success is gauged directly by personal contact with donors. A more realistic way to hold advancement officers accountable is not via dollar goals, but rather by setting "deployment goals" which include an annual number of donor visits with comprehensive follow-throughs and participation in a predetermined number of alumni events. These specific, annual agreements can measurably enhance the operation of the alumni association.[70]

Old skill: Script an effective "ask."
New skill: Build a web of leverage.

4. Rethink union relationships. Presidents and CFOs of stressed colleges and universities need to reach practical agreements with faculty and staff bargaining units through nonadversarial and reasonable negotiation processes. In 1954 more than one-third of all American workers belonged to unions, but by 2002 only about 14 percent did.[71] Even though this percentage continues to drop across the nation, there are still thousands of college and university professors within this shrinking percentage, and members of those bargaining units carefully watch presidents and provosts as they accomplish their administrative agendas.

A number of presidents agreed that their effectiveness in this area is connected to how they work, or do not work, with the union membership between contract negotiations and that this sends the strongest signal that there is a real intent to build a stronger institution. Joseph McNabb, president of Laboure College, a one-hundred-year-old nursing school, believes that "the secret to successful negotiations with unions occurs between contract years. In that period, presidents need to build the trust that they can draw on later. Faculty will listen to a president's language—is it collaborative and collegial?—and, more importantly, they will judge repeatedly whether the president and chief academic officer are advocates for the faculty in the small decisions each week that may go unnoticed by many."[72]

Dennis Berkey echoes this sentiment: "The key is in how the president conducts him or herself between, not during, contract negotiations. Leaders of fragile colleges cannot afford, literally, to fail in negotiations, but it is the relationships that presidents build and nurture with the campus safety officers and carpenters, along with the faculty, that can help save a vulnerable institution when a contract must be signed."[73] One retired president candidly observed about governance woes, "The only way for organizational leaders to achieve trust and respect is by sharing information, keeping promises, apologizing when wrong . . . and avoiding surprises. Trust and respect can only be earned one person at a time, day in and day out."[74]

Old skill: Pacify and stonewall.
New skill: Co-venture.

5. Be tough with everybody. In his final year as president of George Washington University, Stephen Trachtenberg wryly observed that "American universities tend to have a full supply of wisdom and a short supply of courage" when it comes to making difficult decisions about cutting costs, overruling faculty decisions, or pushing back with trustees. In Trachtenberg's view, presidents of fragile universities need to spend less time exploring the implications and ramifications of saying no and more time simply saying it.[75]

Roy Austensen developed a plan with his president and CFO at Valparaiso in 2001 to reject an across-the-board salary increase in order to preserve a 3 percent increase in benefits that was specifically aimed at retaining greater numbers of lower-paying employees at their current levels in the benefits program.[76] Joseph McNabb developed a ten-year plan at Laboure in which long-term health-plan options were capped and the most expensive plans were reserved for present employees and were no longer offered to new staff and faculty.[77]

On the issue of tough decision making, John Sperling, billionaire founder of the for-profit University of Phoenix, bluntly states, "It doesn't make a goddamn bit of difference what people think of me. If I weren't immune to criticism, it would have been impossible to create and protect the University of Phoenix from hostility and legal assaults."[78] Nevertheless, the chief executive officers of some fragile institutions may find that bluster is not as effective as balancing their budgets for two or three years in succession when challenged by an angry faculty senate or a confrontational board committee. Whatever the context, however, it is likely that many of these campus leaders will have to say no much more in the second half of their careers. Trachtenberg summarizes, "Remember to get love from your spouse and children; get respect from your colleagues and adversaries."[79]

Old skill: Be firm while managing decline.
New skill: Be tougher and cut more to save the core.

6. *Recruit trustees unabashedly.* Chief executives who interpret the new skill of recruiting trustees as one in which "the president comes to dominate the selection of new trustees, ending up with a board that is beholden to the president and not disposed to challenge presidential judgment," misjudge its meaning and value.[80] Attempting to find friends who are willing to contribute significant funds to the college and to join its board is an old, relatively transparent skill still cultivated by hundreds, if not thousands, of presidents and advancement officers. Daniel J. Levin, former vice president of the Association of Governing Boards of Universities and Colleges and contributor of the third chapter in this book, explains, "Presidents have always wanted to recruit their own boards, but a delicate balance needs to be maintained so that there is not the perception or the reality that the president has the board in her or his 'hip pocket,' so to speak."[81]

The point is that presidents must identify courageous trustees who will support them rather than recruit friendly trustees who will routinely agree with them. The difference is that friendly trustees, as they always have done, will essentially govern by default—defaulting to what the president wants and to what their colleagues think. Courageous trustees understand that their role is less to challenge the president than to co-venture with him or her in addressing at-risk circumstances. Presidents must still accept that some discussions with board members will be difficult, but as long as courage is valued over friendship, they should recruit new trustees aggressively and unapologetically. Stephen Trachtenberg summarizes, "Presidents need three things from their trustees: money, wisdom, and courage . . . particularly at vulnerable institutions. However, of the three, trustees most need to be courageous."[82]

Old skill: Be candid with the board.
New skill: Think like a trustee.

7. Transform the cabinet. As much as the presidents of fragile colleges and universities critically need their cabinets to continue to improve as administrators, many of the crisis-management skills now necessary at these institutions cannot be learned at a two-day conference or summer retreat: "Real change must be ongoing, systemic, and personal and must align, lead, and engage the workforce."[83] Rosabeth Moss Kanter explains that success "stems from a great deal of consistent hard work to perfect each detail. It is even a little mundane. Win, go back to work, win again."[84]

However, for cabinet members at an institution that is resource poor and slipping downward, a quiet afternoon off-campus or a Saturday morning with the members of a key board committee may be all that is possible and all that can be afforded. In such circumstances presidents will need to develop not only courageous administrators but also accurate forecasters who can process large amounts of data quickly and negotiate often-difficult solutions while leveraging doubt and fear.

Old skill: Encourage consensus.
New skill: Work with doubt and fear.

8. Get ahead of students. Contemporary student life remains an enigma to the senior leadership of many institutions. For two decades or more, presidents and trustees have complained that although the federal government collects a great deal of information from higher education institutions, "policy makers . . . and taxpayers continue to lack key information to enable them to make informed decisions."[85] Reaching this shifting core of learners has become a complex challenge for the busy administrators who are managing at-risk institutions. To begin, "Today's prospective students just don't buy marketing messages delivered on glossy brochures. . . . They rely on their peers' opinions and recommendations on music, movies, and education. And, according to the . . . Pew Internet & American Life Project, 2005, 38 percent of all teens who are online say they read blogs."[86]

A sizable percentage of college administrators might have never seen or participated in a blog until they read a now widely disseminated 2006 article from *Inside Higher Education* titled "The Blog That Ate a Presidency" about troubles and transitions at the State University of New York (SUNY) at Alfred.[87] That article, as much as any other in recent years, caused an entire cross section of professors and administrators to appreciate the power of blogging and to grasp how the rules of engagement for current undergraduates have been revised. The leaders of most institutions, fragile or otherwise, realize that to stay ahead of their incoming classes they need to learn much more about the structure, content, and controls of Facebook, MySpace, and YouTube because these web enterprises offer the real connections and authenticity so highly valued by incoming classes.

Finally, to the extent that these institutions are dedicated to developing lifetime customer relationships with their alumni, they need to expand their faith-based programming and support services. In the wake of the 9/11 terrorist attacks, a continuing war in Iraq, and hostilities in countries such as Lebanon and Israel, many students are turning inward and, according a major study released in 2005 by the Higher Education Research Institute at UCLA, "consider themselves to be on a spiritual quest . . . and . . . find spiritual expression by drawing from the practices and beliefs of several faiths."[88] Learning how to speak to cohorts of students who consider themselves spiritual but not religious is a skill that older presidents and provosts may not have been trained for but that they have come to accept as a primary element in their approach to contemporary student life.

Old skill: Follow student trends.
New skill: Shape lifelong customers.

9. *Define an institutional moment.* Although the development of an effective and lasting brand remains elusive for the majority of American higher education institutions, it is impossible for almost all stressed colleges and universities. Even Standard and Poor's bond-rating agency

has begun to edge toward discussions of brand amid its dry language of fiscal ratios, as noted in a 2005 report: "Standard & Poor's evaluates an institution's demand in the context of a school's niche and the current higher education environment. Demographic trends, the popularity of particular types of programs, and the existence of competing institutions also are incorporated into the rating process."[89] One college counselor lamented in a *U.S. News & World Report* annual college issue, "We've just become so brand conscious—'If I haven't heard of it, it can't be any good.'"[90]

The good news for middle- and lower-tier institutions is that a rising percentage of students appear to be self-selecting out of the race for places at Princeton, Duke, and Wellesley in order to apply to institutions, sometimes far from elite in status, that have developed an individual program that stands out in the field they have chosen as a career. In response, the leaders of some fragile colleges have grasped that within an increasingly competitive marketplace there are still niches to be claimed and that, short of a true brand, these niches can provide much institutional focus and dynamism.

Sometimes a single event can reposition an institution for a generation or more. Higher education marketing specialists can still recall how Boston College transitioned from the status of a local choice focusing on commuters to that of a national top-tier university within a few years after quarterback Doug Flutie connected with Gerard Phelan on a dramatic forty-eight-yard pass with six seconds left to win a 1984 Orange Bowl football game over the University of Miami, 47–45. The following year Boston College's undergraduate admissions spiked upward, and the college has never looked back. In 2006 Boston College was christened one of twenty-five "New Ivies" by *Newsweek*.[91]

In 1998 Valparaiso University made it to the Sweet Sixteen of the National Collegiate Athletic Association's men's basketball tournament. The coach's son was one of the stars of the team. The story of this underrated, plucky program, led by a father-son duo, captured national attention and sympathy well beyond the tournament and even into a second season. Provost Roy Austensen credits these moments in the spotlight as the springboard Valparaiso used not to boost its sports programs but rather to highlight the academic strength and vitality of its mission and curriculum. Emphasizing small-college intimacy within a major university setting and letting its students speak for themselves to the degree possible, Valparaiso also has never looked back at its earlier days as a regional choice among many competitors.[92]

Vulnerable universities and colleges rarely field nationally prominent sports teams, but this skill transcends sports. It involves seizing a moment, often a moment that was not foreseen, and leveraging it boldly into new attention and immediate support for one's institution. Sometimes these moments come only once in a career, and one needs the clarity to realize that this is so and to seize the moment's inherent opportunities without hesitating.

Old skill: Hire a consultant to develop institutional brand.
New skill: Define an institutional moment and leverage it.

10. Exploit new media. For decades the *Chronicle of Higher Education* has presided over the American higher education environment. From our conversations principally with presidents, trustees, provosts, and chief finance officers over the four years spent developing this book, it became clear that at least two more publications are vying for higher education reader trust and loyalty: *Inside Higher Education* and *University Business.* Both journals maintain healthy presences on the World Wide Web; in fact, *Inside Higher Education* is a wholly web-based review. Although both publications are not averse to covering the Ivy League, their stories reflect a continuing interest in the several thousand American colleges and universities that are not ranked highly and do not play football on television but still have long histories and stories worth telling.

At the same time, administrators of institutions at risk can no longer wait patiently for new media to find them. If they do, their first appearance may be negative and beyond their control, as illustrated by SUNY Alfred's profile in "The Blog That Ate a Presidency." Whatever the original motivations behind these new technologies, current students are seeking them out and using them more naturally and readily than the older channels of communication universities still struggle to provide. The editor of the "Weblogs in Higher Education" blog explains, "The faculty may be active, publishing research and innovating in the classroom, but the department webpage often goes unchanged for weeks or months. Multi-million dollar segments of the institution appear to be frozen in time."[93]

Beyond this focus on potentially expensive advances in technology, however, there remain several other forms of under-leveraged, low-tech media that institutions can also exploit at much lower prices. Jim Hightower describes one: "As I've learned from the past dozen years of on-air experience, radio can be a very democratic little box—in part because it's ubiquitous."[94] Also still undiscovered by many higher education marketers are small-market television stations and perhaps the best and least costly investment of all, highway billboards, multiple sites of which can be bundled into one sale-price purchase at slower periods during the advertising year. Overall, this skill is finally that provosts and presidents demonstrate a personal involvement in and understanding of the majority of new media and then actually use one or more in direct support of their students.

Old skill: Write an article for the *Chronicle of Higher Education.*
New skill: Broker articles for new media and new audiences.

Conclusion: Difficult Decisions for Survival

Taken as a group, these ten skills require difficult decision making by presidents and provosts, in particular. Calls to "be tougher and cut more to save the core" or "work with doubt and fear" do not convey the familiar forms of collegiality that many in American higher education can still recall. Yet by 2010 more than 40 percent of the U.S. workforce will reach traditional retirement age, and workers between fifty-five and sixty-four will increase 51 percent to 25 million people.[95] In this transition many familiar ways of thinking about—and leading—higher education institutions will depart with those 25 million individuals. Additionally, although the path to the presidency is still often through the provost's office, colleges and universities are increasingly choosing their presidents from corporate settings.

As greater numbers of these business-trained presidents share campuses with younger, more entrepreneurial faculty members frustrated by the pace of change in an aging, slow-moving culture, decisions will be shaped by new, more competitive principles and will be delivered more swiftly. Yet, as Charles M. Vest, former president of Massachusetts Institute of Technology, cautions, "collaboration may be even more profoundly important than competition in determining the future of higher education. Indeed informal global cooperation is already beginning to create the meta-university that will see the best scholarship and teaching shared worldwide."[96] Thus no matter how many of the indicators on this chapter's at-risk checklist a university or college may demonstrate, in the end a compassionate but clear-eyed approach to budgets and to the people behind them will be critical for survival.

CHAPTER TWO

An International Perspective on the Fragility of Higher Education Institutions and Systems

D. Bruce Johnstone

Fragility, at least of the financial kind, which is arguably the source of all kinds of fragility, is the normal, or default, condition of both institutions and systems of higher education.[1] This chapter will examine some similarities and differences in financial fragility in the United States and in other countries of the world, as well as some similarities and differences in the causes of and appropriate policy strategies in response to financial fragility.

It is true that some institutions and some systems (or the collectivities of public institutions in some countries) are more financially fragile than others, and a few institutions—notably a handful of heavily endowed elite American private colleges and universities—are exceptionally financially robust, but there is some fragility to the financial status of almost all other institutions throughout the world. Even some very well-endowed institutions are having to pare expenses and struggling to maintain revenues, although great wealth gives an institution ways to absorb financial difficulties caused by temporary shortfalls in revenue or unanticipated surges in expenditures without jeopardizing the fundamental mission or character of the institution. The truly at-risk college or university, by contrast, is the institution or, in a macro sense, the higher education system of a state or country that is constantly on the edge of having to compromise its chosen mission or fundamental institutional character because of the inability to consistently raise enough revenue or shed enough expenditures, year after year, to maintain that mission and character.

Financial fragility is the default condition of most colleges and universities in the world not because of pervasive worldwide mismanagement nor because the governments of the world do not care enough about their institutions of higher education, whether public or private. Rather, the fundamental cause is a natural trajectory of costs, or necessary expenditures, that tends in most years and in most countries to outpace the natural trajectory of revenues for institutions and even more for systems. In short, the underlying tendency toward financial fragility

—applies to public and private institutions alike, although the underlying reasons for the shortfalls in revenues for private and public institutions are fundamentally different;

—applies to public institutions and to public systems or to the institutions of entire countries, although some of the solutions at least theoretically available to some public institutions—such as downsizing, shedding high-cost programs, or attracting a more socioeconomically elite population able to pay higher tuition fees—are almost certainly politically unavailable to entire public systems;

—applies to higher-cost research universities, both elite and nonelite, as well as to lower-cost nonresearch, shorter-cycle colleges, also both elite and nonelite, although the vulnerabilities, as well as the solutions, differ considerably;

—is not fundamentally caused by poor management of colleges and universities, although many are poorly managed;

—is not caused by poverty of a country or a state or a province, although poverty clearly exacerbates financial fragility, and wealth gives opportunities for more thoughtful changes and long-term solutions; and

—is dynamic; that is, it is not a function of costs and revenues being out of balance at a point in time, as in a bad year, when revenues may fall short or when there can be unanticipated surges in expenditures, but rather is due to the long-run, natural trajectory of costs exceeding the long-run, natural trajectory of revenues.

A Caveat about International Comparisons

Looking at macro trends even in a single country is treacherous, and the practice is even more so in an international perspective.[2] In the first place, it is necessary to suppress the temptation to perceive what one mainly wishes were happening as actually happening: the all-too-familiar conflation of a generally agreed-upon reform agenda with a reasonable prediction of what will actually be, or the tendency to view as *trends* such seemingly worldwide developments as increased privatization, institutional autonomy, sector diversification, or a diminishing correlation between one's higher education attainment and the circumstances of one's birth simply because these are on the reform agendas of political leaders, governments, and parastatal organizations throughout the world. In short, the fact that most observers want these things to happen and the fact that many political and institutional leaders say that they are happening still do not make them actually happen at all, especially not in extensive and lasting ways.

The second danger in a depiction of international trends in higher education is the tendency to see things through a cultural lens and thus to see similarity and even convergence where reality is much more complex and full of subtle but profound differences. For example, I have been watching for years, with fascination, the halting and deeply contested steps throughout Europe toward a tuition fee: part of a shift in the costs of higher education from an overwhelming reliance on the public taxpayer to costs that are shared.[3] But shared with whom? In the American context a tuition fee rests on the bedrock assumption of an expected parental contribution, at least to the limit of what can reasonably be expected through a common, verifiable test of family financial means or need. However, what we in the United States too often fail to recognize is the peculiarity, especially to a Scandinavian, of the assumption that a college or university undergraduate student should be treated as a financially dependent child rather than the young adult that the Swedes consider him or her to be. The cost of university instruction in Scandinavia is assumed to the responsibility of the state, and the parent's role is finished with the high taxes. Cost sharing to the Swedes, then, does not mean parents facing a tuition bill but students facing the quite considerable costs of living with assistance neither from the government nor from their parents but rather from student loans. This is a little different from the situation in Germany, where the costs of instruction are still thought to be the responsibility of the state, but the costs of student living are assumed to be the financial responsibility of the parent, just as in the United States, with the added encouragement that the German child can take his or her parents to family court if they do not provide this expected support.

There are other differences, both legal and cultural. University students in continental Europe are generally a year or two older than the traditional college-age American student. In many countries they have earned a legal or even a constitutional right to university admission by virtue of their academic high-school diploma: no SATs, college applications, "safe schools," or anxious waits by the mailbox in mid-April.

The Australians have further obscured the financial responsibilities of parents and students by pioneering the device of charging a tuition fee that will never be seen nor even consciously paid for by most students or parents, but will be withheld (with interest) from the students' paychecks after completion, deducted by their employer along with the deductions for income taxes, health insurance, and pension contributions.[4] The Scots have adopted a similar system, and the English (with Wales and Northern Ireland not far behind) are in the process of making this transition, replacing the former United Kingdom tuition fee—which has always been detested by the politically active student leadership and their faculty and parliamentary allies on the far political left—with an additional student debt burden. It is puzzling that a non-means-tested additional loan can be more politically palatable than the means-tested tuition fee it will replace.[5] The point is simply that a system of higher education with underlying costs very similar to the American research university is still embedded in a cultural and political context. The notion that parents are financially responsible for some of the costs of their children's higher education, at least through the undergraduate degree and at least to the extent of their measured ability to pay—which is viewed by Americans as entirely appropriate and equitable—is not necessarily accepted by other countries that Americans believe in most respects to be "just like us."

The Rising Trajectory of Unit Costs

The underlying financial fragility of colleges and universities is due to the naturally diverging trajectories—that is, the tendencies over time—of per-student costs and available revenues. The upward trajectory of institutional unit, or per-student, costs is a function of two main factors.[6] The first is the labor intensity of the enterprise, both of teaching and of scholarship. As a consequence, unit costs in colleges and universities tend to track wages and salaries, essentially unrelieved by the steady substitution of capital for labor and/or by the outsourcing of production to regions or countries with lower wages, lower taxes, and fewer regulations that characterizes the more productive, capital-intensive, goods-producing sectors of the world economy. This is the phenomenon first identified in the economics literature by William Baumol and William Bowen as characteristic of the so-called productivity-immune sectors of the economy, such as live theater, symphony orchestras, social welfare agencies, and education.[7] Because workers in such enterprises, for example, faculty, typically get the same wage and salary increases, at least on average, as those in the capital-intensive sectors of the economy, in which lower labor costs via addi-

tional capital or outsourcing produce real productivity gains and allow
unit-cost increases to be less than compensation increases, the unit-
cost increases in the labor-intensive, productivity-immune service sectors will inevitably exceed those in the capital-intensive, productivity-
receptive, goods-producing sectors. Thus the unit-cost increases in higher
education will, in most years and in most countries, be above average.
Since the rate of inflation in any country is nothing more than a
weighted average of many price increases, it is inevitable that unit
costs in higher education will rise in normal years faster than the rate
of inflation.

Furthermore, if some of these costs are borne by tuition fees, then
these tuition fees must also keep up with the unit-cost increase and
rise faster than the rate of inflation. If the share borne by the government does not keep up, then the tuition fee must rise even faster—
considerably above the underlying rate of inflation—in order to cover
both the tuition's share of the cost increase and the missing governmental share of the increase. It is important to note that these cost and
tuition increases are being incurred even under assumptions of no increases in enrollment, no new expenditures, and no new academic programs that cannot be fully funded by cuts in existing programs—any
of which, if present, will raise the costs and the prices, that is, the tuition fees, even further.

The Perverse Effect of Technology on Higher
Education's Unit Costs

Critics of higher education's rising costs say that this presumed im-
munity from productivity is not immutable and that the application of
new instructional technologies in teaching and learning—multiway distance learning via the Internet, for example, or video- and computer-
assisted self-paced learning—could yield productivity advances if the
professoriate would but allow their introduction. There is some truth to
the view that faculty all over the world, especially in the more elite institutions, are notoriously resistant to acknowledging that their teaching
ought to be made more efficient, or that money is scarce, or that cuts in
faculty or academic programs must occasionally be made. However,
the barriers to higher education cost savings from technology reflect
more than a stubborn, Luddite opposition to technology. Indeed, faculty in the United States and in other advanced industrial nations where
Internet connectivity is most accessible are voracious users of computers, the Internet, and technologically assisted instruction, but the dominant pressure is not to do what has always been done more cheaply, but
to do these traditional academic tasks better with technology. Since

producing considerably more, whether of teaching, learning, scholarship, or service, for only a little more cost is clearly an increase in productivity, there can be little doubt that technology has already increased the productivity of higher education institutions throughout the world, and that this productivity increase can be expected to go on for the foreseeable future; but with few exceptions, technology has still made colleges and universities more, not less, costly.

Market Pressures, Unit Costs, and Rising Prices

The unit-cost increases caused by technology in higher education illustrate the second factor that underlies the inflation of unit costs: the pressure of the market. Far from being complacent, as their critics sometimes claim, higher education leaders are perpetually dissatisfied with its share of the market and its relative prestige ranking. At the same time, the academic profession as a whole, frequently for very different reasons, is also constantly looking for greater scholarly recognition, breakthroughs in research, better ways to teach, and new academic programs. It may be true that this collective faculty drive for improvement is sometimes self-aggrandizing and shows insufficient regard for the good of the institution, and it is not clear that society is necessarily better served by universities all struggling to displace one another on some putative prestige ladder with little or no sensitivity to the public opportunity costs of this quest. Nevertheless, this market-driven drive for betterment—for higher rankings, greater scholarly prestige, a deeper applicant pool, and a greater market share of top students and research contracts—is a major reason that the elite of America's colleges and universities are the envy of the academic world. At the same time, this market-driven competition also drives up top faculty and administrative salaries, the institutionally borne costs of research, and the expensive amenities that attract the most sought-after students (and their parents), and it thus contributes to the steep upward trajectory of higher education costs and to the continuing financial fragility of U.S. colleges and universities.

Of course, market pressures can be a force for lowering costs as well, as markets tend to do in most of the goods-producing sectors of the world economy. Increasing attention to costs and prices can have similar effects in some colleges and universities, at least serving to moderate unit-cost and tuition increases to levels closer to, or even below, the prevailing rate of inflation. Colleges and universities can always cut unit costs when they absolutely must by such techniques as freezing or even lowering faculty and staff compensation, substituting part-time faculty, generally at very low wages, not replenishing library and equipment budgets, or forcing a kind of artificial productivity simply by increasing teaching loads and class sizes. Most of these examples, however, simply yield a cheaper higher education, not necessarily a more productive one. This has been the case throughout the world where public college and university budgets have simply been cut because of the collapse of national economies or of taxing capacities, or where private college and university budgets have had to be cut similarly simply because of insufficient demand.

However, the more likely effect of market pressures on colleges and universities with any semblance of selectivity is to drive costs upward, not downward. This is especially true wherever demand considerably outstrips capacity, where the heavily subsidized price does not begin to cover costs, and where the effective demand is tuition price inelastic. In this way the strong and relatively inelastic demand on the part of most students and parents for the most selective college possible complements the inclinations of the faculty and most academic leaders to provide "more and better," largely without regard to the opportunity costs of these betterments. Thus the college or university will, at least if it is able, provide compensation increases to its faculty and staff even as it consumes more costly inputs such as computing power, library resources, sophisticated scientific and telecommunications equipment, scholarships to assure the best class, space, and especially the best faculty that can be lured from other universities or from outside the academy. Its unit costs will rise in what the faculty and the institutional leaders will genuinely believe to be a proper and even a noble quest for a better product, as well as what the market is demanding.[8]

Rising Enrollments and Cost Pressures on Countries or Systems

As if the nearly inexorable pressure on unit, or per-student, costs was not enough of a problem for institutions of higher education, these cost pressures are magnified at the level of the country or higher education system by increasing enrollment pressures, that is, rising numbers of potential students academically prepared for and desiring to enter a college or university, set against the need for sufficient system capacity and enough families who have the personal financial resources to afford the requisite tuition fees and costs of student living. In the United States and most of the rest of the highly industrialized, high-income countries, increasing enrollment pressures translate to enrollments because there is assumed to be sufficient affordable capacity. Much of the low-income world, however, suffers from insufficient affordable capacity, leaving some students academically prepared but unable to find a place in any affordable public college or university.

Increasing enrollment pressures are a function of four principal phenomena:

1. Increases in the size of the traditional college- and university-going age cohort, that is, the basic demographics of the country, modified—as in the United States and the other major English-speaking higher education systems—by substantial net higher education exporting.[9]

2. Increases in the proportion of this traditional cohort seeking entry into institutions of higher education.

3. Increases in the numbers of college and university participants who are beyond the traditional college-going age but are desirous of and prepared for entry into a tertiary institution.

4. Increases in the number of years (or, more accurately, the number of courses taken) of the average college and university stay.

The basic "enrollment drivers" are the first two listed here: an expanding participation rate of an underlying expanding age cohort. But these two drivers can be accelerated by expanding lengths of stay and still further accelerated by the addition of adults who bypassed higher education participation when they were young. The effect of all these forces on higher education system costs, particularly in low- and middle-income countries with historically high birthrates and historically low participation rates, can be explosive when the naturally increasing trajectory of per-student costs is greatly accelerated by increasing percentages of an increasing population seeking entry to a limited number of higher education institutions.

All these forces have at least theoretical limits. The most basic limit is demographic, the birthrate itself, and birthrates have been declining in much of Western Europe, Russia, and Japan. Participation rates, too, would seem to have a natural limit, although it is hard to conceive of the limit being reached while there are still—as there are in virtually all countries—participation disparities that are associated with socioeconomic class, gender, ethnicity, or language. Yet the acceleration of participation in countries where secondary school is virtually universal and for which financial assistance removes at least most of the financial disincentives to college or university attendance will assuredly slow and, in combination with flat or declining birthrates, can conceivably actually lead to slightly falling college and university enrollments, as may well be the case in Japan, Russia, and some Western European countries Still, in most of the world high birthrates are combining with increasing higher education participation rates to create increasing enrollment pressures.

The increasing level and amount of higher education of by the average student also contributes to enrollment growth even with no increase in the actual number of students, but this source of growth also has limits. The accretion of courses and degrees is a function both of the increasing amount and complexity of knowledge and of the tendency of professions to enhance their status and control competition by requiring more education before entry. A very different sort of multiplier effect—that is, creating additional enrollments from the same number of students—can be observed in countries, such as the United States, that have been experiencing very high rates of attrition or wastage but are seriously engaged in efforts to lessen attrition or to improve persistence. The result is to increase effective enrollment from the same number of entering students.

The Faltering Trajectories of Revenues

We have been examining the phenomenon of rising higher education costs: per-student, or unit, costs in the case of individual institutions, magnified by the additional costs of enrollment increases in the case of higher education systems or entire countries. The other half of the story of pervasive higher education fragility in most years and in most countries is the faltering trajectories of higher education revenue.

For example, at the level of the institution rather than the country or the multicampus system, the upward pressure on unit costs does not mean that all college and university budgets will rise accordingly. In fact, only the most fortunate will be able to find the increased revenue, year after year, to meet these pressures. Others will find the increased revenue, mainly from the state or from tuition or from both, only in some years. In other years these institutions will compensate either by reducing the trajectory of costs—for example, freezing positions, freezing compensation, or simply deferring expenditures—or replacing missing revenue from borrowing or drawing on reserves (i.e., internal borrowing).

The revenues from which naturally increasing higher education costs are paid, whether in a single institution or in a system, come from five sources:

1. Government, or taxpayers,[10] via public budgets

2. Students, via their share of any tuition and fees, financed by part-time employment, by loans, or by savings

3. Parents, via their share of tuition and fees

4. Philanthropists or donors, through current giving or returns on past giving in the form of endowment

5. Purchasers of university goods or services, via research grants, training fees, facilities rental, or the purchase of medical or other clinical services

Revenue from these five sources, together or at least on average, must increase in step with the natural increase in total higher education costs. In what follows, we consider the limits on these various revenue sources for colleges and universities and the ways that they create stressed institutions.

Governments and Taxpayers

Governments everywhere struggle under escalating burdens of pensions and other social welfare costs. Electorates in the highly industrialized countries have been getting more conservative, particularly in their distaste for taxation and government spending. Most Western European countries, with their high social welfare costs and typically spending from one-third to more than one-half of national gross domestic product in the public sector, are trying to shift productive resources to the private sector and to reduce public deficits to comply with the requirements of the European Community and the Euro Zone. Russia, the rest of the countries that have emerged from the former Soviet Union, and the former Communist countries of Central and Eastern Europe all labor under the enormous costs of building an internationally competitive productive infrastructure and weaning a labor force away from its deeply rooted dependence on state enterprises and governmental employment. The United States struggles with an overconsuming, undersaving population that is unwilling to tax itself for the public benefits it demands.

Finally, governments everywhere are contending with politically and socially competing needs for increasingly scarce public dollars. In the United States these may be health care, pensions, elementary and secondary education, or, in recent years, the hugely expensive wars in Iraq and Afghanistan and the seemingly endless war against international terrorism. In the economically and politically transitional worlds in Russia and the other countries that are emerging from the former Soviet Union, the competitors for scarce public revenue include the replacement of decrepit public infrastructure, unfunded pension obligations, the need for a workable social safety net, and the cost of re-

Results of Financial Fragility in Colleges and Universities

The underlying financial fragility of colleges and universities is due to the naturally diverging trajectories of their per-student costs and available revenues. This divergence, also observable in colleges and universities throughout the world, is a function mainly of the labor intensity of the enterprise, both of teaching and of scholarship, compounded by the inclinations of faculty and many academic leaders to provide "more and better," compounded further by the tendency of technology to increase rather than decrease unit costs. These trends have produced these results in higher education systems around the world.

- Slowing the upward trajectory of faculty and staff wages, salaries, and benefits
- Raising tuition and fees
- Turning to philanthropy
- For country systems, encouraging a growing private sector
- For leaders of U.S. public institutions that are financially fragile, insisting on obtaining and then using managerial flexibility to maintain enrollments but also to trim programs and costs
- For leaders of U.S. private institutions that are financially fragile, finding a market niche, being prepared to shed faculty and staff that are peripheral, and not lightly underselling the product with excessive price discounting

versing generations of environmental degradation. In sub-Saharan Africa the competition for the extremely scarce public dollar is truly formidable and includes, in addition to the needs just listed, public health, elementary and secondary education, and assistance to a badly faltering economy. As a result, although the government will continue in the developing world to be the principal revenue source for public higher education, most or even all of whatever limited additional revenue can be squeezed out of the public treasuries will be absorbed by the need to accommodate the inevitably expanding higher education enrollments, leaving little or nothing to accommodate the rising unit, or per-student, costs of the existing university faculty, staff, and facilities.

The problem with public revenue in the United States is faltering state tax revenue, which, unlike federal revenue, cannot be supplemented by deficits, at least not for state operations, and which faces voracious and politically powerful competitors such as elementary and secondary education, Medicare and Medicaid, and corrections. In much of the U.S. South, Southwest, and West, the public systems of higher education are facing severe enrollment pressures stemming from demographics and in-migration on top of increasing public college and university unit-cost trajectories. Still another competitor for already-limited public revenue in the United States is the persistent calls on state and federal levels for tax cuts. These calls—in spite of the fact that the U.S. average tax burden is lighter than in almost any other more highly industrialized country—are in part a reflection of the swing toward political conservatism in the United States that began in the mid-1990s. Along with calls for tax cuts and smaller public sectors in general, the 1980s and 1990s also saw increasing voter skepticism about public higher education and an increasing disinclination to continue annual budget increases at rates above the rate of inflation.

An additional factor in the political vulnerability of public higher education in the United States is the fact that a U.S. multicampus public system is one of the larger items in the typical state operating budget, but the system frequently lacks the passionate political affection associated, for example, with a state flagship university or with state assistance to local schools and so presents a vulnerable target in time of state fiscal stress. That is, a single entry in the annual budget of a state college or university system can carry an effective cut of millions or tens of millions of dollars. Additionally, state multicampus systems have been seeking and generally receiving greater expenditure autonomy, that is, the ability to allocate and reallocate whatever money they ultimately get from the state governor and legislature.

In the end, although state tax revenues will continue in the United States, as in other countries, to be the most important single source of public college and university revenue to cover the costs of instruction, they are a source that will, in most years, fail to keep pace with higher education's rising cost pressures and will therefore require supplementation from nontax sources or expenditure cuts.

Students

The student as a revenue source for a share of the costs of higher education requires accessible part-time jobs for young people or generally available student loans.[11] A student loan program with a substantial recovery rate that includes minimal subsidization and low defaults gives young persons the ability to invest in their own futures and can provide revenue to higher education that, in the absence of borrowing, would presumably not be there at all. With the worldwide spread of cost sharing stemming from the increasing inability of governments and taxpayers to assume all the costs of higher education, the ability of students to bear a portion of these costs but to defer actual payment until they are out of the university and earning income enables participation levels that might be impossible in the absence of borrowing while also providing a third source of revenue to supplement contributions from governments and parents.

There is a large literature on student loan programs.[12] In the context of this chapter, the purpose of which is to document the financial fragility of higher education worldwide, student loans are both an essential and a problematic source of revenue. They are essential because they can at least potentially provide much-needed supplementary revenue for the institutions, as well as for students' living expenses, but they are problematic in their political unpopularity and unreliability in many countries as a substantial and consistent source of revenue. Their unreliability as an income source comes from three essential properties of student borrowing: a high risk of default, often matched by the absence of collateral; the inherently costly nature of small loans that require long repayment periods and high administrative expenses; and the tendency of many governments, for political purposes, to impose insufficient interest charges to cover the true initial cost of money even if defaults are contained. In fact, only the United States and Canada have sufficiently minimal subsidization and sufficiently low default rates that their student loan programs provide a substantial true recovery rate.

In short, students will almost certainly grow in importance as a source of revenue for both instructional and necessary living costs. However, a likely growing political and practical resistance to the very high debt loads that is emerging in countries like the United States, Canada, Sweden, and Japan, coupled with the political and technical difficulties that most low- and middle-income countries have in obtaining a decent recovery rate, probably means that students as a source of higher education revenues will not lessen significantly the financial fragility of colleges and universities worldwide. In the United States, as an example, where the student share of higher education instructional costs is arguably the highest of any country in the world, continuing high debt loads and the broad extent of part- and full-time student employment are nearing a breaking point at which undergraduates will not be able to absorb a significant additional share of higher education's rising instructional costs.

Parents

The effectiveness of parents as a revenue source for college and university expenditures varies by country, partly according to prevailing levels of personal income but also because of culture and tradition, often enshrined in framework laws or even in constitutions that either permit, constrain, or forbid the charging of tuition fees.[13] Within some of the world's high-income and highly industrialized countries it is assumed that parents have an obligation to contribute to the higher education expenses of their children, including both necessary living expenses and whatever portion of underlying instructional costs are to be borne by tuition fees. However, tuition fees are significant only in North America and Japan and to a lesser degree in a few European countries, while officially expected parental contributions toward the underlying costs of instruction are still very low or even nonexistent in most of Europe. In Germany and France parents are expected to cover only food and lodging costs; in Scandinavia they are officially responsible for neither the costs of instruction nor the costs of student living, which are borne by the students themselves via loans. Higher education is still supposed to be free in Russia and most of the newly independent states of the former Soviet Union, as well as the formerly Communist countries of Central and Eastern Europe. However, because of insufficient tax revenue, as well as intensely competing demands for the little revenue that exists, governments in these countries have found a loophole, the dual-tuition policy, through which a limited number of spaces designated as "government sponsored," or tuition free, are allocated by competitive entrance exams and the rest of the spaces are opened to fee-paying or privately sponsored students. This policy permits the government still to claim that it is complying with the law and providing higher education free of charge.[14]

Even in the United States, where parents are used to bearing a heavy cost for their dependent children's undergraduate degrees, the costs of student living are already in the range of $10,000 to $12,000 a year for students who live away from home, before any tuition or fees, leaving limited capacity in most families for any substantially increased parental contributions, particularly among families of middle, lower-middle, and lower socioeconomic status. The inability of these individuals to meet the rising costs of higher education and the accompanying losses in access and affordability play overlooked but discernible roles in the creation of many at-risk colleges and universities.

Other Revenue Sources

In countries that are suffering from faltering revenues of governments or taxpayers and that are also finding little reliable fiscal relief from tuition fees, it is tempting to try to close the revenue gap through the sale of university services and products by seeking corporations, foundations, and government agencies that will purchase research through grants and contracts, or individuals and insurance companies that will purchase medical services and hospital care, or individuals and corporations that will purchase special training in return for tuition fees. These sources in the wealthy countries account for considerable revenue, particularly for larger research universities, and especially for those with academic medical centers. Yet where such volume of revenues is forthcoming, universities that earn these revenues are also incurring enormous additional costs from the activities that generate these revenues. Moreover, it is not clear that these entrepreneurial activities can generate enough of the additional revenue that is needed to help cover the escalating costs of those parts of the university that do not bring in much, if any, of their own nongovernmental revenue.

Philanthropy, although of enormous importance to many private and public U.S. colleges and universities, requires not only great wealth and favorable tax laws but also a tradition and, more important, a culture of giving that is simply not present in most other countries of the world, especially countries in which higher education has long been thought to be the fiscal responsibility of governments and taxpayers.[15] Thus all revenue sources other than government are seriously constrained. Although cost sharing (i.e., the shift of the higher education cost burden increasingly to parents and students), as well as philanthropy and the entrepreneurial activities of colleges and universities, is on the increase in almost all countries, the worldwide trajectory of higher education revenues for individual institutions, multicampus systems, and most national higher education ministries is likely to remain barely sufficient and more frequently insufficient to overcome the powerful drivers of rising per-student costs and expanding enrollments, thus creating fragile circumstances for thousands of colleges and universities, even innovative ones.

Governmental Policies and Financial Fragility: A Dark Horizon

The financial effect of system- or countrywide enrollment pressures on public colleges and universities depends mainly on the degree to which increasing enrollments will also bring increasing revenues—either from FTE (full-time equivalent)-driven budgets or tuition fees—sufficient to cover at least all the additional, or marginal, operating costs of the additional enrollments.[16] From an international perspective this relationship between increasing enrollments and increasing net revenue to public institutions depends on two political decisions of the relevant government: to charge or to increase—or to allow the public college or university itself to charge or to increase—a tuition fee sufficient to cover the marginal costs of expanded enrollments, or to increase the underlying tax-originated revenue to the operating instructional budget more or less proportionally to the increase in enrollments. The underlying default condition of financial fragility of public higher education throughout the world as outlined in this chapter is due to one or more of the following governmental actions or inactions with respect to the connection between expanding enrollments and revenue:

—Failure to increase governmental revenues in proportion to the underlying per-student and/or total institutional cost increase of the expanding enrollment

—Failure of governments to allow institutions to charge a tuition fee at all (e.g., in most of Europe, Africa, and much of the former Communist world) or to allow a tuition-fee increase commensurate with the legitimately underlying cost increases

—Allowing a tuition increase but decreasing the governmental appropriations commensurately

—Insistence by governments that institutional enrollments be increased even in the absence of the requisite additional resources to accommodate them, for example, in continental European universities.

The impact of governments on the financial condition of public colleges and universities is not limited to the effect on trajectories of revenue. Governments can also be responsible both for some of the cost pressures and some of the constraints on the ability of the college or university to deal in the most effective fashion with a cost-revenue squeeze. For example, the ability of the college or university administration to shed staff in low-priority areas is limited not merely by the traditional academic tradition of tenure but frequently by far more restrictive laws of civil service type that guarantee job security to all staff, academic and nonacademic, even without the extensive probationary periods and rigorous selectivity common in most U.S. colleges and universities for the granting of tenure.

In sum, although a fundamental cause of the financial fragility of higher education institutions around the world is insufficient revenue from governments or taxpayers, this fragility is also worsened in many countries by governmental policies that constrain colleges and universities from helping themselves even in the face of potentially costless solutions that do not take away revenues from other appropriately higher-priority public needs.

Conclusion: Lessons for Presidents, Provosts, and Boards

This chapter has examined the endemic financial fragility of universities and colleges and universities through two lenses. The first has been an international perspective that seeks insight from an examination of the financial conditions and trends of colleges and universities elsewhere in the world. The second has been the dual perspective of the institution and the system, even if their challenges are sometimes separate ones.

Four lessons emerge from these perspectives for presidents, chief academic officers, and trustees of institutions at risk:

1. Tuition fees. A consistent stream of dependable revenue from sources other than the government is critical. Obviously, tuition fees will remain the principal source of revenue in the private sector. However, particularly in light of the faltering reliability of governmental revenue, tuition fees can be just as important in higher education's public sectors. What is most important to the maintenance of institutional financial viability is less the level of the tuition fee or even the aggregate amount of net tuition-fee revenue than that the fee be allowed to increase over time in accord with necessary and inevitably increasing costs. A tuition fee that is frozen, most often for strictly political reasons, can seriously aggravate the vulnerability of a vulnerable college or university.

2. Cost-side solutions. Although we have portrayed financial fragility as the default condition of most colleges and universities worldwide, and although we have stressed the paramount need to buttress faltering revenue trajectories and avoid painful cost-side solutions such as cutting, restructuring, and reallocation, these same solutions must remain squarely on the policy table of presidents, CFOs, and provosts. Fond hopes for increased revenues from philanthropy, sponsored research, and additional enrollments of tuition-paying undergraduates are the right aspirations, but they are also all problematic for the majority of higher education institutions. As difficult as cost-side solutions may be, the cost-revenue gap for most institutions will still need to be bridged by reallocation and selective cuts.

3. The access agenda. The agenda of widening participation and promoting higher education access among populations hitherto underrepresented requires system advocacy and oversight. In spite of the widespread American perception of the academy as liberal and politically leftist, universities worldwide tend to be highly meritocratic and frequently not well suited to provide the kind of tertiary-level education wanted and needed by most youth. Presidents, chancellors, and chief academic and student affairs officers must carry much of the responsibility to advocate for the necessary resources and to execute the appropriate policies and programs of the access agenda.

4. Institutional diversification. College and university leaders must curb the inclinations of their institutions, particularly their faculty members, to overfocus only on scholarly prestige and student selectivity. There must be room and resources for excellence in other, less costly dimensions of quality such as teaching effectiveness, student retention, community service, and continuing professional development. In summary, financial fragility may be higher education's default condition, but this does not mean that the condition is without solutions.

CHAPTER THREE

A View from Washington: Trouble Signs for At-Risk Universities and Colleges

Daniel J. Levin

One thing the national associations, think tanks, and public policy organizations in Washington, D.C., are good at is producing reports about the state of higher education and the daunting challenges the nation faces. Typically an organization receives a foundation grant and recruits a panel of high-profile, experienced academic, political, and business leaders to consider various aspects of a problem and recommend solutions. The goal invariably is to produce an influential report that proposes ways to address a "crisis," reform national policies, or transform certain aspects of higher education. Over the course of several months or a year, the organization's staff and a hired writer research and investigate the issues, often citing evidence gathered in similar efforts, to substantiate the report's findings and recommendations. At the outset the panel's august chair insists that the product of the commission or task force or committee should not be "just another report that gathers dust on a bookshelf," although a better metaphor nowadays may be "dissolves in the Internet's ether."

For the higher education community in the nation's capital—professionals who work in the numerous national associations housed in One Dupont Circle and environs, as well as officials in the U.S. Department of Education and staff members of congressional committees—scanning the report and digesting its executive summary are about all that can be expected. Increasingly it is difficult to keep up. This only slightly cynical scenario aside, these reports often contain compelling information and recommendations, and although no national commission or task force has to date directly addressed the specific challenges for at-risk colleges and universities, it is also fair to say that such reports often are highly relevant to these financially and academically struggling institutions, their students, and their professional communities.

As an example, fragile colleges and universities are constantly monitoring their competitiveness, or lack thereof, in disciplines related to science and technology. Thus many paid special attention to a 2006 report from the National Academies (the National Academy of Sciences, the National Academy of Engineering, and the Institute of Medicine), *Rising above the Gathering Storm*. Capitol Hill lawmakers had asked the National Academies to recommend "the top ten actions, in priority order, that federal policymakers could take to enhance the science and technology enterprise so that the United States can successfully compete, prosper, and be secure."[1] The National Academies created the Committee on Prospering in the Global Economy of the 21st Century, which identified two key challenges: "Creating high-quality jobs . . . and responding to the nation's need for clean, affordable, and reliable energy."[2]

American Vulnerabilities

The report of the National Academies cited a number of alarming statistics that confirmed for public policy makers the vulnerability of many of our colleges and universities:

—In South Korea 38 percent of all undergraduates receive their degrees in natural science or engineering. In France the figure is 47 percent, in China, 50 percent, and in Singapore, 67 percent. In the United States the figure is 15 percent.

—More than one-third of all doctoral degrees in the natural sciences and more than one-half of doctoral degrees in engineering in the United States are awarded to foreign-born students.

—About one-third of U.S. students intending to major in engineering switch majors before graduating.

—Almost twice as many bachelor's degrees in physics were awarded to American students in 1956 as in 2004.

Perhaps more alarming, although the challenges the report documented surely are no surprise to many presidents and provosts who are competing to attract students to their resource-challenged programs, it may be the case that a rising percentage of administrators, faculty, and trustees have begun to tune out such reports and report cards (if they ever were tuned in), even as the national conversation about stressed institutions intensifies.

One report no one seems to have missed, however, is *A Test of Leadership*, the report of the National Commission on the Future of Higher Education, more commonly known as the Spellings Commission, after U.S. Secretary of Education Margaret Spellings. Formally announced in September 2005, the nineteen-member commission was chaired by Charles Miller, a Texas investor and former chair of the state's board of regents. Over the course of a year, Miller presided over six formal public sessions in various locations around the country that attracted audiences of a hundred or more. As the process unfolded, it became clear to many observers that this was not going to be just another Washington report. Miller's sheer force of personality and will ensured that the report would be noticed. Commission member Robert Zemsky, in perhaps the most revealing account of the panel's work, wrote, "No one really knew whether higher education's products were any good or not. What, if anything, students were learning was anybody's guess. There was no accountability. Accreditation wasn't working. No governmental body—federal, state, or local—could know if it was getting its money's worth. In an era of heightened global competition, business as usual would not suffice."[3]

As provocative as Miller wanted to be, Zemsky explained in a January 2007 *Chronicle of Higher Education* article, the Texan wanted a polite, civil discussion that recognized the real problems and suggested daring solutions. However, in Zemsky's view, a first draft of the document's preamble and findings played the "blame game" and was inflammatory. It slammed colleges and universities for the cost and quality of the product, grade inflation, and binge drinking. The process had become politicized, which is exactly what many in higher education had feared when Spellings established the commission and named Miller chair. The national dialogue commission members had sought was turning nasty, and some observers thought that their initial fears that the commission's preordained agenda was to recommend standardized national tests for baccalaureate degrees would be realized. "What was missing in the discussions of change and transformation," Zemsky asserted, "was a workable strategy for getting large numbers of colleges to do things differently. Miller would argue that he did, in fact, have a strategy, the first step of which was getting higher education's attention. The way to do that was to use what he called 'strong language,' forcefully identifying the enterprise's many flaws and broken parts—in short, a strategy of jolt and shame, or roughly the educational equivalent of shock and awe."[4]

As various advocates on the panel softened the rough edges, the tone of the final document shifted. Zemsky concluded, "Instead of a

Three Emerging Trends

- The legacy of the 2006 National Commission on the Future of Higher Education is a prodding of the higher education community to cooperate in finding ways to measure what their students have learned. Colleges and universities that can prove that their graduates have learned and improved from the time they entered to the time they graduated are more likely to succeed than those that resist this trend.
- The federal government is unwilling and unable to help solve at-risk colleges' persistent financial and strategic problems. Increased federal aid in the form of additional funding for Pell Grants is likely to be only incremental and of marginal help to tuition-dependent institutions.
- Demands for transparency with students, parents, and elected officials will continue to increase in key areas such as governançe, tuition levels, fundraising, and spending.

shot across its bow, what higher education got was a mild scolding couched in civilized language that proposed little that was new and much that was neither possible nor likely. . . . What remains to be seen is whether we had in fact begun a national dialogue leading to the transformation of American higher education."[5] To be sure, the report of the Spellings Commission, like others issued over the past few years, fairly documented higher education's shortcomings, particularly for fragile institutions without the resources or will to overcome a set of stiff new challenges. The report's recommendations, although certainly not radical, did ignite national discussion about how best to measure what students have learned and how to hold colleges and universities accountable. Such conversations had been taking place within the academic community for quite some time, but the legacy of the Spellings Commission may well be that it fomented action on ways to measure what students have learned and on accreditation reform.

Ten Challenges for At-Risk Institutions

A January 2007 report from Moody's Investors Service identified four types of institutions that were most likely to struggle in the future: (1) small private colleges with limited geographic draw, particularly those in rural areas or with small endowments; (2) private colleges with ambitious strategic plans and spending to improve national reputation; (3) regional public universities in weaker demographic areas that compete heavily with community colleges; and (4) community college districts in economically stagnant areas.[6]

"Over the long term," notes the report's executive summary, "we believe the sector faces increasing challenges that will build gradually in most cases. These challenges are related to shifts in student demand in some areas, reduced affordability, asset/liability management, federal and state support and oversight, and governance reform which will necessitate increasingly sophisticated management and governance structures."[7]

The report also identified ten key issues that will affect higher education as a whole, and vulnerable institutions even more acutely, in the future:[8]

1. *Adapting to changing student demand and preferences.* Shifting demographics will change enrollment patterns for many institutions. Some states can expect to see continued growth, while others will face certain declines. The proportion of students from low socioeconomic backgrounds is expected to grow, as is the number of nontraditional students. This will force many institutions to become more flexible and even risk-oriented in developing and delivering new programs.

2. *Determining appropriate pricing strategies and policies.* Many fragile colleges and universities will have difficulty sustaining net tuition revenues while remaining accessible and affordable. Key will be how effectively an institution can balance need-based and merit-based financial aid and the degree of tuition discounting the school believes is necessary to sustain critical enrollment levels.

3. *Improving governance and management.* As public universities and colleges face continued funding and other competitive pressures, states will need to update and define their approaches to governance. In public and private higher institutions alike, improved governance effectiveness will be essential.

4. *Increasingly complex balance-sheet management strategies.* Balancing risk and reward tolerance and determining how best to monitor institutional investments will be an increasing challenge for already-stressed institutions.

5. *Enhancing operational management.* Colleges and universities unprepared for slower revenue growth and increasing competitive pressures will need to improve their operations and focus more on where to invest their limited resources.

6. *Determining appropriate levels of operational and capital spending.* As competitive pressures continue to drive spending decisions, at-risk institutions will face major levels of new financial stress unless and until they distinguish one or more market niches for new program development and broad brand enhancement.

7. *Mission positioning.* In attempting to attract students, donors, and government funding, fragile institutions in particular will need to articulate and promote new and more distinctive missions. Most notably, struggling private colleges with high tuition will need to make an aggressive case to both parents and students that the benefits of attending their institution outweigh the cost.

8. *Shifting governmental funding.* As all colleges and universities experience volatile shifts in their levels of public support, attracting significant levels of private support will be both more competitive and more essential.

9. *Implications of increasing wealth concentration.* Only top-tier institutions will be able to continue to make substantial investments in facilities, programs, salaries, and financial aid. With few exceptions, fragile colleges and universities will need to focus much more of their resources on mission positioning and strategic spending in the coming decade.

10. *Heightened demand for transparency and questions about the sector's nonprofit status.* As these colleges and universities inevitably raise tuition levels, mount unprecedented fund-raising campaigns, and grow their endowments, pressure will increase to communicate more fully and more candidly with their students, parents, and elected officials.

Healthy colleges and universities will also need to address the implications of these issues and adapt to the challenges they pose over the coming decade, but for many stressed institutions that are straining to attract students, maintain quality, balance budgets, and plan strategically, these issues will determine whether they survive as freestanding entities.

Causes of Fragility

At a national meeting of college and university finance officers, planners, and facilities officers in 2006, Michael S. Strauss, the chief economist and chief operating officer of Commonfund, explained why

---

Three Best Practices

- Strengthen the board of trustees. An effective president who operates in partnership with the board is essential.
- Ensure the perception of academic quality. Fragile colleges cannot be excellent across the board, but a college's leadership must identify and develop academic quality in key strategic areas tied to the institution's mission.
- Maintain morale by sustaining a positive view of the institution's strengths, hopes, and expectations for success. Start a significant new initiative or project to lay the groundwork for the next success and engage all stakeholders, including local community institutions, in the planning process.

---

the rich will get richer and the poor will continue to struggle.[9] Colleges and universities with small endowments and high degrees of liquidity will be at a distinct disadvantage over the next two decades, Strauss argued. He predicted that institutions with endowments larger than $1 billion would find an average return on investment of 9.8 percent, compared with 8.4 percent for institutions with endowments between $51 million and $100 million. If these rates of return prove accurate, he said, nearly two-thirds of the better-endowed institutions will be able to provide the same level of service they do today, compared with less than half of the less well-endowed schools.

In fact, Strauss said, the investment performance of the larger endowments may be as much as 4 percentage points higher, partly because of their reduced liquidity. For example, 55 percent of the assets of the largest endowments are liquid, compared with 82 percent of the assets of the smaller endowments. The endowment levels of the increasing cohort of American colleges and universities best described as at risk, however, might as well be in the stratosphere because many of them lack the wherewithal to supplement their operating budgets with almost any additional revenues or earned income. Clearly, if access to revenues from sources other than tuition remains limited, the institution will continue to struggle.

How do presidents and chairs of fragile schools know whether their college is merely muddling through difficult circumstances or is in serious decline? The more the institution can apply indicators from its own strategic plan, the better, writes Kent John Chabotar, president of Guilford College in North Carolina.[10] Such indicators provide a rationale and consistency and allow for standardized reporting and controls. Chabotar also cautions that "small sporadic deficits are not cause for alarm, nor is a large deficit in one year—if there are sufficient reserves or endowment to cover it."[11] However, when deficits increase in consecutive years or are greater than 5 percent to 10 percent of operating revenues, then it is time to take aggressive, even intrusive, action, in his view.

John D. Sellars, appointed president of Drury College in Missouri in 2005, has analyzed the results of surveys on institutional decline he conducted in 1992 and 2002 of more than thirteen hundred senior administrators and board chairs at 132 private colleges in two articles published a decade apart in *Trusteeship* magazine.[12] As a result, he learned that some of the reasons for decline were controllable, and others were intractable. Key controllable reasons included perception of academic quality, percentage of the budget allocated to student aid, the size of the student body, and the percentage of annual revenue from gift and endowment income. Uncontrollable reasons included regional demographics and economics, age of the institution, population of the local community, and, for church-affiliated institutions, extent of church support. The strongest predictors, Sellars found, were the perception of academic quality and the size of the student body. Institutions that allocated a higher percentage of their budgets to grant aid and earned relatively higher income from gifts and endowment revenues fared better, and those with large tuition discounts proved less able to maintain high-quality academic programs and services.

An additional controllable reason for institutional decline is the quality of the governing board. In an unusually frank article published in 2003, Robert E. Lowdermilk III, president of Wood College in Mississippi, told the inside story of an institution that struggled with financial stability and a changing higher education market. The school lost its accreditation at one point and recovered by rebuilding its board over a seven-year period. Lowdermilk explained:

> The governing boards that served Wood College for much or more of the past two decades, though stocked with many capable and well-intentioned individuals, in my view were inadequately attuned to the urgent and continuing implications of financial neglect. Nor were they conversant with the relevant higher education issues affecting the college. Succession plans providing for new trustees who possessed a knowledge of and commitment to fiscal responsibility and fund-raising were inadequate. Rather than advocacy or tenacity, apathy was the mark of these boards. Inatten-

---

**The Single Most Important Piece of Advice
for a Leader of an At-Risk Institution**

- Everything you do should focus on the goal of restoring financial stability. In particular, focus on strengthening the board, adopting a strategic plan that the entire community endorses, improving academic quality, and rebranding the college.

---

tion to what I would call "the things that matter" immobilized their capacity to govern effectively. . . . It was evident that the governing board over time was neither fully equipped nor adequately motivated to ask the difficult questions and respond with answers that would ensure the institution's future. Some issues that may not have been immediately detrimental to its long-term health, but nevertheless required attention to help the institution comply with the customary operations of modern colleges, escaped the board's direct or peripheral vision. Other issues that were avoided or ignored altogether had a cumulative negative effect on the college and required substantial, if not superhuman efforts to compensate for dangerously long neglect.[13]

As president, Lowdermilk came to believe that the board was inattentive to the college's true financial picture, and he became convinced that many Wood trustees were unaware of the manner in which the institution's budget was developed and funded. Few board members asked serious questions about the budget or shortfalls in tuition, gift, and endowment income and the resultant strains on the college's fiscal stability. "Over time, board complacency became even more visible as operating deficits were disregarded as serious indicators of the college's financial position," he acknowledged. "Key issues that emerged from the results of financial audits were often overlooked, though the audits were accepted each year by the board. Rather than engage in active fund-raising and advocacy, the typical board response to budget shortfalls was to borrow to meet operational needs."[14]

To compound its problems, the college was losing students to an emergent community college system as the board hesitated to fund a systematic effort to promote the school's distinctiveness. Lowdermilk admitted that this was part of a pattern of inadequate attention on the part of trustees to the responsibilities and requirements of trusteeship. "Trustee accountability for service to the institution," he writes, "was a new idea to many board members."[15]

Things did not turn around overnight. It took several years to reconstitute the board with well-informed and committed trustees and to change members' attitudes. The board approved a profile of a "desirable" trustee, and talented individuals eventually came forward to help the college through this challenging period. Trustee giving has increased substantially, and Lowdermilk now maintains that the transformed board understands the consequences of failing to address issues of financial instability and good governance and that it has positioned itself effectively to overcome its at-risk circumstances.

Turning Things Around: Seven Steps

As candid as Lowdermilk was about the shortcomings of his board, a newly engaged, more focused group of trustees is only one element of the equation for a university or college that is struggling to achieve equilibrium. An effective president who operates in partnership with the board is also essential. Indeed, no institution that is facing financial and strategic challenges can possibly hope to improve itself if it lacks a strong and engaged leader who has earned board support. This point was driven home by the 2006 report of the Association of Governing Boards of Universities and Colleges (AGB) Task Force on the State of the Presidency in American Higher Education, which called for "leadership that links the president and governing board closely together in an environment of support, candor, and accountability."[16]

This panel of academic chief executives, trustees, and business and political leaders convened by the AGB contends that institutions that are able to attain a new style of collaborative yet decisive leadership will be best positioned to surmount the challenges that will face higher education in the next decade. Regardless of whether the vulnerable institution is a multicampus community college, a large flagship university, or a small liberal arts college, its president "must exert a presence that is purposeful and consultative, deliberative yet decisive, and capable of course corrections as new challenges emerge," according to the task force's report. "Integral leadership succeeds in fulfilling the multiple, disparate strands of presidential responsibility and conceives of these responsibilities as parts of a coherent whole. Leadership of this sort links the president, the faculty, and the board together in a well-functioning partnership."[17]

Although the task force's report was meant to offer inspiration to presidents and board members, perhaps its greater value over the long term is in its practical suggestions. Similarly, John Sellars summarized his decade of research on institutional fragility and seven steps to reverse it:[18]

What Presidents Should Do Differently

- The public policy debates in the nation's capital should not preoccupy presidents of fragile institutions. Ten minutes a morning with the online editions of the *Chronicle of Higher Education* or insidehighered.com should be sufficient to stay abreast of important developments.

---

1. Strengthen the board of trustees and increase volunteer involvement. During periods of vulnerability the board must look more deeply at how it operates. Does it evaluate its own policies at least once per year and assign at least four members to assess the board's specific outcomes?

2. Ensure the perception of academic quality. It is impossible for fragile colleges and universities to be excellent across the board, but it is also essential to identify niche program areas and develop academic quality in all of them. Establishing a demand for such programs enables the institution to sustain a higher net tuition price, attract better faculty and more qualified students, raise more funds, and even attract a share of research dollars. Of course, expanded marketing of academic program niches is also a necessity for prospective students to learn about the institution's evolving mission.

3. Decentralize decision making. When the ideas of vice presidents and deans dominate the way the college operates, this dominance can curtail needed innovation, decrease the trust of the faculty, and increase resistance to change. Additionally, communication channels may become restricted, participation may decrease, and those leaders become vulnerable as scapegoats. Decentralized decision making encourages an institution's flexibility and enhances its ability to address at-risk circumstances.

4. Maintain morale. To stem employee turnover, leaders must find ways to retain talented faculty and staff by including them in decision making, communicating more openly with them, involving them in strategic planning, and rewarding commitment, achievement, and improvement.

5. Broaden the resource base. Leaders must diversify the resource base by building deeper, more active relationships with alumni, governmental units, corporations, and foundations. Doing so provides opportunities to enhance fund-raising, provide ancillary educational programs, and attract larger grants and contracts for services that, in turn, broaden the institution's resource base.

6. *Plan strategically.* Vulnerable colleges and universities need to assess changing student and employer preferences more effectively in order to adapt program choices and stabilize institutional revenues. Including a wide range of campus constituents in an authentic strategic planning process fosters a greater sense of shared mission and encourages candid discussion of emerging trends and their implications for the institution.

7. *Prioritize spending cuts.* Declining resources can produce destructive internal competition for annual budget allocations. Avoiding across-the-board cuts and reallocating resources to new programs and growth areas are crucial for institutional vitality. Discontinuing programs that are academically or financially weak and not mission driven, although always complex for the faculty and the chief academic officer, allows a fragile community to enhance the academic quality of its remaining programs. In working through this process, it is key to understand the specific revenue level each academic program generates annually, as well as all the specific costs of operating that program.

In closing, unfortunately, campus leaders should remain wary of the adage "I'm from Washington, and I'm here to help you." Sadly, presidents, board chairs, provosts, and faculty members who are working diligently to sustain their institutions had better come to grips with that classic Big Lie because no one from Washington is coming to help.

II

Analyzing Risk via the Leadership Team: New Approaches, New Results

There was the general experience of lots of small cuts in the budget that may not have made a major difference individually, but when viewed together conveyed a sense of loss across the institution. In retrospect, I would say, ask more questions, no matter what your position at the institution. Be more aggressive about getting information directly when concerns arise, and do not be afraid to be candid with your community, even when the news is negative.

> —Jason Terry, former assistant professor of art at Mount Senario College, Wisconsin, in a telephone interview with James Martin, 30 May 2007

We were not interested in expanding but in maximizing the space we did have, and to demonstrate that we were serious about making the most of what we had. We went to a seven-day schedule and started a weekend college. We converted the president's office to a classroom, and I worked out of a storage closet.

> —Will Austin, president of Warren County Community College, New Jersey, in a telephone interview with James Martin and James E. Samels, 18 July 2007

CHAPTER FOUR

Leading Stressed Institutions: What Works and What Does Not

Charles R. Middleton

The novelist Henry Fielding, observing life through his character Squire Allworthy in the novel *Tom Jones, a Foundling*, and U.S. House of Representatives Speaker Thomas P. "Tip" O'Neill, from Massachusetts, seemingly had little in common. Both, however, knew that all politics are local and that influence and ability to achieve the results that leaders seek are grounded in effective local engagement. For university presidents, the corollary is clear: the effectiveness of a presidency and a president's ability to move the institution depend in the first instance on how well the president leads the leaders. This imperative is most pronounced in stressed institutions, where the pace and intensity of change, and thus success, are directly proportional to the president's personal involvement in setting new directions across numerous areas of activity.

Much has been written on presidential leadership.[1] The focus of this literature, however, is largely on strategic decision making, legislative relations, dealing with various constituencies such as the faculty or alumni, and similar global topics. This chapter is concerned primarily with the internal dynamics of presidential leadership at a fragile college or university. It focuses on the importance of developing and then leading a cabinet of campus leaders whose successes individually will contribute to the attainment of overall institutional well-being and progress. The president also has to provide leadership, as appropriate, to the board, but that is a matter covered in chapter 5 by William Weary in this book, and I will make only focused observations on it in this chapter in the context of issues that affect the leadership team, cabinet, or executive council, as that body is variously described. As a disclaimer, no example given here relates exclusively to any individual or institution, and all examples have been selected for the purpose of providing insight into an issue under discussion via their general applicability and, where pertinent, their at-risk factors.

The Cabinet: Who Are These People and Why Are They Here?

The period between the formal announcement of a new president's appointment and his or her arrival on campus includes opportunities in person, electronically, and by phone to interact with key community members, but the challenge of building an effective leadership team begins in earnest when presidents convene their first cabinet meeting, which usually occurs during the first few days of a presidency. Those who would advise new presidents, and they are many, are uniformly of the opinion that decisions on who should remain on the leadership team and who should be asked to step down, particularly in fragile circumstances, are best taken quickly. This means that these decisions must be guided largely by what others have observed about individual performance and ability, supplemented in part by the new president's initial reactions based on personal, although limited, and random discussions in the interim period.

An extreme application of this principle occurs, sometimes driven by financial circumstances, when a new president asks for the resignation of the whole cabinet of the past president and then selectively either reappoints some among them or allows all to continue in office but keeps the resignation letters on hand for future use. This practice is, in my view, unnecessarily disruptive and a clumsy way to make clear the obvious, namely, that the new president wants his or her own team and holds the authority to create it. Worse, it also puts on edge all other administrative leaders in the institution, especially academic deans and directors of major divisions in finance and student affairs, and has the side effect of focusing these key leaders on their own professional futures precisely at the moment when the institution most needs them to be working collaboratively to address common issues.

Then there is the matter of what kind of leadership style the new president wants to convey. Most first-time presidents, perhaps remembering what it felt like when they were dean or vice president and a new president arrived on campus, prefer to follow a slower approach. They consider that it is better to give incumbents the opportunity to adjust to the new direction of the institution and to commit to its future as envisioned by the new president than to assume that they will be unable or unwilling to do so. On balance this is an effective way to proceed, and most often the advice of the experts is set aside. Overall, by giving senior colleagues from the previous administration an opportunity to adjust to changed circumstances, the new president conveys to the institution as a whole a commitment to treat people fairly and to give them an opportunity to contribute to the future of the institution before making changes. When that proves to be too generous a decision in individual cases, or when the institution's budget may be constrained by fragile conditions, departures occur in a context that nearly everyone understands is essential for the benefit of the college or university.

Contemporary cabinets typically include all individuals whose presence is necessary to ensure that institutional deliberations are comprehensive, such as all vice presidents and all those whose work directly connects to the president, such as chief of staff, college or university counsel, and the public relations officer. Perhaps the most important factor, however, and one that is especially important at fragile colleges and universities, is how closely the new president must be involved in making decisions about the future. The greater the involvement, the larger the cabinet must be and the greater the challenge of building an effective leadership team becomes. Over time the size of the cabinet can shrink, but initially it is advisable to be as inclusive as necessary to establish the presidential writ over all activities that really matter if the institution is to prosper.

Performance Evaluations at Fragile Institutions: Who Goes, Who Stays, and Why?

Few things are more certain in the life of a higher education institution than the fact that the leadership team will evolve over time. Sometimes the changes come fairly quickly, sometimes more slowly. Strategies vary on how to proceed, but in my experience, gradual evolution has been preferable to dramatic change because at stressed institutions it takes time for a new president to assess fully the issues that the institution faces and to determine how they are interrelated. The first year, indeed, may be largely given over to this assessment and to weighing what is learned against what was revealed during the interview process. The establishment of a deeper understanding than any superficial examination of the issues may entail is essential, and new presidents are often surprised to find that things are not as portrayed in the interview process, and where they are different, they are not for the better. These observations, of course, are based on the assumption that no crisis, such as a major budget shortfall, materializes. If it does, then immediate and sometimes-dramatic personnel changes become essential, but if there is a more orderly progression of affairs, new presidents are well advised to learn the rhythms of their campuses and to assess cabinet-level leadership as part of that learning process.

Three Best Practices

- Effective presidential leadership at stressed institutions depends on thoughtful creation of a senior leadership team to work directly with the president on developing strategic initiatives and then leading their implementation.
- Presidents should be purposeful in building the leadership team, taking care to retain senior officers from the previous administration in continuing or new roles where feasible while not hesitating to hire new talent where change is necessary to ensure success.
- Assuring diversity within the leadership team is an essential ingredient of long-term success because it provides the best assurance that multiple perspectives will be achieved.

The first component of this assessment is to decide whether the managerial skills of the incumbents in key areas of expertise are sufficient to enable them to lead the forthcoming changes competently. When I arrived at Roosevelt University in 2002, I thought it best to be explicit about this expectation, and I immediately proceeded to evaluate the incumbent vice presidents against a standard of competence that was benchmarked against performance by similarly situated leaders I admired in previous institutions in which I had served. The leadership principle is that all members of the cabinet must perform their duties as leaders in their own division in at least a competent manner. Since the definition of competence will expand under the new president as her or his agenda begins to be implemented, this is a baseline judgment that must be made in the initial months by any president.

Three outcomes emerge with regard to continuing vice-presidential appointments. Whatever the outcome in particular cases, these colleagues deserve professional respect, and even when they are being asked to vacate their position, they should be permitted to leave with dignity.

First option: Replacement. The first option for leadership development in a fragile environment is replacement of inherited incumbents. Assessment of performance and potential growth in the context of changing circumstances is particularly critical for the positions of provost or chief academic officer (CAO) and the vice president for finance or chief financial officer (CFO). Others in particular circumstances, such as the vice president for enrollment services if enrollments are declining, could be equally critical, but as a general rule the CAO and the CFO especially must share the values and aspirations of the president if the campus is to be well led internally and fragile financial conditions, in particular, are to be resolved.

Less clear in these circumstances is that often the president must make a comparative decision regarding which of these officers, all of whom were appointed by the previous president, to retain and which to replace. Replacing both at once or at the same time can be unwise because vacancies and the ensuing interim appointments in both positions may deprive the college or university of too much high-level experience and breadth of understanding. The continuation of at least one incumbent while searching for a replacement for the other usually provides for a more orderly transition. It also gives the continuing appointee time to grow into the new order of things if she or he can.

It is hardly surprising that since the majority of presidents are still selected from people with academic leadership experience, changes in provosts are, in my experience, more likely than changes in financial officers, rightly or wrongly. The primary reason is clear: a president can backstop more easily in an area in which he or she has held the position. Nonacademics may prefer to retain the CAO, whose knowledge of the academic rhythms of the institution will be difficult to replace. Presidential management of a significant portfolio through an interim appointee may well be one of the stabilizing ingredients that underlies emergence from fragility.

An additional oddity in higher education practice can sometimes occur: a CAO who was an unsuccessful candidate for the presidency may elect to stay on. Despite some examples of successful transitions, in my view, this does not work, at least for long. A quick departure back to the faculty or assistance from the new president in the CAO's search for a position elsewhere is wise. In the latter case the institution may lose an able leader, but the fit may have been wrong for the new leader, and the former CAO's career will also be enhanced in the process.

Second option: Transfer to a new position. A second option for leadership change is moving individuals into new positions. In these cases the president's assessment is that incumbents will be better suited for other assignments. Sometimes the ground for change is prepared by sending the incumbent to participate in a national leadership program either for few weeks or for an academic year. These "assignments" broaden the knowledge of talented individuals who can then be reassigned to new or alternative portfolios of responsibility after they return to campus. This practice expedites change in the organization while taking advantage of the knowledge that continuing employees can bring to new tasks. It should be used sparingly and usually not in filling the most senior management positions, which are better filled via national searches if the college can afford them.

Third option: Leave in place. The third option, and usually the preferred one, is to leave an individual in place. Searches for new leadership are expensive and fraught with uncertainty, particularly for fragile, resource-poor institutions. Anyone who has ever served on a search committee realizes that pools of applicants are often far shallower than the numbers of applicants would suggest, especially today when baby-boom retirees are expected to outnumber qualified replacements in all levels of university management and leadership.[2] Experienced presidents also all know from experience that candidates who look really wonderful on paper too often disappoint in person once the interview process is under way. I once sat on a search committee whose top candidate for a dean's position arrived for the intake interview of a two-day visit not only disheveled but disorganized in thought and speech. What was supposed to be a largely ceremonial beginning of the process quickly disintegrated into a series of short answers to broad questions as we sought unsuccessfully to create a solid foundation for the events to follow. Word spreads quickly on campuses, and in this case the attendance at subsequent public sessions was far less than expected as people avoided the pain of having to sit through interviews that clearly were going nowhere.

Presidents know these truths better than most, and this explains in part why in every institutional category—private to public, two- to four-year, single campus to multicampus systems—there is always a core of individuals who serve from administration to administration. What may not be as well understood but is certainly observed in all contexts is that some continuing appointees are there precisely because they are skilled in adjusting to new initiatives. Many who have served at multiple institutions over the course of a career most likely recall numerous colleagues who epitomize these characteristics and are still in place years later.

Managerial Competence and Strategic Engagement on Vulnerable Campuses

At a fragile university or college it is extremely important that every incumbent, from department chairs to deans and up to vice presidents, be able both to demonstrate an understanding of the current strategic directions of the institution and to set aside local interests to support the broader purposes of that plan. Deans must ask chairs to work together as a group to assure the overall success of the plan even though that success may well play out differently for various, sometimes-competing, departments. Provosts and vice presidents must similarly ask their deans and directors to set aside or at least delay implementation of local priorities in support of broader possibilities. The most effective leaders avoid setting goals that privilege one set of units or activities on a permanent basis, but there are always occasions, learned about in the early administrative assignments of every president, when advantage in the short run falls to some over others. A key example occurs annually at many institutions when a dean authorizes faculty searches in some departments and not in others.

In stressed institutional environments vice presidents must be able to grasp the broad picture of their institution and put aside turf struggles because it is not only appropriate but essential for the president to expect that all his or her cabinet members will both understand and help sustain the broader strategic directions of the institution. This is such a critical responsibility that it deserves more thorough and public discussion on campuses than it frequently receives. To begin, in recruiting or retaining vice presidents, presidents must devise effective ways to discuss with candidates and incumbents alike their views on the essential purposes of the academy. These conversations are not only interesting but are also critical for two reasons. First, they enable a president to gauge the extent to which competent managers understand how their divisions both contribute to and are dependent on successes found elsewhere in the institution. Second, they reveal the extent to which each vice president will be able to contribute to the conceptual thinking that is shaping the strategic direction of the institution.

Two examples suffice to demonstrate the point: One long-serving CFO is a wizard at financial management and has balanced the budget annually despite the annual occurrence of uncertain revenue streams coupled with the vigorous pursuit of an ambitious agenda for change led by a highly successful president. This CFO's technical ability to manage investments and monitor expenditures has long impressed everyone on campus, including the incumbent president and his predecessor. In cabinet deliberations, however, rarely does this individual comment, and then only to worry about how to fund some of the ideas that others put forth.

A CFO at a different institution faces similar challenges and has attained the same successes. He is also seen on campus as a "financial type" who keeps a free-spending president's imaginative agenda under control, but in reality, in cabinet deliberations this individual is one of the most thoughtful discussants in every strategic debate, using financial

---

"From Survival to Recovery to Renewal": Tulane University's Response to Hurricane Katrina

Scott S. Cowen, Cynthia Cherrey, and Yvette Jones

On 27 August 2005, the day on which more than 1,700 students and their families arrived at Tulane University to start their fall semester, the university was in "full hurricane mode," even though twelve hours earlier this had seemed inconceivable because Hurricane Katrina, then bound for the Florida Panhandle, was not perceived as a major threat to university operations.[3] Unfortunately, the storm rapidly changed its direction, and it was soon to hit Greater New Orleans with enough force to become one of the most destructive hurricanes in the nation's history.

President Scott S. Cowen and his senior leadership team decided to allow students to check into their residence halls before evacuating the campus on more than sixty buses to the Jackson State University gymnasium in Jackson, Mississippi. With an immediate plan established, Cowen, a few key administrators, and essential buildings and grounds personnel stayed behind as the rest of the institution left the area. The rest of the story, as written by members of the Tulane community and the national media, is history: By Tuesday, 30 August, 50 percent of the campus was submerged, and the administrators then living in the Reily Student Recreation Center had no power, no water or sewer pressure, and no communications. Cell-phone text messaging was the only way, they discovered, for them to speak with family members and the university community.[4]

---

information to buttress the conceptual arguments in favor of critical programmatic development. Both of these individuals remain secure in their positions, and both of their presidents report great satisfaction with their performance as financial advisors and managers, but as each approaches retirement, only the president who works with the second individual worries about finding a replacement.

Vulnerable institutions often retain cabinets that fall short of the ideal advocated in this section. These institutions often include examples in which standards were not met, with predictable results. Notwithstanding exceptions, however, the ideal remains. Given the importance of cabinet discussions in shaping the strategic directions, and sometimes the survival plans, of a fragile campus or a system, the ultimate effectiveness of those deliberations depends on having more rather than fewer members of the group contribute ideas. Although the

---

"From Survival to Recovery to Renewal": Tulane University's Response to Hurricane Katrina *(cont'd)*

President Scott S. Cowen, Cynthia Cherrey, Tulane's chief student affairs officer, and Yvette Jones, the university's senior vice president for external affairs, offered these leadership lessons from the storm in a 2006 interview with James Martin and James E. Samels:

> We have learned over time that you cannot become a great dean or president until you reach the point at which you do not care whether you are one or not. It is the nature of things to compromise, to cut corners, or to try to, but there comes at time when one simply must stand up and say: This is the way we should do it. One must develop an incredibly thick skin, but at times like this, presidents must do the right thing regardless of what the consequences may be personally.
>
> Many leaders become afraid to make decisions because of the consequences. By the time we get to these positions in life, we have proven ourselves many times. This does not mean that one should refuse advice, but one also cannot become immobilized. There is a balance one needs to achieve, and one way to achieve it is in hiring and surrounding oneself with the kind of people who will not be afraid, in the right moment, to tell a leader he or she is wrong. Good leaders need to be surrounded by good leaders.
>
> Finally, it is critical to make the necessary changes to the organization before a crisis occurs. Organizational strengths and weaknesses are amplified during a crisis. In fact, during a crisis these shortcomings can become magnified and create additional obstacles.[5]

---

president in the final analysis must articulate these initiatives, they are refined and strengthened by the give-and-take that takes place at the cabinet level. These discussions help the president sharpen the options to be presented for community-wide debate. Broad participation by the leadership team is essential for the success of fragile institutions.

Shaping the New Leadership Team: Difficult Choices

One of the lessons new presidents must learn, and sometimes the hard way, is that it takes more time to put together an effective cabinet than one might expect. The assessment of the inherited leadership is the easier part, and although it may take a while to make changes, most presidents early on determine where opportunity to do so lies and where it does not.

What cannot be hurried, however, cannot be hurried, nor do even the current deliberative processes always lead to success. It is said that nature abhors a vacuum. So, too, do academic communities. Most of all, presidents are eager to find new leadership so that they can get on with developing the broader purposes of their presidency. When I was at the University System of Maryland, I once overheard one regent say to another regent that it was always his practice in business to terminate quickly and to hire slowly and that he could not understand why the university followed any other principle. As noted earlier, presidents often get it wrong, terminating slowly and hiring at a glacial pace. Slowness of deliberation is a hallmark of our work. In my own efforts to help Roosevelt trustees understand this better, I rhetorically ask, "Why do something in two months when it can perfectly well be done in six or seven?"

Under these circumstances one might think that success inevitably follows, but experience teaches otherwise. In the law there is the concept of the mistrial. It might well have a useful analogue in higher education, the missearch. One mark of presidential leadership is the capacity to be patient, and nowhere is this ability more needed than in restarting a search when merely acceptable candidates remain at the end of a year-long process. At vulnerable colleges and universities with little resources to spend, this can be a particularly acute problem. Sometimes presidents have to settle, of course, because the managerial imperative to fill a position outweighs all other considerations, but when that is not so, and particularly in senior appointments such as CAO, conducting a second search can be preferable if one takes the long view.

Still, this takes time, and presidents are very often in a hurry, so they settle for whomever they can get rather than holding out for the candidate they desire. Although this might occasionally be satisfactory at stronger institutions, in at-risk environments it often contributes directly to leadership problems. Thus waiting a second semester or even a second year for the prospect of an optimal candidate seems the preferable option if it can be taken, although it will slow the full development of the leadership team.

Presidents of fragile universities most likely inherit organizational structures that are less than optimal for the emerging needs of their institutions. All administrative arrangements are historical artifacts at some level. They reflect ongoing and common divisions, as well as local peculiarities that are explainable only if one knows the history of the office or the comparative power of previous administrators. No president can escape the historical administrative residue of her or his predecessors, and the chief executive officer must grasp these past developments as fully as possible if successful change is to occur, a point

---

Three Emerging Trends

- Presidents appointed to positions at stressed institutions must plan on spending a greater percentage of their time in the first few years than they may have anticipated dealing with internal management issues.
- There is a growing shortage of highly qualified individuals to fill senior positions that is compounded by the uncertainties of working for at-risk institutions. As a result, presidents will need to take more time to develop less experienced individuals.
- At-risk institutions require longer commitments from their presidents.

---

that the distinguished librarian of Congress Daniel Boorstin once reinforced when he "said that trying to plan for the future without a sense of the past is like trying to plant cut flowers."[6]

Two Reorganization Models

Two major models of reorganization need to be considered. The first is caused by the creation of new divisions to bring into the president's inner circle a leader in an operational area critical to the institution's future direction. Such an area may have been located in a vice-presidential division or even outsourced and managed through contracts, such as information technology (IT). In at-risk institutions, bringing IT in-house and recruiting a vice president to lead the area reflects the president's understanding that this resource must be more strategically allocated in support of all institutional areas. The appointment of a cabinet-level officer in IT who reports directly to the president increases the likelihood of this and also signals to the institutional community the importance that the president places on the uses of technology to support and often drive institutional change. Finally, it places the technology budget closer to the president, where it can be more carefully monitored and managed.

A second source of reorganization is more difficult to implement and involves carving out of a current vice president's portfolio an area that normally might not be worthy of direct presidential leadership. The imperatives of fragile institutions, however, sometimes elevate areas that normally function quite well as part of a larger division to separate status. At Roosevelt, where our human resources (HR) functions needed significant upgrades and state-of-the-art implementation, the retirement of the director of human resources who reported to the

---

Single Most Important Piece of Advice

- Tackle the most critical challenges first, build some success, and never underestimate the power of continuity.

CFO gave me an opportunity to hire a vice president with years of experience to lead an institution-wide rethinking of how better to use human capital in support of attaining our goals.

Presidential decisions to reorganize also sometimes involve transferring these subunits from one vice-presidential area to another. When this transfer is done, usually it is to the CAO. In these cases, however, the overarching presidential goal may be to create a strong provost model so that internal management of the institution unambiguously lies with that officer, thus freeing the president to focus on external needs. In other cases, and especially in fragile institutions where the functions of the transferred unit are closely related to the specific work of the president, the transfer can be to another vice president. At Roosevelt the reassignment of the Marketing Department, which had been very successful in the narrowly focused tasks of enrollment management, to a broader Office of University Communications led by a vice president who works directly with me on government and community relations issues has opened up new possibilities for greater strategic use of this resource for broader university purposes.

On other occasions, the issue may be nothing more than rationalization of a historical anomaly such as moving the public relations office from institutional advancement to government and community relations. Again, whatever the specific operational area, the creation of a new cabinet-level leadership position signals the enhanced importance of that area to institutional strategic success. A corollary benefit sometimes also arises out of these reorganizational options. The proposed changes, helpfully discussed in advance with the vice president who will no longer have responsibility for the area, can lead to revealing responses. In my experience, some vice presidents will work to help the president make the transition and even encourage it; others will resist the inevitable. These discussions, therefore, are another opportunity to gauge how well one's senior leaders understand the importance of collaboration and their commitment to a common goal as a measure of leadership performance.

The One Thing I Would Do Differently

■ Assess the abilities of the senior team members inherited from one's predecessor and make changes more expeditiously.

Moving Forward: Challenges for the Cabinet

Finally, the day comes when the new cabinet meets and all present realize that they are there because the president has completed assembly of the new leadership team. In well-functioning institutions this could take two years; at stressed institutions, however, as much as new leadership may be crucial, the new team-building process can take even longer because of constrained resources, failed searches, and other uncertainties. As well, the new cabinet may now be larger than its predecessor and more diverse.

Typically, new cabinet members will bring a variety of divergent views and experiences, a difference of generations, and, increasingly, experience from outside higher education in corporate settings. The reality is that tough as it is to assemble a diverse group of able managers, forging them into a cohesive team is even more challenging. Effective presidents, even at vulnerable institutions, come to realize at some point that one of their greatest challenges is to lead the leaders. Presidential leadership begins in the cabinet room. Precisely at the moment when the president realizes that all of the colleagues at the table are his or her appointees comes the moment when the work of making the collective more than the sum of its parts begins, and this work may be more idiosyncratic than building the team initially was.

Nevertheless, certain patterns will emerge. Foremost among them will be those cases in which the CAO, and occasionally the CFO, facilitate team building. How extensive a role these two individuals play often depends on the confidence of the president in their ability to do so and the president's willingness to unite confidence with authority by allowing them to make some decisions without consultation with the president. Even so, the president may be at work behind the scenes, regularly consulting with the CAO, sharing ideas, mapping out strategies, and weighing options about major issues. Even in these circumstances the president will be more present than he or she appears to be, but less personal time will be required, which will free her or him to focus on CEO matters such as board relations and major donors.

In some instances at a college or university at risk, this delegation may not be fully possible. Faculty members often look to engage the president personally, especially on issues for which institutional change is both imperative and nerve-wracking. In these fragile environments the personal involvement of the president can be critical for several reasons. Hands-on presidential management of some matters may be essential if fundamental changes in the institution's direction are to be initiated and even sustained. Strengthening vulnerable institutions requires significant, bold change in the termination of outdated practices and the creation of new ones, sometimes with declining or depleted resources. Therefore, although other senior leaders can and should manage the details of these changes, presidents must remain active on stressed campuses in articulating both the strategic goals that are driving them and the advantages that will accrue when they are made. Effective presidents also lead the board forward in this context through close collaboration with the chair, senior trustees, and trustee committee chairs. Board understanding of the major strategic drivers and of the speed of change even on small, resource-poor campuses today can facilitate the work of a new cabinet more than its members may initially realize.

Finally, as a clear indication that the new cabinet is working effectively as a team, the president openly relies on these colleagues for some of the most imaginative ideas to shape the institution's future. Savvy presidents realize that although many of their ideas early on may emanate from a careful reading of sources and conversations with presidential peers, once the cabinet is set, more and more reliance can and should be placed on its creative solutions.

CHAPTER FIVE

Fragile Universities and Colleges: The Role of the Board

William A. Weary

The role of the board, always critical to long-term institutional health, assumes even greater importance for fragile universities and colleges in each institutional category nationally. "Fragility" can be defined in many ways; one, perhaps somewhat jokingly, is "one mistake away from bankruptcy." Although standard measures tend to be financial—such as endowment and operating expenses, discount rate, and dependence on tuition—many others figure significantly as well, including the structure and function of the board. Good analysis also recognizes that institutions may be fragile in only one or a small number of areas and may also move in and out of those varieties of fragility over time.

Consider some of the possible forms of fragility:

—Funding is inadequate for needs in program, compensation, facilities, technology, staffing, and enrolling the students the institution most desires. Serious compromises occur at every step of the way.

—For a number of possible reasons—such as program quality and reputation, relevance of programs to student interests, location, image, or facilities—the competition is overwhelmingly strong and the institution comparatively weak.

—The administration is dysfunctional and working in silos.

—Internal governance structures and procedures cannot or will not respond to necessary change or reach timely decisions.

—The board presents some combination of imprisonment in trivia and domination by a chair determined to "run this university like a business."

—The institution has been unable to define its distinctiveness and create a brand.

—The institution has allowed potential ties to its external community—major donors, friends, alumni, local leaders, legislators and politicians, and former members of the board—to atrophy and individual members to become distant or alienated.

—Affiliated constituent groups, such as an alumni association and foundation, advance their own agendas and work independently of the institution and its duly constituted authorities.

—Actions of the board and the president have so damaged governance and the presidency as to gut their clout. No one and everyone is in charge.

—For any number of reasons, public perceptions of the institution have become so negative as to encourage legislators, politicians, and donors to withdraw their moral support and reduce funding.

—There is a scandal.[1]

For the board to play its role constructively, strengthen the administration, defend the institution, and help lift it from vulnerability, a wide range of approaches is required. In this chapter those approaches that are helpful at the moment a board fully recognizes its institution's weakness—or as the institution enters a crisis—precede a more generalized set of remedies capable of preventing fragility in the first place.[2]

Most institutions, at one moment or another, descend into fragility, however briefly and perhaps in only a few areas. Even highly prestigious universities display at-risk behaviors when no one within can or will speak to the work the university intends to perform or the agreed-upon roles of the board, the president, and colleges in advancing it. Others prove surprisingly healthy in the face of exceptional pressures, speaking clearly about their challenges, addressing their issues, and continuing to hold their heads high.

Turning Things Around: Thirteen Steps

1. Prepare, review, and use a code of conduct for members of the board. A code of conduct for members of the board makes clear just what their responsibilities are and how to behave in the face of queries and concerns. A well-written code not only allows members to tell others about their responsibilities but also makes possible board correction of wayward individual members. The document is best made available on the institution's website, handed out to prospective members, and discussed with any public appointing body (such as the governor's office). In orientation sessions new members review the document carefully and receive instruction in how to listen without comment, refer individuals to the chair and/or president, and express solid support for the institution.[3]

Such counsel in how to respond to concerns also can figure within meetings of the board—as politically advisable—along with background materials to provide concerned outsiders with a broader and probably more accurate perspective than those that appear in the media and circulate as gossip.

2. Make sure that there is a clear and fact-filled "message" about the institution and that structures are in place to communicate it internally and externally, with the board playing its part. Forthright disclosure of the institution's challenges and accomplishments is one of the keys to increased confidence and lowered anxieties. The regular press coverage of Tulane University after Hurricane Katrina has been a model of such honesty.[4] Each member of the board must be able to speak the same truths and even to know the same truths. Of course, these truths also must figure on the website, in regular press releases, in statements from leadership, and in careful communication to all of the institution's constituents. A strong and effective communications office is not only rare but also essential.

3. Identify the specific authorities upon which the board may have to rely in the months and years to come. Advance and shared knowledge must exist with respect to the following issues:

—The exact authority of the executive committee, the board chair, the president, and the vice presidents and other administrators; what the executive committee may do and not do on its own; what requires full board approval; and what authority the board has over vice presidents.

—The precise legal relationship of the institution to any sponsoring or affiliated body, whether government, church, alumni association, foundation, bargaining unit, or other entity.

—The president's contract: How long does it run? When must it be renewed if it is to be renewed? What does it require of each party? What escape clauses for both parties exist within it? What are the potential costs of different decisions?

—The board's right to terminate an individual's membership and/ or censor him or her; also, the board's ability to remove officers and the procedure for doing so.

—The definition of "financial exigency" and the policy on who declares it and under what circumstances.

—Existing policies and annual declarations of conflict of interest (sometimes now also called mutuality of interest).[5]

—Policies and their implementation with respect to IRS regulations on compensation ("intermediate sanctions") whose violation exposes board members of independent institutions to potentially significant financial risks.[6] Do appropriate policies exist? Has a peer group been assembled? Are there policies for presidential assessment, and have they been implemented?

—How the board assesses the president's performance and its own.[7] In associated fashion, what the board and president have agreed the president's and board's jobs each year will be and toward what ends.

4. Assess the institution's basic fiscal condition. At least five pieces of information are required:

1. A reliable cash-flow analysis for the coming year. All action depends upon the results. Projections of "nose just above the water" too often, for fragile institutions, become "nose frequently under the water," since every institution, and especially a fragile one, encounters unexpected difficulties on a regular basis.

2. That portion of the endowment over which the board has control.[8]

3. The institution's total indebtedness, terms of repayment, carrying costs, dates of any balloon payments, formally available credit, and probable bonding limit.

4. Any bond covenants that require annual contributions of specified sums or ratios.

5. The names of board members and institutional friends capable of underwriting debt, if necessary, and at what sums.

5. Charge a committee on governance with a quick review of best practices. Check obvious resources on governance for signs of egregious structure and/or function or evidence that could be used against the in-

---

**Three Best Practices for Board Members of Fragile
Universities and Colleges**

- Keep board meetings focused on the big issues.
- Hold annual planning retreats with the president and key administrators.
- Insist on a powerful governance committee.

---

stitution by its "antagonists."[9] Read through a series of several current books and articles and check for relevance. What changes appear to be advisable or even necessary? What would a harsh critic seize upon as evidence of board malfeasance?

6. Schedule a retreat of board and administration to assess the institution's recent history, current situation, and future prospects and to set board and presidential goals for the year ahead. An external facilitator skilled in work with the academy spends several days in interviews of constituents, makes a preliminary report to the board, and both designs and facilitates the retreat. Designed to generate a shared understanding of the institution's circumstances and an overview of the board's structure and function, the retreat concludes with a list of tasks the institution must address over the year or years to come.

An initial retreat should be followed by one for the entire administration and then by one(s) for faculty, students, alumni, and the broader community. The basis of a strategic plan lies within their shared results. Such retreats, conducted under the board's leadership each year and with an external facilitator every several years, build sound habits of internal exchange of views to address major issues, keep them in the forefront, and focus upon the vision.

7. Establish and use a network of influential friends and potential friends of the institution. With a group of board leaders, identify a group of twenty or so individuals within the institution's community, the legislature and state, banks and foundations, media, philanthropic circles, and alumni whose support can help strengthen the institution. Included in this list are individuals who may have expressed some skepticism in the past and need new information and perspectives. Members of the board and the broader institution's community are selected to meet regularly with these opinion makers. The message and information developed in step 2 and the results of the retreat(s) form the basis for communication. The task force on communication meets regularly to report on meetings with the individuals.

8. *Ask up front whether the institution should be closed.* Some stressed colleges and universities in difficult straits do well to ask about closing or merging with another institution. No matter how the discussion ends, it is healthy to raise it. Assigning as board reading Rabbi Edwin Friedman's classic work on cross-generational dysfunction in a synagogue will draw out some of its potential applicability to fragile higher education institutions:[10]

Symptoms of Institutional Anxiety

—High levels of reactivity

—Herding (making sure everyone thinks just the same way)

—Blaming

—Looking for the quick fix

—Confusion of feelings and opinions

Symptoms of a "Stuck" System

—Repeated failed attempts to correct the system

—More new answers to old questions (rather than new questions)

—Polarization

—Inability to learn from experience

What Keeps Leaders from Forward Movement

—Placing a higher value on data than on decisions

—Focusing on feelings rather than responsibilities

—Thinking that a strong self is autocratic rather than acting out of integrity

What Makes for Great Leaders

—Low reactivity

—Clear boundaries of where they end and others begin

—Ability to hear and engage all voices and maintain their own

—Willingness to be vulnerable.

Moreover, significant advance planning and resource allocations are required to shut the doors even after a decision has been made: The issue must be addressed early. Being forced to announce in February cessation of operations the following September adds insult to injury and may well result in additional litigation. Questions to raise in the discussion include the following:

—If we close the institution, will our students find other institutional and program placements readily and be comparably served?

—How much passion does our institution generate? How many people will truly extend themselves for us? How much money do they have to give? Are they willing to give?

—How distinctive are we? What difference do we make? What are our unique results?

—If we ceased operations next year, would a similar institution emerge within several years? What advantages would it have over ours?

—Could we provide at least a year's compensation for faculty, administration, and staff unable to find other positions after closure?

—Is there a worthy nonprofit group in the area with a related mission that could make a significant difference, given our resources?

9. *Verify that the institution has effective legal counsel experienced in higher education.* During all the previous steps expert legal counsel is essential, not only to help interpret the institution's key documents but also to offer wise perspectives on alternative courses of action. For some institutions, in-house counsel suffices, but many supplement such skills with outside specialists. Sole reliance on the expertise of attorneys who are members of the board, however, is unprofessional and dangerous. These issues are discussed in more detail in chapter 13 of this volume on legal challenges for fragile institutions.

10. *Commission a full governance audit.* Retain the services of an outside expert to make a thorough and honest study of the way the institution does business. In this audit the institution's defining legal documents receive special scrutiny, but lengthy interviews with members of

> ## Three Emerging Trends for Board Members at Fragile Institutions
>
> - Rising demands for accountability throughout American society ensure that if boards and presidents do not set their own goals and assess their performance according to them, others will do so for them.
> - The historic and essential role of governing bodies in the history of American higher education today largely is unknown or ignored. Increasingly, boards are tarred with the brushes of corporate governance, with the public ready to blame them, whether deservedly or not.
> - With the retirement of the baby boomers, new generations of students, parents, and alumni are posing significant opportunities and challenges for institutions of higher education.

the board and key administrators are essential, as is a survey of their perspectives, prepared after conclusion of the interviews. Observation of board and committee meetings generates invaluable information as well. Overall, the board's fundamental capacity to add value to its institution is assessed.

Every several years relatively easy and rapid assessment can occur through administration of a survey like the venerable "board self-study" of the Association of Governing Boards of Universities and Colleges (AGB). A retreat with an external facilitator then processes the results with the board. However, for any institution with significant issues to address—and any institution that has never conducted a governance audit—the full review is a requirement.

For institutions that are demonstrating serious symptoms of fragility, a number of related issues normally benefit from attention. An executive committee generally acquires power through the duration of a crisis. A handful of loyal members may keep speaking, working, touching base with each other, and holding the institution together, but the rest of the board may become distant and disengaged, even as the executive committee itself becomes exhausted and angered at carrying the load. Committees may atrophy, strategic discussions may disappear, and years can be required to reignite real board engagement. Special attention may be required in these difficult moments to keep those committees functioning as they face large and relevant questions of strategy and to keep the board alive.

11. Make sure key databases are in place and sound. The profusion of data available to our institutions today offers advantages that were simply unavailable even ten years ago. For stressed universities or colleges, the benefits of such knowledge can be exceptional. A standard set of variables includes the following:

—Admission "funnel" statistics by program, graduate and undergraduate: numbers of inquiries, applications, acceptances, and enrollments in raw numbers and percentages

—Retention from first to second year, also with appropriate breakouts

—Graduation rates, with breakouts

—Cost per student per program

—Discount rates for financial assistance

—Compensation

—Percentage of alumni participation in the annual fund

—Annual fund receipts, also presented as a percentage of budget

—Board giving to the annual fund as a percentage of the annual fund

—Average board-member gift

—Endowment and endowment per student

—Rate of return on endowment

—Deferred maintenance and deferred maintenance as a percentage of plant value

12. Collect other essential bodies of information not as easily gathered.

• Academic Program Development

One of the greatest threats to fragile institutions is a catalogue full of aging, dated academic programs about which students have lost interest. A standard board requirement is knowledge of which of the institution's academic programs are strong, which are weak, and what each needs to achieve excellence. Accreditation alone does not suffice since it assumes that existing programs should continue and only need to be improved in specified ways. The issue of whether to cut and where does not arise. Thus the board must insist that appropriate review procedures are in place and that they allow for the kind of prioritization carefully delineated by Robert C. Dickeson.[11] Simply assembling policies for full program review can take a year or more. Implementation comes later. Although some universities have managed to complete the process in a year, there are advantages if a school is able to work calmly and reflectively through their departments before the crises hit. In the midst of severe institutional pressures, effective decisions on program rationalization may not even prove possible. Could the rapid, creative work of Scott Cowen and his leadership team at Tulane after Hurricane Katrina have occurred without prior review?[12]

• Student Life

With enrollments declining at many fragile institutions, what will the implications be for mission, programs, and facilities? Must another niche be carved?[13] Successful board work requires an understanding of the institution's niche and brand distinctiveness. What are key competitors doing? How well does the institution compete? What are students, faculty, and administrators saying about competitors, and what does this say about those institutions?

• Financial Management and Controls

Particularly given widespread worries over financial mismanagement, the board must understand how the institution's financial operations function and be satisfied that appropriate staffing, technology, risk management, and controls are in place. At institutions in all categories and geographic factors, and in spite of increasingly tight fiscal pressures, budgeting procedures still may date from an era of greater prosperity. Does the finance office collect appropriate information throughout the institution, link it to institutional planning and program quality, and allocate sums wisely? In a crisis, would it impose standard, across-the-board cuts? Would it know how to do otherwise?

• Endowment

Most board members know the dollar value of their institution's endowment. Appropriate leverage also comes from knowing, as noted before, that specific proportion of the endowment that the board itself can spend as it pleases. However, "endowment" covers numerous categories. Individual funds must be grouped by various combinations of donor intent and board flexibility. The issue is not always trivial, since some funds may have been created so far in the past and with such vagueness as to defy normal sorting today. Sometimes lengthy research stands between the board and the answer. On stressed campuses this information is indispensable, and court action may be required to break the terms of bequests and other gifts from those long deceased. Naturally, any board will wish to satisfy itself that current endowment funds are clearly written in this regard: For many institutions, a board policy that tilts the scales toward unrestricted use makes excellent sense. Boards also should verify that proper oversight of the endowment is in place in written and implemented policies, that returns are in line with those of other institutions, and that policies for payout are current, reasonable, and defensible.[14]

- Compensation

Colleges and universities in general are awakening to the impact the passage of the baby-boom generation will have on them, not only in reduced numbers of potential successors but also in terms of the successor generation's shifting expectations of work.[15] Those who are thinking far into the future may begin reflecting on the impact of the millennial generation as employees, managers, and professors on higher education institutions. Many faculty and administrators are expected to retire within five years of this writing.

Given a thorough understanding of the census of its faculty, staff, and administration, how much flexibility does the institution have? What will the likely financial impact and opportunities be? What can be accomplished now to prepare? Managers of fragile infrastructures will need to answer many difficult questions: How do the results of the faculty census correspond to emerging plans with respect to new, potential, and no-longer-relevant programs and to new pedagogies and technology? What possibilities emerge? Where do possibilities of a wide range of early retirement programs fit? Also, how do salaries and benefits compare with those at peer institutions? Are they sufficient to hire worthy replacements?

- Institutional Management and Succession

Especially in stressed environments the board needs to know that the president's administration works as a team, that it operates according to well-defined procedures and policies, that its members support each other, and that knowledge is shared and built upon collaboratively. Although there is some disagreement on the meaning of long-term succession planning within institutions of higher education, the board should also know which individual within the administration is capable, if necessary, of standing in for the president. Especially important in today's increasingly litigious environment are effective

---

The Single Most Important Piece of Advice for Board Members of a Fragile University or College

■ Remain on the board only if you continue to possess passion and hope.

---

grievance procedures that set high standards for access to the board and make clear that the board, if brought in, serves as an appellate court and reviews only whether existing policies were followed.

• Philanthropy and External Relations

A committee on advancement, working in tandem with the vice president for it, is well positioned not only to analyze the institution's philanthropic statistics but also to build a larger understanding of the field.[16] How well staffed is the office in both numbers and quality? As well, the sensitive management of the college or university's alumni network can make a critical difference for a vulnerable board leadership. Key questions that will need to be answered include the following:

—The degree to which alumni are engaged with the life of the institution

—The institution's success in differentiating programs to meet the expectations of younger alumni and donors

—The numbers of major donor prospects

—The adequacy and depth of donor files and office records

—The extent to which constituents are cultivated

—The status of major and planned-giving programs

—The sufficiency of technology to support the office's work

—The success of the last campaign and readiness for the next one

• Internal Morale

Particularly at weakened institutions, critics and the politically motivated can be heard to say, "Morale is at an all-time low." Board members, normally somewhat removed from campus life and worried about their institution, too often take such comments as accurate, and damaging decisions can result. Savvy boards arrange for dinners and other meals, receptions, and interviews with members of constituent bodies. They also avoid the serious trap of appointing constituent "representatives" to their boards and asking them to speak for those groups.

Assessments of the president's performance every five years also allow an external consultant to interview a broad cross section of constituents on a series of general and specific criteria and report back to the board.[17] These assessments should include a number of constituent interviews, and they should not be conducted by board members who informally ask strangers, "So how is the president doing?" Not only do board members normally lack the professional skills for interviewing, they also are unaccustomed to "reading" academic institutions and knowing how to handle personally interested attempts to manipulate their conclusions.

• The Broader Context of Higher Education

The thorough and comprehensive reporting available to boards today through general journals like the *Chronicle of Higher Education* and *Trusteeship* allows members to stay in touch with trends and best practices. Presidents can help by distributing relevant articles to members, providing them with useful feeds and alerts from the Internet, and sending them to appropriate conferences. Some boards also take out subscriptions to key journals for their members and even assign some subscriptions by committee.

• The Committee on Governance

Many crises occur because of failure to practice sound governance and build up appropriate policy and habits, particularly at universities and colleges already weakened by lack of student and financial resources. A governance committee can offer a thorough and meaningful orientation to these challenges for new and inexperienced trustees. Boards that talk about their work and continuously assess it tend to improve. Late in the spring semester the committee should revisit the goals prepared one year previously, lead a discussion of the board's performance on them, and suggest goals for the year to come. More thorough reviews every few years and a governance audit every decade or so are essential further supports of best practice.

Increasingly, good boards also assess the performance of their individual members on the basis of the board's approved code of conduct.[18] In related fashion some governance committees make a point of touching base with each board member each year, inquiring about her or his satisfaction with board service and collecting suggestions for better meetings, for example. Such habits are powerful tools for holding a board together in times of stress. Of course, the governance committee also keeps a current list of professional skills the board requires, measures current membership against it, and seeks members to fill those missing characteristics. In public institutions that receive members gubernatorially nominated and legislatively approved, smart boards still have governance committees that, in addition to taking time to address the many questions of best practice, also brief the governor and staff on the kinds of persons required for the institution's advance and even may suggest particularly appropriate individuals for consideration.

• Presidential Assessment and Search Vehicles

Any board must know objectively how well its president is doing on the basis of mutually agreed-upon goals, linked to a strategic plan that grows out of campus consultation, but a clear assessment of the president's performance can be much more difficult in a crisis or a period of extended stress. Thus it is wise to structure a multiyear assessment model because policies and procedures to assess presidential performance take some time to assemble and, when well designed, play out over a period of five or more years, since, in addition to ongoing assessment, there are annual and periodic reviews.[19] Annually set goals for presidential performance, linked to the board's performance, allow the president to report at each meeting (and between meetings) on progress against them. Each spring the president's self-assessment on the basis of those goals permits a small assessment committee of board members to sit with the president, review the statement, generate new goals, and come back to the board with a report. Included in that report are recommendations for adjustments to the president's compensation and the results of the board's annual study of the compensation of peers.

Boards that regularly engage in goal setting and assessment according to well-conceived policies also are ready for the moment when a new president must be found. Thorough knowledge of the institution, familiarity with the challenges the outgoing president has addressed, and a shared vision and agenda of work ahead make preparation of a leadership statement quick and easy. They also present candidates for the position with a uniform and accurate sense of its challenges and opportunities.[20] A presidential search at a fragile college or university can generate anxiety-driven, politically motivated demands for participation in the process. In moments of calm, boards should write their own policy and ensure widespread and appropriate constituent engagement, productive selection of the search committee, and a final de-

---

A Key Decision You Would Make Differently with the Benefit of Later Thinking

- Insist on defining an institutional peer group and its benchmarks.

---

cision by the board. Of course, careful and external preparation of a contract is also essential.

- Strategic Planning Practices

A shared vision for the institution's future—particularly for one with a mission at risk—is a foundation of long-term institutional health. Boards need to know where the institution is headed and why, and they must play a determinative role in the process. That knowledge reduces and even can eliminate partisan politics and narrow, uncoordinated decision making. The plan itself does not create the necessary certainty. Rather, it is the written outcome of a careful process that engages the entire community in a review of the institution's recent history, current situation, and future prospects.[21] If board and president fail to set the agenda—their most powerful tool for institutional health—others most likely will, potentially at significant cost to the institution.

- Campus Communication Channels

A board's effectiveness increases considerably during periods of fragility if it has sound internal and external communication. An annual spring retreat at which the board sets its own goals and those of its committees, all in the context of the strategic plan, is a key element in addressing at-risk circumstances, as are regular meetings of individual committees in the company of the entire board. Each board member needs to know what the board and its parts are doing, why, and with what intended results. Between meetings boards benefit greatly from regular and detailed e-mails from the president, particularly about troubling areas of operation reviewed in previous meetings.

In this regard one of a board's greatest opportunities for making a positive difference in its institution's health lies in building and solidifying relationships with the broader community. An external affairs committee requires an annual generation of a list of individuals and groups to be cultivated, assigns members specific tasks with respect to them, and reports back on the results. Legislators, politicians, opinion makers, media stars, major donors, bankers, alumni associations, foundation and corporate leaders, and significant neighbors all figure within such lists. With a list of such individuals and groups, boards can use their ambassadorial authority to create a wide web of understanding and supportive institutional friends. At all points in an institution's history, such bonds can be of exceptional benefit. In periods of fragility and stress, they can be pivotal.

13. Make the most of meetings of the board. Finally, all the preceding steps should come together in the meetings of the board and its committees. Proper structuring of those meetings provides the institutional framework within which knowledge is generated, spread, and acted upon, even during periods of fragility. Too often, however, meetings can become merely a series of presentations of lengthy and trivial reports from committees essentially uncertain about what they are to be doing about the difficulties and shortcomings they have observed. Particularly damaging in vulnerable periods are reports to the board from constituent members who are speaking for their constituencies. Often these representatives will send e-mails to their membership in advance of the meeting, collect the negative responses of those with time and desire to compose them, and present their conclusions as representative. Effective boards do not want to be manipulated, and these attempts should not be confused with the effective models of communication described previously.

A concluding executive session with the board's executive agent, the president, in attendance is a powerful tool for raising questions and concerns, sharing information, beginning to set future directions, correcting mistaken impressions, eliminating gossip, modeling direct communication, and building goodwill and trust.

Most higher education institutions descend into fragility at some point in their histories, and many could be described on a consistent basis as fragile in one or more areas. However, in this era of competitive institutional rankings and accountability, too many colleges and universities are convinced that a handful of friendly statistics spell safety, or that a few warning signs spell disaster. The real keys to long-term strength and success lie in sound governance, careful policies, and informed, thoughtful leadership. At stressed institutions these all must be demonstrated at the board level.

CHAPTER SIX

Preserving and Extending the Academic Mission of Vulnerable Institutions: Best Practices for Chief Academic Officers

Patricia Cormier

Colleges and universities across the nation are entering a new era of competition that may rewrite the history of American higher education. Most important, these institutions face a prolonged and unprecedented shift in the number and type of students they serve. Nontraditional students, immigrants who speak a multitude of languages from different cultural traditions, the growth of the for-profit sector, and the impact of new technologies on teaching and learning are all shaping an environment of intense competition with increasing limitations on the resources of institutions in all categories, whether two-year, four-year, or graduate level. In addition, the country faces a turbulent economic environment with the changing nature and outsourcing of jobs, massive federal deficits set against the background of structural changes in the economy, and the continuing threat of terrorism.

Declining support for higher education at both the federal and state levels is not likely to be reversed in this uncertain economic environment as the competition for resources within higher education becomes even more relentless. In this environment the challenges faced by stressed universities and colleges are especially formidable, and the roles that the chief academic officer plays in sustaining the vitality of the institution are pivotal. This chapter will outline how effective academic leadership makes the difference at fragile institutions.

Vulnerable or stressed colleges are often defined as those in financial difficulty and with declining enrollments, but a fragile college may also exhibit other signs of stress, such as an ambiguous or dated mission, high student attrition, and unacceptable levels of faculty and staff turnover. Budget constraints clearly rank at the top of the list. A provost or vice president of academic affairs does not have much control over how much money the institution has, but she or he will often have much control over where that money is spent, and where those resources are used will greatly affect how the institution is perceived. Alumni with pride in the institution are the best asset it can have, not only for their financial gifts but, as importantly, for their continuing accolades. This chapter will focus specifically on what the chief academic officer can do to enhance a college or university's reputation and to improve the quality of its educational product, that is, well-rounded, civic-minded graduates. Although the focus will principally be on institutions in immediate danger, these recommendations can be used to make less fragile institutions stronger as well. An annotated literature review on these issues appears as the first note of this chapter.[1]

Six areas will be discussed that offer opportunities to revitalize a campus: living the academic mission; establishing an academically supportive environment; redefining the roles and responsibilities of the faculty; identifying and cultivating new student populations; developing partnerships with internal and external communities; and taking calculated risks. Eight institutions are highlighted in which these strategies have helped move the college or university from vulnerability to strength. Some examples involve public institutions, others involve private institutions, and the choices represent a cross section of geographic areas. Schools were chosen for their abilities to prevail against, not just survive, troubling circumstances, and each case study demonstrates the essential synergy that must exist between the president and the chief academic officer; one cannot accomplish the desired goals without the other.

Penson Associates, a Florida consulting firm, has been conducting research for several years on skill sets for academic leaders. In examining over 250 institutions, it has identified several skill clusters essential to successful leadership; the most recently added cluster is termed "entrepreneurship."[2] In a fast-moving academic environment the ability of academic leaders to be agile and flexible and to seize opportunities is essential to success, particularly when a college or university requires restructuring. In *First among Equals: The Role of the Chief Academic Officer*, James Martin and James E. Samels identify ten characteristics that are necessary ingredients for the modern-day chief academic officer, at least half of which are relevant to entrepreneurship: being an expert with ambiguity, a champion of new technologies, a supporter of selected excellences, the shaper of a new consensus, and a visionary pragmatist.[3]

Chief academic officers must be astute in identifying signs of financial stress, particularly those related to academic programs, such as declining or burgeoning numbers of majors in particular programs and the need to reassign faculty positions on the basis of those numbers. As a part of strategic planning, the chief academic officer must weigh educational program costs against revenue to make the best use of resources available to the institution. In this context wise decisions by provosts and vice presidents of academic affairs determine the ultimate success or failure of the institution.

An Academic Action Plan for Vulnerable Institutions: Six Steps

Live the Mission

Some, but not all, of the institutions studied affirmed the need to stay true to their missions in the face of adversity. In our experience, mission drift is common when an institution is faced with financial difficulty and too few resources to deliver a high-quality educational product. Academic officers need to understand and believe in the mission and constantly to align available resources to accomplish it. New or repackaged programs must capitalize on the strengths and expertise of the faculty. It may be necessary to refocus the curriculum to meet an emerging regional workforce-driven need. Examples might be redefining the basic sciences into a preprofessional allied health-care focus, or the preparation of science educators for schools, or reorienting history and political science into a prelaw program. The liberal arts and sciences remain but are marketed differently to prospective students.

Infusing the mission into the campus culture is one of the great challenges for academic affairs in a fragile environment. The responsibility of the chief academic officer is to make the mission authentic for the institution's key constituents. Faculty recruitment must focus on finding individuals who comfortably convey a belief in the purpose and goals of the college or university. If the emphasis, for example, is on public engagement, faculty must perceive the importance of that goal in their work. In addition, professional development that enhances the mission must be supported. Faculty roles and responsibilities, as reflected in tenure and promotion guidelines, must also reinforce the mission. In the institutions we examined, the chief academic officer played the central role in examining, reflecting, and restating the mission and essential values of the institution.

The better defined the mission is, the better the opportunity for students to identify with the institution. Students can recognize authenticity or the lack thereof very quickly, and disconnect themselves from the life of the campus if they sense that the institution is becoming less

Three Emerging Trends

- Significant reconsideration and rethinking of faculty roles
- Expansion of the range of academic services offered to a region
- Identification of new student populations

focused and more derivative. The mission statement must be reexamined on a regular, publicly announced schedule in order for it to reflect what is actually occurring on campus and to remain relevant to the student body it serves. David Leslie and E. K. Fretwell point out that a mission should be distinctive, but they also emphasize that a mission may be too specialized and therefore have limited appeal.[4] In two cases in our study, refocusing institutional mission was the mechanism for survival and resulted in tangibly revitalized institutions. An institution that never looks at its mission critically is exhibiting a key condition of vulnerability. Thus the chief academic officer must ensure that the mission is the unifying and driving force within the institutional community as reflected in every educational policy, budget development, and student life report and planning document.

Create an Academically Supportive Environment

The transition between high school and college is difficult for many students, in part because college students are suddenly expected to retain specifics that may be discussed only once during a course, and they must learn to manage their own time to a far greater extent. In addition, increasing numbers of students present complex challenges to institutions to provide academic support for a variety of needs—learning disabilities, cultural orientation, language and mathematical deficits, intercollegiate athletic conflicts, psychological problems, and familial nonsupport or the reverse, family intrusion. External pressures to fit in can result in drug and alcohol dependency, sexual misconduct, and an array of other social problems. Rising percentages of students work part- or even full-time while attending college. All these needs force universities and colleges to support mechanisms to promote academic success.

Stressed institutions, however, must be even more aggressive in providing academic support than institutions that enroll highly motivated, well-prepared students. As fragile colleges develop new student populations, mechanisms to support those students are essential. These mechanisms necessitate close cooperation between academic and student affairs because much student learning takes place outside the classroom. In turn, student affairs must create a safe and inspiring environment that contributes to the total development of each student.

The literature is replete with research that demonstrates the importance of student engagement, and this is particularly true of support for underrepresented students. New chief academic officers learn how costly it is to have to replace a single student, so student retention becomes viewed as inseparable from efforts to increase enrollment. As one response, faculty-student interaction results uniformly in better grades and college graduation rates. The 2006 National Survey of Student Engagement found that "student engagement had a measurable impact on grades and students' likelihood of returning for a second year of college, particularly among underserved minority populations. . . . Data indicated that activities such as collaborating with peers on projects inside and outside the classroom helped students overcome previous educational disadvantages."[5] In addition, the survey demonstrated that both adults and distance learners learned better when they engaged in group projects and meaningful educational experiences. The implications of these findings speak to the need for chief academic officers to encourage experiential learning opportunities outside the classroom and to work closely with student affairs officers in developing a climate of support for students. Exemplary advising and academic support centers continue to be crucial to student retention.

Redefine Faculty Roles and Responsibilities

Eighty percent of the budget of many higher education institutions is devoted to personnel. Within the budgets of chief academic officers, that percentage is often higher. Flexibility in faculty recruitment and retention is another key for vulnerable institutions to remain nimble and responsive to the shifting demands of the marketplace. Faculty tenure is often blamed as the primary reason that an institution cannot make progress and therefore suffers declining enrollment and financial distress. To some extent this may be true, but the institutions we studied found ways of redefining roles and responsibilities that added to the distinctiveness of the mission and allowed the institution to reconstitute itself. Institutional leaders of Florida Gulf Coast University claimed significant success because it has no tenure, yet it has no problem recruiting and retaining faculty. Academic officers in these institutions worked with faculty to define their roles differently, and it was in large part the faculty's willingness to reengineer their roles and their programs that resulted in successful outcomes.

Cultivate New Student Populations

Most of the vulnerable institutions we interviewed were actively recruiting new areas of the student market, particularly adult students, single mothers with children, specific ethnic groups, gifted children, and inner-city and rural populations. At all eight institutions chief academic officers were challenged to develop curricula and delivery systems to accommodate differences in learning styles and the personal needs of these populations. They also seized opportunities to garner resources for these initiatives that were new to the institution—foundation, corporate, and federal support. These new students also provided new kinds of needed visibility and distinctiveness for each institution. In each instance the provost or vice president for academic affairs had to exhibit high levels of flexibility and a willingness to take risks. Sometimes their efforts faltered, as detailed later, but not without adding to the arsenal of strategies to make the next set of choices more successful. Some institutions found that by attracting more students they could become more selective. Increased selectiveness, in turn, continued to attract a rising number of students and allowed the institution to upgrade its student body in terms of high-school GPA scores and representation from foreign countries, thus diversifying the educational experience for its entire community.

Develop Collaborative Partnerships with Internal
and External Constituents

Developing collaborative partnerships with internal and external constituents is perhaps the most important step in restructuring fragile institutions to ensure success. New partnerships between academic and student affairs have already been mentioned, but linkages with the offices of finance, administration, instructional technology, and facilities management can also be developed. Synergy among these units helps both to further the mission externally and to foster an enhanced climate of communication and trust internally. At more than one institution interviewed, we noted that if the members of the faculty are included in these discussions, they will feel a sense of ownership, will actively integrate the concepts of the mission into their syllabi, and, most important, will model these values as they interact with students. Likewise, if students are included in these discussions, they will feel a sense of inclusion and empowerment. Faculty and students who are encouraged to become involved feel that they are part of the process, often even if what they argued for turns out to be the minority opinion. Admitting that there are problems to address or announcing that certain changes must occur is a choice that must be taken in order for positive change to occur. Over the long term the chief academic officer is the primary campus facilitator of these exchanges among the faculty and students. He or she knows that constructive debate about the core values behind the mission of an institution will result in a healthy, adaptable environment. University communities who fight their way back from the brink of failure tend to be those whose constituencies have been honest with each other, in our view.

External partnerships must be fostered as well. The community that surrounds an institution may sometimes feel excluded or competitive, and effective outreaches can include alumni advisory boards, parent councils, corporate and K–12 school councils, and community advisory groups that directly serve the president and chief academic officer. Institutions should welcome these contributions from various constituencies because they can produce increased understanding of the needs and challenges for an at-risk institution. They also result in more support for the institution over time. Education involves the exchange of ideas on many levels, and institutions that prevail are inevitably those that invite and act on advice from their members and the broader community on a regular basis.

Several of the institutions we studied described their relationships with both on-campus constituencies and external audiences as crucial to their success. In one case the external community was broadly defined to encompass a major metropolitan area. In another the community spanned two countries. The importance of forging alliances and recognizing the value of cooperative ventures was stressed by several campus leaders as vital to increasing enrollment and establishing a sustainable marketing niche. When institutions were implementing bold initiatives, support and acceptance from the community were key elements in achieving institutional success.

Take Calculated Risks

Vulnerable institutions must begin their self-examinations with several unavoidable questions: How much change is needed? Where should major changes begin? How much will these changes cost? How likely is their success? Restructuring the institution becomes a reality, and that often necessitates strategic reallocations.[6] Clearly this is an area where the president must provide leadership, often by relying on the provost or vice president for academic affairs for strategy, planning, and implementation. Good institutional research must inform the decisions, and the president and chief academic officer, along with the chief financial officer, must know what questions to ask to ensure

---

Three Best Practices for CAOs

- Create multiple learning environments to ensure student success.
- Develop institutional partnerships with both internal and external communities to leverage resources and achieve new economies.
- Live the mission.

---

the right answers. In sum, effective strategic planning at fragile institutions is characterized by inclusiveness of both internal and external constituencies, is based on institutional values, and is informed by reliable data. Reallocation of resources requires careful attention to preserving the core mission because "strategic" planning now often means that some areas of the institution will be strengthened and others may be eliminated.

In more than one of the institutions highlighted later, bold decisions by the president and chief academic officer resulted in a major turnaround for the institution. In one case the core mission was recast to meet the new and emerging population shift within a region. In another the institution gambled on a dramatic alteration in the delivery of its curriculum. In fact, in every case the leadership of the institution leaned on innovation and new ways of conducting its business to overcome fragility. None chose to stand pat. Also, in all cases the chief academic officer was the point person to effect change. Although the president often pointed the way, the provost or vice president for academic affairs had to sell the idea to key constituents and then find ways to support and implement it. Every president with whom we spoke emphasized that strong leadership in academic affairs was a make-or-break difference in the turnaround of her or his institution.

Achieving Success at Eight Institutions: The Role of Academic Leadership

Alverno College

Alverno College, a private institution located in Wisconsin, was established in 1887 and is now the product of the merger of a nursing school, a music college, and a teachers' college.[7] Only women are admitted to the undergraduate program. The college was intertwined culturally and financially with the religious order of the School Sisters of St. Francis, and in 1969 the administration of the order made a decision to separate the order from the college. It also decided to accept into the order only women who already had college degrees and encouraged those who were new members to return to their homes to get their degrees. This caused the college enrollment to drop by about 50 percent. Around that same time the order decided to assign the collective debt to the college, effectively placing the institution in a fragile position.

Even before the critical changes that occurred in 1969, the professors at Alverno had begun looking at innovative teaching methodologies. The sudden and serious financial danger became a catalyst for further innovation. The faculty felt free to experiment since the college was on the edge of disaster, and they managed to turn a challenge into a fundamental strength. This attitude of making do with less became embedded in the campus culture and is still evident today. President Mary J. Meehan notes, "People have always stepped up to the plate. We have no money but we're very creative. It's almost this pride thing. We don't need a lot. Just work with what you have because we are creative and innovative and we can make this work. That is a very prevalent spirit when you walk on the campus." By 1973 a new curriculum was implemented that emphasized four abilities with explicit learning-outcome criteria. Each course, besides being responsible for content, also fits into one of these levels of ability.

Constant, perpetual self-examination and reflection are integral parts of the academic community at Alverno. Students are even required to assess and document their own abilities and progress. This also means that faculty members cross the traditional borders of discipline and work together. The pervasive attitude that assessment is constant also has the positive effect of taking the sting out of criticism; the attitude is that "we are always striving to become better; we are not finished yet, and we never will be." Senior Vice President for Academic Affairs Sister Kathleen O'Brien, who has been at the institution since 1976, says that a big lesson others can learn from Alverno is not to "wait until everybody is ready. You're not going to design it to be the perfect system until you try it out. You're going to have to make it run at some point. So just go and do it. Not everybody felt ready, but we were told to go and do it and learn from your experience."

The college's sense of community is very strong, at least partly because the faculty all meet every Friday afternoon to make decisions about the institution and discuss pertinent topics, no small feat since the college has 115 full-time faculty. It serves more than 2,200 women and now boasts a weekend college and a graduate program, as well as its undergraduate program. This clearly indicates a commitment to

providing an academically supportive environment, as well as to cultivating new and distinct student populations.

Wilberforce University

Wilberforce University is the nation's oldest historically black university, established in 1856 and located in Ohio.[8] In 2002 the university was facing $5 million in debt, and the board requested that the
Reverend Dr. Floyd Flake, a former U.S. congressman and Wilberforce
alumnus, become the new president. The university was very much at
risk; it was deep in debt, and financial auditing had not been done in
three years, so the board of the university was even unsure exactly
how far in debt it was. Maintenance had been deferred for so long
that in the first year the university had to put in a new heating and air-
conditioning system because it could not risk going into the winter
without it. Flake aggressively sought federal and private funding, cut
staff, slashed salaries, and increased faculty workload. The institution
is financially sound at this point. There were more than fifty majors
when Flake took office; Wilberforce now has seventeen majors for its
roughly one thousand students. Flake is currently serving what he describes as his "fifth year of a one-year commitment."

Flake understands the importance of establishing a supportive environment. Within three days after he became president, FBI agents
came to speak with him about concerns regarding firearms and drugs
on campus. Under his leadership the Wilberforce community addressed
those issues, and as a result the quality of the student body has improved over time. "These kids are tired of seeing the killings and
gangs. Many of them are so happy to be out here in the wilderness
because they're not running for their lives," Flake asserts. He and his
executive vice president have made it their practice to go to the cafe-
teria on a daily basis and speak directly with students. He has worked
to encourage the understanding among faculty that "whatever impacts one area negatively impacts all of us." Flake advises institutions
in similar fragile circumstances to develop what he calls "transactional leadership models," through which decisions can be made
more quickly: "You've got to basically identify your problem and
then come up with a solution and implement. At Wilberforce, we
could only take about three steps. I think if you're in a situation like
the one I inherited, that's about all the time one has." He also believes that ongoing accountability must be integrated into the campus culture and that presidents trained in the corporate sector can in
some cases bring a welcome emphasis on sound business practices to
higher education.

Single Most Important Piece of Advice

- Take a calculated risk.

Florida Gulf Coast University

Florida Gulf Coast University (FGCU), a major public institution, was established in 1991, and its first student was admitted in 1997.[9] The university emphasizes school-to-career training and has built partnerships with General Motors and Ford, among others. It currently serves 8,400 students. The student/faculty ratio is 17:1. William Merwin became president of FGCU in July 1999. In his almost eight years in this position, he worked hard to encourage the feeling that the university is a family, an especially difficult feat when the family is so large.

From its founding FGCU has addressed its potential vulnerability via an innovative faculty development model: a virtually tenureless faculty. As of 2006 there were 325 faculty, and only 18 of them were tenured. These 18 have been there since the school's inception and were tenured when they were hired; no new tenure-track positions have been created. From the beginning, advertising for faculty focused on FGCU's emphasis on creativity and innovation, a concentration on distance learning, interdisciplinary and team teaching, and being the university for the twenty-first century. Not offering tenure was certainly taking a risk, but faculty came and stayed. They are given multiyear contracts of either three or five years. Without this division between junior and senior faculty, barriers have dropped, and the campus working environment is a collegial one.

If individual faculty members get an evaluation that is below standard, they are placed on a three-year continuing contract and are given help to improve. Faculty are evaluated and assessed on an annual basis, and students participate in this evaluation. FGCU does have the traditional titles for its faculty and appropriate financial incentives to make promotion desirable: the stipend for moving from assistant to associate professor is a 10 percent increment, and moving from associate to full professor is a 15 percent increment. The university's attrition rate for faculty is less than 15 percent. As in the other seven institutions interviewed, the chief academic officer in this setting has considerable opportunity to recruit and retain faculty who support the mission.

Northern Kentucky University

Northern Kentucky University (NKU) is a fourteen-thousand-student public institution established in 1968.[10] Jim Votruba has been the president at NKU since August 1997, when he found himself at an institution that lacked focus and had established what he calls "a culture of poverty." At NKU the belief among community members that they were underfunded gave them the global excuse to avoid any major, potentially transformative initiative. Votruba tried to determine what the larger public's aspirations were for the institution, and then he tried to realign the university with those goals. A strategic planning process called "Vision, Values, and Voices" was developed. Several weeks after Votruba's arrival in 1997, a committee representing faculty, staff, students, and community members had conversations with small groups of fifteen to twenty people about the university's current strengths and weaknesses, as well as the direction that it ought to take. The committee participated in a retreat where it developed a set of core values and a set of six strategic priorities with a five-year horizon. Every spring Votruba convenes a "town meeting" during which he informs the community about the priorities and discusses what has been accomplished.

NKU is now much more engaged with the public, as was demonstrated by public involvement with the "Making Place Matter" project in which four universities "developed stewardship 'roadmaps' consistent with their missions, governance, and regional agendas, providing diverse examples of regional stewardship." Votruba says of civic engagement, "It goes to the heart of how I think universities have to define themselves. Not as ends in themselves, but as a means to a broader set of, in our case, regional and secondarily statewide purposes." Public engagement is one of the criteria used to evaluate faculty; however, NKU does not say that each faculty member must meet the same criteria. "What we said was we don't expect every faculty member to be doing engagement, but we do expect the department in aggregate to be serving the full breadth of admission, including engagement," Votruba explains.

The administration spends a great deal of time annually with departmental chairs defining effective workload models. The chief academic officer works directly with the university's deans to link promotion and tenure criteria to the mission and goals of public engagement. When asked for advice for leaders of fragile institutions, Votruba commented:

> I think that to engage one's base, to engage the constituents in defining a future and really setting out very explicitly to differentiate oneself from

other institutions in a metropolitan environment was at least a key for us. But it was engaging the stakeholders in a way that made it their voice. The vision and core values, strategic priorities for us, started with the voices of those who would make it happen. That was terribly important. I think that it is also important to dream very big dreams, because that's what motivates people to want to act. And those dreams very rarely involve money.

Christopher Newport University

Paul Trible became the president of Christopher Newport University (CNU) in Virginia in 1996 when it was already seriously at risk and losing enrollment each year.[11] It had become too dependent on a part-time nontraditional student population. Trible explains, "CNU was really in trouble. We had no sense of direction, falling enrollments, lack of financial resources. Key staff positions were empty. . . . Our campus facilities were mundane, ordinary, and uninspiring." CNU decided to take a calculated risk based on a carefully developed strategic plan. Campus planners identified five key values: students first; great teaching; liberal learning that encouraged leadership, honor, and civic engagement; access; and opportunity. They established a Budget Advisory Committee composed of equal numbers of faculty and administrators, which is chaired by a senior tenured faculty member. They eliminated more than fifty positions, three professional programs, and three graduate programs. (Since that time the university has added seventy-five new full-time faculty positions.) State and local leaders were persuaded to support the school; the state contributed $5 million, and the city of Newport News pledged another $5.6 million. This money allowed the university to move forward, and that forward momentum extended to the attitude on the campus. A football team was established with the idea that it would contribute to campus spirit and culture.

Over the past decade SAT scores have consistently risen. "What we chose to do was return to our roots," Trible states. "We said we're going to emphasize, once again, the liberal arts and sciences. We're going to reach out to traditional students, and we're going to place our emphasis on things like great teaching and small classes and undergraduate education." Once a branch campus of the College of William and Mary, the university had about 200 students living on campus in 1996. CNU now has 3,000 students living on campus and a total enrollment of almost 4,800. This institution took a calculated risk, and when the president was asked, he admitted that he had never considered failure a possibility:

I think that's the power of great dreams. Each of us in our lives has to have a dream or a vision so powerful and so strong that it allows us to overcome the obstacles and the detractors and the dissenters—those people who say it's an impossible dream. I really spend a lot of time with our students in saying don't waste you life on small dreams. Don't allow other people to define your life and your aspirations.

Wilson College

In 1979 Wilson College, a Pennsylvania women's college, faced extinction when enrollment dropped from 700 to 250.[12] Serving new and distinct student populations in an academically supportive environment was the challenge for its chief academic officer. In the early 1980s Wilson opened its doors to adult learners with its continuing-education program. Wilson is well known for an equestrian program, which began around the same time, in part because the college acquired an equestrian center as part of its expansion in the early 1970s. By the early 1990s Wilson had begun partnering with Presbyterian colleges abroad, starting with two Korean colleges, and today it has international students from seventeen different countries and is embarking on a "Global Citizenship Initiative" that brings international students to the institution from seventeen countries, as well as sending its own students to other countries for service learning opportunities. In 1995 Wilson started its "Women and Children" program, which enables students to live on campus with their children near a child-care center. As of 2006 the college enrolled more than 775 students and boasted an adult learning program, a teacher intern program, and its first graduate program, an M.A. in teaching. Wilson also has developed the Fulton Center for Environmental Sustainability and hosts an international conference on sustainable living every two years. Having led the development of a recent institutional strategic plan, titled "Enduring Mission, Expanding Visions," President Lorna Edmundson asserts that "the hardest thing is to move the curriculum in a direction that is truly perceived by the market as being distinctive."

University of Texas at El Paso

In 1971, when Diana S. Natalicio came to the University of Texas at El Paso (UTEP), located near the Mexican border, its slogan was "Harvard on the Border."[13] Because the standard it set for itself was so high, the university had become aware of its inability to achieve that level of success, and overall institutional confidence had suffered. Natalicio did not become president of the university until 1988, but by then she had certainly noticed a disparity between the makeup of the

---

One Thing That Should Be Done Differently

■ Do not wait until everybody is ready for change.

---

surrounding community's high schools and the student population of UTEP. She made a concerted effort to have the institution reach out to students who had been told that they were not "college material." Now the school's twenty thousand students are 72 percent Mexican American, and 82 percent of them come from El Paso County. The university currently offers thirteen doctoral degree programs, has developed a joint enrollment option with a local community college, and is one of the Documenting Effective Educational Practice (DEEP) institutions highlighted in *Student Success in College*.

Tapping into the local Mexican American student base was a controversial direction to take, but this new direction made the institution eligible for special funding from both state and federal governments. More than half of UTEP's undergraduates are the first in their families to attend college, and one-third of its students report that their family's annual income is $20,000 or less. Natalicio believes strongly in being committed to both access and excellence. When asked for advice for the president of an at-risk university, she cautioned, "I'm always hesitant because I think that every situation is unique, but maybe that's the answer. It seems to me that it is about understanding at a deep level who you are as an institution and whom you are attempting to serve. How do you differentiate yourself from everybody else? Be as authentic as you can and true to your mission."

Mary Baldwin College

Mary Baldwin College is a private institution affiliated with the Presbyterian Church, is located in Virginia, and has an enrollment of 2,200 students.[14] All of its undergraduates are female. It obtained the property and buildings of a former military academy in 1976 when the institution was experiencing negative trends in both enrollment and finances. The Adult Degree Program, created in 1977, was coeducational from the beginning but now is 85 percent female. The college maintains campuses at five additional locations and has operated the Program for the Exceptionally Gifted since 1985, which fully matriculates women as young as thirteen into the college experience and is the only program in the country to do so. The inquiry-based master of arts in teaching was created in 1992 and features instruction from a faculty member working side by side with a practicing teacher. The Virginia Women's Institute for Leadership was established in 1995 at the request of attorneys for the Commonwealth of Virginia. It is the only all-female cadet corps in the country; more than 40 percent of the cadets achieve a commission in the armed forces.

Pamela Fox, Mary Baldwin's current president, believes that a key to the college's recent success has been its focus on reinforcing its core undergraduate program and enhancing the academic excellence of its residential college. In 2005–2006, Mary Baldwin received the highest number of applicants in the history of the college, and between 2004 and 2006 its retention improved 10 percentage points. Fox contends that her institution's turnaround has been primarily driven by two factors: "the conscious purposeful diversification of programs and revenue streams while remaining central to the mission" and "seizing opportunities." She describes Mary Baldwin's changes as "extending our mission to different audiences, including graduate students, but it was centered on the mission and on the existing academic strengths of the college." Fox advises that "you have to be observant of the kinds of opportunities that might be a good fit for your institution, but you also have to be very honest about how much the institution can bear in terms of change. That's a delicate balance. Then you have to, at some point, just take the plunge."

Conclusion: Back from the Brink

It may be difficult to change the way a vulnerable institution is perceived and even harder to change the way it operates, but often these changes are necessary in order for a college or university to survive. Higher education presidents may place such a high value on tradition that their institutions can become resistant to change, and this may lead to the conditions for fragile institutions. In order to change those institutions, presidents and faculties need to challenge policies that have become outdated or create a new direction to establish a marketing niche. Although the desired outcomes and currency are different for higher education than for business, financial concerns are a factor that cannot be ignored; often changes must be made to sell the "product." Making any of the changes mentioned in this chapter, such as creating a new mission statement, serving a new and distinct student population, or being honest with the community about shortcomings, will undoubtedly meet with some and perhaps much opposition. However, challenging the status quo is finally necessary when prior decisions have ultimately pushed the institution in an at-risk direction.

When successful corporations describe formulas for success, they often center on concurrence by all in the organization on mission, vision, and values. The same is true for the higher education institutions we studied. Accomplishments at the institutions were measured by how well they supported the mission overall and, more precisely, by how clearly members of the faculty, administration, board, and student body understood the expectations for their performance.

The formula for success for fragile institutions is not uniform or simple; however, it requires academic leaders who are aligned with and rooted in institutional values, who can articulate and live their institutional missions, who have highly refined communication skills, who are skilled in best practices in student recruitment and retention, and who have a high threshold for ambiguity and change. The vice president for academic affairs realizes that constructive debate about core values, mission, and vision of the institution will result in a healthier environment even when he or she must wear a cheerleader's costume to sustain its momentum. College and university communities that work their way back from the brink of failure are inevitably those that are honest with each other and make the continuous, concerted effort to find ways to strengthen their institutions. Finally, the most important job of the CAO is to be the guiding force who listens to the community and encourages it to enact positive, steady change.

CHAPTER SEVEN

The Challenge for Student Affairs in Stressed Institutions

Lori Reesor, Steven LaNasa, and Patricia Long

Senior student affairs officers (SSAOs) and student affairs units confront a unique set of challenges at stressed institutions. Within these colleges and universities SSAOs must contend with the same problems that face senior administrators of almost all institutions while also using their authority and influence to establish a tone for students and student leaders—as well as providing a buffering function—to ensure that the work of student affairs professionals continues to be reviewed as a priority within such fragile circumstances.[1] Too often, however, at fragile schools the Office of Student Life is viewed as an add-on rather than a core function, and this leads presidents and provosts to look first to this area for cost savings. This chapter provides an investigation of this trend along with strategies and solutions for the SSAOs of fragile institutions.

Unlike other major units such as academic affairs, administrative affairs, and development, within at-risk college and university structures, student affairs divisions can face heightened scrutiny of their purpose, needs, and resources. This tendency might be viewed as counterintuitive and especially problematic for the SSAO because the student affairs function, through effective enrollment management leadership, often provides a critical path out of vulnerable circumstances.[2] In this environment the SSAO assumes additional responsibility for institutional success because enrollment growth and student retention, even in competitive markets and amid challenging public relations or image problems, provide increased revenue and security for the university or college.

Thus the Office of Student Life may be looked to for the potential to improve institutional standing while it may simultaneously be viewed as an unnecessary activity or, at a minimum, a set of activities that can take place with fewer resources. These two perspectives are not mutually exclusive and, in fact, appear to be quite common.[3] However, these opposing themes of prospective value versus latent doubt often take on a more problematic and explicit role within stressed institutions and create a set of challenges that affect the student affairs unit and its leadership and staff, as well as potentially affecting students negatively through a decline in the overall quality of student life.

As institutional fragility becomes more commonplace nationally among higher education institutions because of factors such as increased competition, declining resources, and changing student preferences, student affairs leaders must be prepared to confront these challenges with several new strategies. To do so, SSAOs must position their units to weather the unique situations faced by student affairs on these campuses. This chapter provides an overview of the impact of institutional fragility on student affairs units and personnel and concludes with recommendations for SSAOs who are currently addressing these challenges at their institutions. In addition to defining the most common adversities faced, emphasis is placed on successful techniques politically, on how practitioners can contend with the emotional impact on themselves and their professional staffs, and, finally, on the steps practitioners must take to keep the student affairs mission central to their campus operations.

This chapter offers case studies of student affairs divisions at several stressed institutions. Structured interviews were conducted with senior student affairs professionals that focused on the impact these circumstances had on their units, and how they faced critical situations. In addition, midlevel managers and students were interviewed at the same institutions to determine the impact of fragility on their experiences.[4] Colleges and universities selected for this study represented varied sizes, geographic locations, demographics, and missions. A commonality shared across the institutions, however, was the fact that each operated within a fragile environment, and this fragility severely affected the student affairs unit.

How a Stressed Environment Affects Student Affairs

Although each institution's story was somewhat different, the internal impact was often the same: declining resources negatively and severely affected student affairs units. At these institutions severe to moderate budgetary reductions resulted in student affairs offices returning significant portions of their budgets, sacrificing programs, and holding positions vacant, even the position of the senior student affairs officer at two institutions. These financial challenges also coincided with heightened institutional scrutiny of the student affairs office's mission, purposes, and overall value within the institution. In at least two institutions this scrutiny was openly contentious and resulted in an intense, politically charged environment that dramatically affected senior leadership and staff members.

Additionally problematic was the need for the SSAO to triage the unit, which David Leslie and E. K. Fretwell consider a common practice within potentially expendable units within fiscally vulnerable institutions.[5] The most troublesome result for these SSAOs was the accompanying discussion of where within the organizational structure student affairs fit best. The focus of some of these discussions actually concentrated on the elimination of the SSAO position, on the placement of student affairs under academic affairs, and on the parceling of traditional student affairs activities among other institutional executives. Thus in addition to the financial hardships faced throughout the institution, student affairs faced additional crises of purpose and prestige within institutional settings. Several professionals interviewed spoke of the tremendous loss in status and professionalism experienced throughout their units when their leader was no longer considered an executive on a par with the other divisions at the university.

Many institutions that face budgetary concerns are also faced with the convergence of numerous additional factors that lead to crisis or fragility. This was certainly the case among the SSAOs we interviewed.[6] A major commonality across the institutions—both a cause and a symptom—was the pronounced turnover of the institution's senior leadership, most dramatically felt by the "revolving door of the Provost's Office," as described by one senior student affairs director, and the institution's president or chancellor.[7] Typical turnover at these institutions averaged four chief academic officers and three presidents in a ten-year period.

A critical struggle within all the institutions examined for this chapter was the substantial shifting of institutional purpose that often occurred with senior leadership turnover. Similarly, it was common for SSAOs and their units as a whole to suffer from a crisis of purpose that focused on the role of the student affairs unit within each institutional context. Although some units faced this crisis because of new leadership that applied what might be described as a perspective of a business/industry model, others were presented with the crisis because of significant retrenchment within the state's funding processes. Regardless of the route, the SSAO was called on to navigate multiple issues that were fundamentally interrelated with the purposes and values of student affairs as a profession.

Three Emerging Trends

- New reporting structures for student affairs, including reorganization and/ or redistribution throughout the institution.
- In difficult fiscal periods, offices of student affairs are more intensely scrutinized, which increases the need for data and assessment to demonstrate effectiveness.
- Turnover of senior leadership at at-risk institutions requires ongoing education and information about student affairs and its role.

Turnover at the top also served to reinforce the scrutiny of the student affairs unit because new leadership typically brought new ideas and new way of doing things. Alternatively, some new faces often had no ideas regarding student affairs and even a general lack of understanding of the function itself. This was especially problematic when it left student affairs to drift while sending both implicit and explicit messages throughout the institution about the purpose and value of the unit. In addition, a new leader's ideas often presented the institution with a new focus or a departure from previous missions. In some cases these transitional uncertainties over the purpose and lack of permanence of leadership left many with the impression that the institution was adrift and that everyone was following his or her own agenda.

How Fragility Affects Student Affairs as an Organization

One way fragility affected each of the institutions studied for this chapter was through the reporting structure of student affairs. A. Sandeen and M. J. Barr discuss the various models through which student affairs can report in a college or university.[8] At all the institutions the actual or potential change in reporting lines created significant stress and anxiety for the unit and the staff. In two institutions the reporting structures were changed in a way that resulted in elimination of the SSAO. This change not only affected the individuals who were in those positions (one left the institution and the other assumed different responsibilities at the institution) but resulted in a disassembling of the Division of Student Affairs as those professionals knew it. The units had to develop new and creative means of communicating, collaborating, and accomplishing their goals and mission.

Another stressed university felt that the threat of reorganization would actually happen, and this created immediate turmoil and uncertainty for many of the administrators in student affairs. Managing the dislocations at the institution's upper levels while also maintaining day-to-day operations and services for students became an increasing challenge. One leader described the experience as "not being rooted" or existing in "shifting sand."[9] The feeling of not being grounded resulted in additional stress and a heightened focus to prove the importance of student affairs work. Student affairs as a profession has traditionally struggled with its role in the academy;[10] the student affairs professionals we interviewed felt this even more significantly because of the fragility of their institutions and a change or potential change in reporting structure. One individual interviewed for this study described student affairs as the "friendly partners, always happy to help."[11] When the questions and, in some cases, criticism focused on the usefulness and even the value of student affairs, the unit spent increased time and energy attempting to prove the critics wrong and provide justification for its existence. In reflection, some of the leaders interviewed questioned this strategy and its effectiveness with comments such as the following: "We bent over too much. We lost our backbone. We lost the sense of all we have to offer and our importance to the university. We showed we were even weaker and we are still suffering from that [approach]. We have become reactive."[12]

How Fragility Affects Student Affairs Professionals

The role of the student affairs leadership team in fragile colleges and universities, especially those with frequent leadership changes, is significant and often overlooked. One administrator described it as "a lot of starts and stops with frequent shuffling of people."[13] Another senior student affairs officer spent tremendous time educating or reeducating these administrators about student affairs work and its value at the institution. Another vice president felt that it was best to align with the transitional leaders(s) to form a "positional allegiance" so that the work of the institution could move forward.[14]

One of the challenges of working at a vulnerable college or university is balancing day-to-day tasks with unforeseen crises. Some of the leaders interviewed for this study described feeling that their primary job was crisis management and putting out fires. For some this work was acceptable, but one individual also described it as "meaningless and not advancing the institution."[15] A number of individuals talked about the process of reviewing their current position and their career path and considering leaving their positions. Some felt constantly threatened and wondered if they would be asked to leave. Others felt that they needed to leave a poisonous culture and seek opportunities elsewhere. They described it as extremely taxing to feel that "you are on the brink of losing your job every day" and also noted an increase in the level of stress felt at the prospect of adding the work of conducting a job search to managing a difficult position.[16]

Most of the individuals discussed how they all simply worked harder and harder, year after year. A "frenetic" pace was one term used to describe the culture in student affairs.[17] Whether it was related to protecting one's turf, justifying one's existence, or simply employing a coping mechanism, the professionals who were interviewed discussed the many additional hours worked by most staff members who were already going above and beyond what was required. The competition for resources added an extra layer of tension and responsibility to existing workloads. In our interviews no one talked about working smarter, only harder. Few talked about prioritizing tasks or doing more with less. The overarching theme was simply to work harder in hopes of proving to others that they were indeed valuable.

Although this frenetic pace seemed necessary for the maintenance of the SSAO's position, it had a physical and emotional toll on the student affairs staff as individuals. They used words such as "angry," "frustrated," "disillusioned," and "tired." Another individual talked about how she looked around the room at a directors' meeting, noticing the bags under everyone's eyes and recognizing that there was a total lack of energy among the group: "My heart ached for the people and the incredible amount of work they did."[18] This pain often brought a group close and forced individuals to support each other in every way possible: "There was a sense of holding hands; anything I could do for you, I would."[19] Others felt useless and that they could not contribute in a positive way to the organization anymore. For some the only way to survive was to leave the institution, something they really did not want to do but saw as the only choice.

Trust and Tension: Navigating through Fragility

The heart of student affairs work is the students; thus when the student affairs unit is negatively affected, there is a strong potential that students will suffer the consequences. In our research it was strongly evident that professionals wanted to make sure students' lives were not negatively affected and that they were able to get the support and services they needed to have a quality education: "We worked even harder because we didn't want students to suffer."[20] Most felt that students, whether prospective or current, were not aware of the vulnerability of their institution and that business for them went on as usual. However, some discussed the impact on student leaders, especially those involved with

---

Three Best Practices

- Maintain professional connections and resources.
- Recognize, organize, and utilize student affairs' broad constituents more ambitiously.
- Establish a team whom you trust, to whom you can delegate, and who are supportive of the institution's evolving mission.

---

student government. The mission and goals of some student leaders were dictated by the goals of the current administration, and if those goals were in flux, the students were in flux as well. At one stressed institution the SSAO was removed from the president's cabinet; when this occurred, many individuals began to wonder whether students' needs were being represented properly and if the student voice had been lost. Although this dramatic move might be viewed as administrative belt-tightening, it reinforced staff insecurity and added to morale issues.

Although it is common to engage students to help reach goals or as advocates for an office or cause, there can be a fine line between educating students and manipulating them. Stories were shared that students were being used to advance the agendas of various campus factions and that the students did not always know what the real truth was. The stories and contexts from these institutions suggest that despite the numerous and varied causes of fragility, SSAOs and student affairs units are likely to be affected in several basic ways:

- Crisis of purpose: What is the role that student affairs plays at the institution?

- Calls to demonstrate value added: How central is student affairs to the campus mission?

- Reconfiguration of unit: Can other executives more effectively manage it?

- Staff morale issues: How much do student affairs staff members contribute to the mission of the campus?

Often it is too late to start establishing relationships during difficult times. Having a strong base before a crisis allows leaders to draw on this goodwill for strength and support: "My personal relationships were broad and deep. I had established meaningful and expansive connections with faculty, students, staff, and community leaders prior to the crisis. I had

an established pattern of acting with integrity and I was known as someone people could trust."[21] Others discussed the importance of establishing relationships but noted that when there was such constant turnover,
it was difficult to establish loyalty, especially if the person did not hire
you in the first place. Trust was a value discussed by most of the leaders.
It was important for the senior student affairs leader to create an environment of trust both within the organization and externally. As the
SSAO, this leader needs to have a small team of individuals whom the
person can trust and confide in. One leader "tightened the circle of next-
level leaders" and formed a smaller team to have a place to communicate
both information and feelings as openly as possible.[22]

The senior student affairs leader may also have to deal with limitations of power and influence.[23] Leaders are typically used to being productive and high achievers, but in times of crisis, feelings of impotence,
powerlessness, and helplessness can occur. Leaders discussed the physical and emotional impact the crisis had on them as individuals. One
person acknowledged not taking care of his personal well-being and
eventually needing to take some time away from the institution. Another commented on how difficult it was to leave campus and the accompanying crisis for his professional development. However, by not
leaving campus, this leader had a harder time maintaining outside connections and felt that he lacked a strong external support system that
might have helped him get through the difficult times. In reflection, all
who were interviewed acknowledged the importance of knowing one's
limits and taking care of oneself.

Many of the leaders also discussed the tension between being open
and limiting how much information was shared. SSAOs set the tone by
conveying a positive attitude that things will be fine. It was noted that
it is important to have open communication with one's supervisor so
that when a staff member needs clarification about what is occurring,
he or she trusts the information. Communication among staff, although
especially important in times of fragility, also has the potential to lead
to more conflict.[24] One student affairs leader described updating staff
about the campus crisis at the same time another staff member was
soft-pedaling the same information. In further discussion the two individuals considered how sharing too much of the information with lower-
level staff members could increase their stress level and result in unnecessary worrying when their jobs were actually safe. Although this
leader cited the importance of communication, she also noted the tension
experienced in having to decide how and what to communicate in order to keep people informed but still protect the staff. Ultimately this director chose the balance of remaining open at times but also protecting

---

Single Most Important Piece of Advice for SSAOs

- Regardless of where student affairs is located in the organization, constantly reaffirm that students are central to your work.

---

staff so that the day-to-day operations could still occur without additional stress or pressure.

An interesting dynamic discussed by a few of the individuals interviewed was how one's personality type (Myers-Briggs Type Indicator) affected their response to the crisis. A "feeler" described the situation as difficult and painful because so many individuals were struggling and going through emotional problems. Another personality type sought less discussion on the emotional impact of the situation and more concentration on accomplishing specific, practical goals and projects even when things were chaotic. One senior administrator who was reflecting on her SSAO's leadership during the more stressful times emphasized that being "open about the negative, but not dwelling on it" was comforting and helped reinforce a tone that worked well in his department.[25]

Nine Action Steps for At-Risk Environments

After evaluating both the successes and missteps shared by these student affairs leaders, we conclude with nine recommendations for those who are managing at-risk circumstances on their campuses:

1. Maintain professional connections and resources. As evidenced by the interviews in this chapter, these issues and challenges are increasingly commonplace. Professional associations are keenly aware of this trend, as are colleagues in the profession. Maintenance of close contact with other student affairs professionals was identified by many who were interviewed as a key form of support and source of professional guidance in difficult times.

2. Routinely evaluate your trust scores. In part because of the nature of the profession, student affairs professionals seek to place a high level of trust in others, just as they do with students. Unfortunately, within the politically charged environments of threatened institutions, SSAOs must negotiate the realities of human nature in the contexts of competition and power. A key support for the professionals interviewed for this

What SSAOs Should Do Differently

- Communicate more candidly about the resources of the Office of Student Affairs internally.

chapter was the ability to share with others the struggles that they faced. As mentioned previously, the opinions of colleagues with perspectives from other institutional settings were important when they were coupled with the support of those familiar with the inner workings of one's own institution. SSAOs must be cautious about this, however, and carefully evaluate the trust they place in others. In several of the institutions examined, the collegial relationship of peers was converted to that of supervisor and direct report, leaving lingering questions about what might have been revealed.

3. Delegate but maintain a strong presence. It is critical that SSAOs stay in touch with their units. Building a strong cadre of directors and support staff is central to the ability to be away from the day-to-day operations, but presence has been identified as especially critical for SSAOs in fragile settings where the worth and impact of student affairs work may have been called into question. Presence and engaged leadership help lower- and midlevel student affairs staff members continue to feel valued within their institutions.

4. Communicate strongly about the unit both internally and externally. SSAOs repeatedly shared that one of the toughest lessons learned was how critical it was for them to communicate strongly what the unit was doing for students and especially what the unit was doing for the institution overall. Very often those who were interviewed explained that they failed to note that other campus senior executives did not see the results of their efforts. The SSAO holds the explicit responsibility to convey unit contributions, and starting this communication after fragility takes hold is too late.

5. Be explicit about personal values, the values of the unit, and the relationships between them. Values are central to the profession of student affairs, and living by them and then successfully communicating this were identified as powerful forms of motivation by student affairs staff members, especially in vulnerable circumstances. Staff members acknowledged that they need to understand and then respect the values of their SSAO.

6. Do not allow anyone to forget that students are central. Student affairs professionals at stressed institutions need to continue to provide services and opportunities for students and to educate student leaders, in particular, about campus dynamics so these younger leaders can be successful in their own circles. SSAOs have the responsibility to carry the student voice forward on decisions that affect students' experiences.

7. Differentiate among forms of support and "presence" offered to staff. It is important to be aware that individuals will respond differently in times of crisis, and effective leaders need to provide multiple forms of support and guidance to meet the needs of their staff members.

8. Do not be shocked by the need to justify yourself. SSAOs must be prepared to confront the need to justify the purpose and place of student affairs on several levels of the college or university structure: executive leadership, professional staff, faculty, and even influential undergraduates.

9. Recognize and use student affairs networks. It is important for SSAOs to use their existing networks internally and externally to obtain information and, to the degree feasible, shape policies and campus culture. SSAOs should actively develop collaborations among faculty, alumni, trustees, and state legislative delegations to gather information and learn different perspectives.

Working in stressed college and university environments is an extremely difficult situation for any campus executive, but senior student affairs administrators may be more vulnerable than the other members of the institutional leadership team. Some SSAOs will survive and even thrive, but many will not. One individual said that "we always think, this won't happen to me,"[26] but evidence confirms that increasingly it is happening even to senior student affairs professionals. A quality student affairs team and organizational model can exert tremendous positive force on a weakened mission and infrastructure, so it behooves senior campus leadership teams to collaborate and recognize their important contributions.

III

Who Is at Risk and Why:
The Financial Factors

Some maintenance could not be deferred, and allowing too many students not to pay their bills for too long a time caused the financial ratios to crash. Student life had to be supported, but we could not catch up and find enough money to operate.

> —Pastor George W. Freyberger, former college chaplain and dean of students at Upsala College, New Jersey, in a telephone interview with James Martin, 10 May 2007

We ran out of money. We could not pay the bills. People tend to assume someone else will pay for things.

> —Reverend Owen Jones, former president of Rose Hill College, South Carolina, in a telephone interview with James Martin, 10 May 2007

CHAPTER EIGHT

Effective Financial Leadership of Stressed Colleges and Universities

Michael Townsley

Financial data suggest that a large proportion of small and medium-sized private higher education institutions live on the edge of financial viability. Those institutions that live closest to the edge lack resources to provide a credible education for their enrollees and are forced to troll for students with a paucity of academic skills or personal motivation. Unforeseen events and mistakes can force these institutions to close their doors. Even though these conditions can also prevail at public higher education institutions, they are more typically assured of their continuance, subject to the politics of the moment. Still, despite fears that dramatic shifts in demographics or cuts in federal or state support will compel the closure of hundreds of schools each year, most at-risk institutions somehow survive in the face of severe financial threats. The evidence indicates that on average only seven institutions a year have closed their doors during the past thirty-five years, according to the *Digest of Education Statistics*.[1] Thus it would appear that survival for most at-risk institutions is a matter of pluck and luck and help from alumni, the government, or windfalls at the last minute.

The fragility of the finances at private institutions is most evident when investment returns fall dramatically, as happened in 2001 and 2002, when more than 50 percent of a set of private institutions reported deficits (table 8.1; data for the two years included 608 small [fewer than 1,000 full-time-equivalent (FTE) students], medium [1,000 to 2,000 FTE students], and large [more than 2,000 FTE students] institutions).[2] When investment returns are removed from net income and the reporting period is extended into the economic recovery of 2003 and 2004, the fragile condition of small and medium-sized private institutions is particularly noticeable (table 8.2). Thirty-eight to

Table 8.1. Percentage of Private Institutions Reporting Deficits with Unrealized Gains and Losses

Institution Size	Number	2000	2001	2002	2003	2004
Small	165	24.2%	47.3%	55.2%	45.5%	17.6%
Medium	263	10.3%	45.2%	57.4%	35.7%	4.9%
Large	180	6.1%	35.0%	53.9%	27.8%	1.7%

Source: Data provided by the Austen Group, Eagle, Colorado, 2006.

56 percent of those institutions continued to report deficits for each of the four years. These proportions are consistent with an earlier study that included the years 1999 and 2000, when economic conditions were very strong.[3] A substantial proportion of large private institutions also reported deficits during this period. However, the string of operating deficits for these institutions tapered off after the market slide of 2001 and 2002.

The implication of the data is that most private institutions, especially small and medium-sized ones, operate very close to the margin. Table 8.2, which excludes investment returns, illustrates that the average net income between 2000 and 2004 for the sample ranged from 4 percent to −3 percent for small institutions, from 4 percent to −4 percent for medium-sized institutions, and from 3 percent to 0 percent for large institutions. More telling is that when investment returns are excluded, small institutions had operating deficits for three of the five years and medium institutions had deficits for two of the five years. This suggests that when the financial buffer of investment returns is removed during dismal periods like the years 2001 and 2002, net income for many private institutions immediately becomes problematic. Small and medium-sized institutions, in particular, creep along a fine line between positive and negative net income, never quite building the reserves needed to survive periods of uncertainty or change. Figure 8.1 shows this effect for small and medium-sized private colleges. Large private institutions usually ride much higher above the line, but they too are vulnerable to deficits, as noted earlier, when financial markets turn negative, because they lose endowment income and gift income falls.

The risky condition of many American institutions, both private and public, is supported by the "2007 Higher Education Outlook" published by Moody's. It reported that the risk of declining revenues

Table 8.2. Percentage of Private Institutions Reporting Deficits after Unrealized Gains and Losses Are Deducted

Institution Size	Number	2000	2001	2002	2003	2004
Small	165	48.5%	51.5%	50.9%	55.8%	47.9%
Medium	263	39.5%	47.1%	50.6%	52.1%	41.1%
Large	180	37.2%	38.9%	45.6%	45.0%	38.3%

Source: Data provided by the Austen Group, Eagle, Colorado, 2006.

associated with declining enrollments over the next decade would become apparent in 2007 when enrollment grew only 1 percent, compared with double that growth rate annually between 1998 and 2004.[4] Susan Fitzgerald believes that four types of institutions will be at greatest risk: midtier private institutions that are pursuing improved reputations, small rural colleges, regional public universities where population is falling, and community colleges in "economically stagnant areas."[5] The combination of real risks in the economy and finance of higher education—major reshaping of demographics in large regions of the United States, the cost of delivering education or research, debt loads, financial aid, and declining tuition revenue—will push colleges that live on the edge of fiscal health. The threats noted by Moody's will further undermine the financial integrity of both private and public institutions that already live day-to-day and are unable to build financial reserves without a large influx of debt to protect and strengthen their financial condition.

Effective fiscal management is imperative for an institution's strategic condition because it records whether it produces and husbands the resources needed to achieve its mission. As a result, institutional leaders must treat finance as more than mere number crunching. It should be seen as the lifeline of the institution, and its vital signs should be constantly monitored to assure that the institution can maintain and strengthen its ability to provide services that yield significant value to students and society. Moody's noted in its 2007 outlook report that institutions of higher education must develop "realistic financial plans" if they want to survive.[6]

Although private institutions are as susceptible as public institutions to changes in governmental support, most private institutions must navigate rough economic waters on their own without recourse to state coffers. Since public institutions can face at-risk conditions similar to those at many private institutions, the actions suggested here also apply to them. However, the long-term financial welfare of a public institution is dependent on the political savvy of their presidents and boards to acquire state funds to support their institution. State funding may bring enormous competitive advantages to public institutions, but it also contains very high costs in the form of regulations and funding criteria that constrain the scope of their decisions.

Quite simply, effective management for at-risk higher education institutions means ending the at-risk condition. If they have to dance around the condition, they will remain at risk, with the associated threats of continued decline, inability to keep pace with change, and, by implication, shortchanging their students. This chapter provides ways to strengthen these public and private institutions through guidelines and commentary as they develop strategies and management tools to reach a financial state in which they have the flexibility and strength to deal with their own institutional economics and finances.

The Economics of At-Risk Institutions

The economic model for at-risk institutions is no different from that of other institutions of higher education in which price as a market-clearing mechanism is distorted by their not-for-profit status and internal or external subsidies in the form of financial aid or endowment

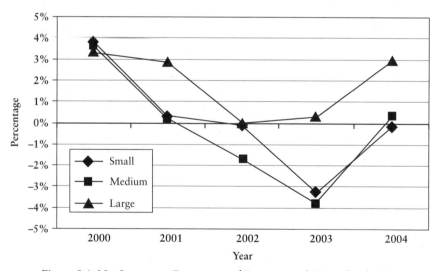

Figure 8.1. Net Income as Percentage of Revenue with Unrealized Gains or Losses Deducted

---

Three Emerging Trends

- Major demographic trends clearly show shrinking traditional student pools in the Northeast and Midwest; expanding student pools in the Southeast, Southwest, and West; and fewer students prepared for the academic rigors of a college education in all regions. The Northwest and Midwest will experience downward pressure on tuition revenue. All regions will see upward pressure on financial aid and the cost of education for academic services because of the decline in academic skills.
- Tight markets and declining government support will increase tuition dependency, causing many private and even some public institutions to change their business models.
- Small colleges, particularly rural or religious ones, will be forced over the brink by the government, auditors, accrediting agencies, lenders, and student markets.

---

income.[7] The governance structure in higher education further aggravates economic distortions because the cumbersome hierarchical and consensual decision-making structure is slow to react, is unable to clearly articulate its goals, and selects inefficient technologies to deliver its services. Pricing and governance impose a double impact on higher education institutions because long-term financial equilibrium is nearly impossible to achieve. The inability to achieve financial equilibrium reduces their financial resilience because they do not have sufficient liquidity for daily operations, much less the reserves that are needed to respond to unexpected events. Financial equilibrium in which revenue and expense growth rates are in balance, given that revenue exceeds expenses, is the sine qua non of financial strategy.[8]

Just what is risk? Risk under most financial definitions is simply the deviation from the probability that a set of expected events will occur. Risk for institutions of higher education has been defined by D. Collier and C. Patrick as "the potential for financial difficulties, which is inherent either in the institution's capital structure or in the way it carries out its operations."[9] Capital structure refers to debt load, endowments, and liquidity. A college or university is at financial risk when normal operations, endowment income, or liquidity reserves are insufficient to fully cover debt service, payroll expenses, vendor payments, or unexpected emergencies.[10] The risk now becomes real because conditions in debt instruments may require full and immediate payment of outstanding balances, employees can sue for nonpayment of services,

---

Three Best Practices

- Build financial reserves—cash, unrestricted investments, and endowments.
- Install a financial and administrative system that precisely records and reports the condition of the institution on a real-time basis.
- Set performance objectives, track performance continuously, and make strategic changes when the market or performance fails to achieve objectives.

---

or vendors can also sue or place a lien on the property that could prevent short-term borrowing.

There are usually three types of risks: general economic risks, institutional-sector risks, and specific institutional risks. A general economic risk is produced by a change in the economy, for example, higher interest rates, new regulations, or changes in economic performance. An institutional-sector risk occurs when economic changes specifically affect a certain sector of higher education, for example, changes in demand nationally or regionally for engineers, nurses, or teachers. Examples of specific institutional risk are a strike by part-time faculty, a change in the student market for the institution, or a rise in the number of competitors. Nathan Dickmeyer suggests a variety of risks that institutions of higher education may encounter, such as fluctuations in applications, grant awards, research productivity, utility rates, success of athletic teams, academic preparation of students, or retention rates.[11]

Risks can lead to either better-than-expected amounts of net income and growth in the capital structure or worse-than-expected changes in net income or the capital structure. It is important to note in this context that risk is both good and bad. It is good when actual events are better than estimated, and obviously it is bad if actual events are worse than expected. For purposes of this chapter, only negative risk will be considered since it generates substantial short-term and long-term problems that can adversely affect the operational stability of the institution.

Strategic Planning for At-Risk Institutions

Most presidents and key leaders of an at-risk college or university are all too aware of the deteriorating condition of their institution if it has a history of deficits, declining enrollment, costs rising faster than revenues, or ever-increasing levels of short-term debt to cover daily cash requirements. They have learned the hard way that the institution is in trouble because they have had to beg or borrow to secure necessary funds—or ignore complaints from numerous employees, vendors, and banks. These presidents have learned to cope with decline; whether they are successful at coping is another issue. In many cases the board and president are surprised by how the "severity of decline affects the speed with which responses are formulated and implemented."[12] Presidents who have mainly experienced long periods of growth earlier in their careers can be shocked by the pace of decision making needed to deal with unexpected, persistent, and deep decline in financial condition.[13]

Changing the direction of a college frequently calls for major shifts in mission, structure, and personnel. The literature shows that the typical response to continuing financial problems is piecemeal retrenchment, which does little to change the dynamics that put the institution in an at-risk state.[14] David Whetten sees several reasons that strategic responses lack boldness and vitality: personal stress, the innovation-resistant structure of higher education, the difficulty of quantifying educational excellence, the tendency for the best to leave first, and the tendency for traditional values to checkmate change.[15]

George Keller, an early leading advocate of strategic planning in higher education and author of the widely influential *Academic Strategy: The Management Revolution in American Higher Education* (1983), asserts that the president is essential to encouraging, prodding, and pressing for the kind of change that pushes an institution out of its at-risk state.[16] A president learns quickly that she or he must convince institutional leaders that the likelihood of a successful strategy increases to the extent that they apply self-discipline, market sensitivity, foresight, and prudent ground rules of acceptable behavior to the problem.

Strategy incorporates the assumption that a rational approach to problem solving and decision making can yield a viable and flexible strategic plan. The classic rational approach to strategic planning is based on gathering raw data, converting data into usable information, identifying strategic options, recognizing the consequences of the options, and understanding the chances of success or failure of a particular consequence. The commonly accepted steps in strategic financial planning include the following:

1. Prepare a data book with sections on finance, markets, academic programs, information technology, and management policies.

2. Isolate critical internal strengths and weaknesses and external threats and opportunities.

3. Determine factors that are central to avoiding or moving out of a state of risk.

4. Identify strategic options and test their short- and long-term potential.

5. Select the strategic options with the greatest probability of success.

6. Develop the strategic package, which should include goals, action plans, and monitoring procedures.

A strategic plan must do more than build buffers against contingencies. Strategies must make the institution flexible and responsive to the market. Financial reserves are only valuable if they feed an efficiently run operation so that the institution can serve its market. Otherwise reserves will only survive until the next crisis, in which panic planning again becomes the norm.

Commentary on the Strategic Guidelines

Financial strategy is dependent on effective strategic analysis.[17] It must take a comprehensive view of the institution because the institution's future is contingent on these factors that drive its financial condition: markets, academic programs, and management resources. Isolating critical internal and external factors calls for a thorough analysis of internal operations. Since the main problem is financial risk, the institution must have a clear picture of how it generates income, expends funds, and uses its financial reserves. This understanding is contingent on recognizing that financial management is not the cause of financial stability. Rather, finance is the scorecard that shows how well the institution is responding to demand and producing services.

Determining what is critical to avoiding or ending a fragile financial condition must be more comprehensive than finding what immediate steps should be taken to eliminate deficits. The college or university must build the financial resources and financial buffers to avoid the vagaries of the moment, which means that it must find a mission, market, and services that will increase financial reserves.[18] Strengths, weaknesses, opportunities, and threats (SWOT) analysis is an excellent instrument for capturing the internal and external factors that determine the university's strategic condition. The university itself is the focus of the strengths and weaknesses components, while factors external to the university are the focus of the opportunities and threats components. The advantage of this process is that it forces the analysis to look beyond the immediate daily concerns of survival to consider the larger issues that are causing the vulnerability of the institution. It is within the

---

Single Most Important Piece of Advice for Presidents

- Presidents must lead from the front if they are to turn around an institution that is at risk financially. A president cannot wait to mollify all factions, resolve every policy dispute, or hope that financial resources will magically appear to save the day. Financial stability is driven by decisions, and leadership is at the core of a successful turnaround.

SWOT context that market, financial, and operational analysis can be most fruitful in figuring out how to design and implement the strategic plan.

A SWOT analysis can generate literally thousands of factors that are likely candidates for either creating problems or solving problems, but it will not indicate their relative value. The analysis should glean those internal weaknesses or external threats that have had the greatest impact in producing the current condition or have the potential to amplify the threats substantially. Financial analysis is a key component of a broader SWOT analysis because it points to the fiscal factors that are placing the institution at risk, but financial solutions alone may not be able to resolve some issues; the strategic plan must show how it will overcome those weaknesses. The next section focuses on how financial analysis will identify those financial factors, and it will suggest their impact on designing a strategy for recovery.

The first task is to convert opportunities and strengths from the SWOT analysis into strategic options that target the critical list of weaknesses and threats. These options will need to be rigorously tested against a reliable and comprehensive financial model that incorporates basic financial performance and investment criteria. Rigor means more than a well-drafted model; it means that the options must be realistic. Here is where the president must insist on precision and candor during the design and testing of strategic options. These tests must tell the news, good, bad, or indifferent, regarding the potential of a particular option to alter the financial condition of the college or university.

Once a realistic set of options is selected, the next stage is to turn them into an articulated plan that specifies goals, actions, responsibilities, timelines, and resources. Goals are the single most important component of the action plan because they will define success or indicate that major or minor modifications must be made in the strategic plan. The goals have to be measurable and accepted by all the sectors in the institutional community—the board, chief administrators, faculty, and others who have to sanction and implement the plan.

Just as goals are imperative for the action plan, a rigorous performance-monitoring system is indispensable to determine if the strategy is working or not. Monitoring systems should be designed to determine how well the institution is doing at three levels: strategic goals, internal performance, and external benchmarks (other institutions or industrial averages).[19] The monitoring system also should link directly with strategic planning to refine action plans when performance fails to meet goals. Strategic plans are only as good as their implementation. A strong plan can be waylaid if implementation is half-hearted or if it is not continually monitored and if refinements are not expeditiously made. Time, as much as money, is a resource very easily depleted in assuring that performance achieves the goals of the plan.

Strategic Options: Making the Economics Work

Colleges and universities that are working strenuously to remove a reputation for fragility must examine the realities of the market, how they can most effectively serve that market, and the resources that are needed to reenter the market as a strong rather than weak player. There are a variety of approaches taken over the past decade that an institution can test as a viable strategic option. However, time, demographics, and resources will eliminate some of those options. For example, it is very late in the game for some colleges to turn to working adults as their financial savior because many baby boomers have now reached the age at which it is no longer economically feasible to make an investment in higher education. Also, if the institution is not now offering a continuing-education program, and if every institution, for-profit or not-for-profit, within twenty miles is doing so, the market is most likely fully absorbed. Timing is key in responding to market demands. This is where market sensitivity earns a premium because plans that do not acknowledge the realities of the marketplace will waste the meager resources available to a struggling college or even a well-known university.

Table 8.3 presents conditions that should be considered for different types of strategic options. They must be adapted to the exigencies that face the institution. There is also one concept, online education, that will be discussed separately in some detail because many institutions are either considering this option or have begun to invest in what is believed to be its potential to add a huge flow of new revenues to the annual budget.

Table 8.3. Guidelines for Strategic Options

General Rules

1. Test all projects with a multiyear cash-flow budget.
2. Band the outcomes with high and low estimates based on the potential of positive or negative events.
3. Use net present value to rank-order projects.
4. Clearly lay out rules governing projections and related assumptions.
5. Design incentives for program managers to find new revenue or cut expenses.

New Revenue Sources

1. Generate positive cash flows within three years.
2. Study the competition—how can you do better?
3. Find out what employers or graduate schools expect of your graduates—how can you provide those skills?
4. What is working in other parts of the country?
5. What are the high-paying fields for graduates; can you offer programs in those areas?
6. Charge for new services that you offer students.
7. Raise money from alumni by offering expanded services.
8. Lay out detailed marketing, pricing, academic, and service plans.

(table continues)

When a college or university begins to consider strategic options, it should review a comprehensive list of reasonable options. Investment analysis avoids selecting the first option that comes to mind because it may not produce the results that another option could have generated if a broader sweep and analysis had been conducted. Strategic analysis tests each option with a full study of market demand and its financial requirements. The analysis should involve collecting data on market potential, conducting surveys and focus groups of potential students, holding meetings with employers, and assessing the direction the competition has taken with the idea of producing a better product than anyone else is offering. The same presumption about rigorous testing is true for the financial analysis; this should include a five-year estimate of cash flows and investment requirements. Cash flows should be used to estimate the net present value of the project, and the projects should

---

Table 8.3. Guidelines for Strategic Options (*continued*)

Expense Reductions and Management Efficiencies

1. Use computer services to replace administrative offices.
2. Compare costs with those of best-practice competitors.
3. Increase the number of chairs in classrooms.
4. Rent or use space that is not being used currently.
5. Cut utility costs.
6. Reduce paper use.
7. Add new staff judiciously.
8. Avoid off-budget hiring.
9. Do a staff utilization study to determine whether personnel are used efficiently.
10. Refinance debt when interest rates fall.

Outsourcing and Joint Ventures

1. Outsource anything that will cut costs, for example, security, custodial services, maintenance, parking, transportation, copying, bookstores, food services, information technology, or dormitories.
2. Find partners for new capital projects to offset cost and depreciation.
3. Develop joint ventures with other institutions that complement your programs.
4. Develop joint ventures with community colleges, high schools, vocational schools, or other training institutions.

---

be ranked in order of the computed values.[20] Then the market and net-present-value rankings should be compared to determine what is realistically feasible and select those projects that have the highest probability of success and of producing solid returns for the institution.

Colleges and universities that are considering online education initiatives need to approach them in a disciplined, hard-nosed fashion because the investments are substantial and competition is accelerating. Online projects are not simply plugging programs into the web. Major changes in policies, procedures, information technology, and communication systems must be instituted if the institution expects the project to have any chance of success.[21] The problems that must be resolved are myriad, but they are resolvable if the president, key administrators, and faculty are willing to cooperate and do the tough slogging to make online education work. The following are just a few examples of the procedural and policy problems that will need to be addressed: registration procedures, timely completion of classes, class standards for teaching, access to libraries, the distribution of books, and the reliability of the network. The financial analysis of the online project will need to follow a model that fully encompasses the expenses in preparing courses, delivering courses, and supporting students. Table 8.4 outlines the major factors that must be considered in estimating the value of an online project.

A Financial Diagnosis for At-Risk Colleges and Universities

Since at-risk institutions are by definition financially unsound, financial analysis is a critical element of their strategic analysis. This analysis must provide the following elements:

—The current and long-term financial condition of the institution, given existing strategies, plans, and practices

—The leverage points in the financial system for alleviating financial risk

—Models for testing strategic plans

—Indicators of performance

A major financial challenge for higher education is the lack of standard indicators that are accepted as signals to the industry that the financial condition of a particular institution or institutions is taking a turn for the worse.[22] Many reasons exist for the dearth of indicators. One reason is that indicator values are not widely published. Second, national data sources, such as the Integrated Postsecondary Education Data System (IPEDS), do not include data for variables needed to compute sophisticated indicators of financial health like the Composite Financial Index. As a result, information about financial health is spotty at best and usually localized to the institutions and possibly a few peers that are studying the problem of financial health. Thus individual schools usually are not aware of major changes in their condition until those changes have transpired. Even institutions that employ sophisticated financial planning models often are working with linear models based on historic data that drive the model in one direction. Also, there are no common measures used to indicate future value of the institution, such as price per share or market share. As a result, institutions are left with painstaking and expensive research efforts to estimate their future financial condition that often founder on the assumptions built into the model. For fragile universities and colleges, this can be an expensive use of precious money and energy. Nevertheless, if colleges or universities,

Table 8.4. Guidelines for Estimating Financial Impact of Online Programs

General Rules: Online Education

1. Basic questions: is the program acting as support for existing courses, or is it conducted solely on the web but taken only by campus students, or is it conducted solely on the web but taken by noncampus students?
2. What infrastructure is needed to support the program?
3. How reliable is the current infrastructure?
4. Is additional support staff needed to maintain the infrastructure twenty-four hours a day?
5. Are there adequate academic supporting resources, for example, library materials?
6. Who will develop the courses, or will they be purchased?
7. Are there copyright issues?
8. If the program is based on continuous or cohort enrollments, is it supported by appropriate registration, billing, and financial procedures and administrative policies?

Budget Planning

1. Design a budget model that forecasts revenue, expenses, and cash flow. Use the following items to develop the model.
2. Enrollment projections that include attrition and graduation rates.
3. Pricing policies: is the price based on prices for regular courses, or will there be a low-price/high-volume strategy?
4. Cost of course development and courseware licenses.
5. Space-allocation costs.
6. Training instructors for online course delivery.
7. Operational and capital cost of information technology.
8. Operational and capital cost of communication systems.
9. Operational and capital cost of backup systems.
10. Cost of online library support.
11. Marketing and advertising.
12. Admissions, financial aid, and registrar support.
13. Administrative, staff, and faculty compensation.
14. Office supplies and equipment.

Source: Dennis Jones and Frank Jewett, "Procedures for Calculating the Costs of Alternative Modes of Instructional Delivery," in *Dollars, Distance, and Online Education,* ed. Martin J. Finkelstein, Carol Frances, Frank I. Jewett, and Bernhard W. Scholtz (Phoenix, AZ: Oryx Press, 2000), 227–28 (budget-planning guidelines).

regardless of size, want to turn around their fragile status, they must expend the effort and funds, or they will be subject to the whims of the market and significant upcoming changes in demographics.

Financial analysis rests on a reliable data set.[23] This may seem an obvious and uncontestable stipulation, but the structure and definition of financial data and the data that feed the books are not always consistent. Accounting rules, policies, and variations in how the data are defined among offices can change dramatically from year to year. Several examples will illustrate the issues. One is that data problems can exist in the transition year when new Federal Standards Board of Accounting (FSBA) rules are introduced. In the past decade there have been major changes in rules on depreciation, gifts, and the structure of financial reports. Other changes of this form happen all the time and must be taken into account when multiyear data sets are being tested. Another example is how the registrar's and the billing offices define a student. The former may define an FTE student as anyone enrolled after the drop-add date, while the latter may discount an FTE student based on the amount of refund that is set out in financial aid policies. The number of students will have to be reconciled between the two offices for the analysis because the reference point of financial data should be the audited financial reports. Use of other reports means that timing issues come into question and the accuracy of the analysis may become an issue. Audited reports are a good benchmark for analysis because a third party has reviewed the records, and the data in the report provide a firm point of reference. Once the data issues are resolved, the analytic tools can be applied.

There are many different analytic tools that are commonly employed to parse the financial condition of an institution and point to the leverage points for change. Before any tools are employed, it is wise for institutional leaders to remember that financial analysis is not a precise science in which an equation leads to a recognized and accepted answer. The best way to approach the analysis is to apply several indicators. The initial findings will indicate where to drill deeper to find the problem.[24] What follows is a multistep analysis that applies different tools to locate risks and leverage points in the financial system. Anyone who is conducting a financial analysis may want to modify these tools or add other tools that could be deemed to have a better chance of isolating problems, risks, and solutions.

Step 1. Baseline data are needed to place where the institution stands and to act as a yardstick when strategic change is measured. The data should be comprehensive and not limited to finance alone, and they should examine flows from inside and outside that generate revenue,

What a President Should Do Differently

■ Institutions in a constant state of financial risk often force presidents to make suboptimal hiring or retention decisions because the best employees cost too much money. Successful turnarounds are directly dependent on the quality of three key positions: academic, finance, and information systems. Hiring or keeping the best-qualified person can often mean the difference between a turnaround that succeeds and one that fails miserably.

result in expenditures, or shape financial reserves. The baseline should contain at least three to five years so that trends can be noted.

The first component of baseline data works with audited statements of activities, financial position, and cash. In addition, admissions and academic program data, such as student-faculty ratios and classrooms plus personnel counts, should be part of the baseline. The audited data should be presented in dollar amounts and as percentages of a common base, for example, revenue and expenses as a percentage of total revenue, assets, liabilities, and net assets as a percentage of total assets, and cash as a percentage of total cash. Placing the data in percentage format removes the obscuring effect of changes in scale. Dollar amounts and percentage tables provide easy indicators of the direction and pace of major changes. Another first-line tool is to compute one-year percentage increases and compound rates of change.

The analysis should proceed by first looking at one-year changes to see if changes fit expectations and to determine the impact between two years on financial condition. Cross-year changes either in absolute terms or percentage changes can indicate trends, relative scale of changes, and where problems may exist. For instance, if net tuition is shrinking over time, then the data might show if that change is caused by falling tuition revenue, rising tuition assistance, or a combination of the two. Marginal analysis provides a second component of baseline data because it indicates how new money is flowing into and through the system. All that needs to be done is to take the absolute dollar differences between two or more years and determine which revenue categories contributed to changes in revenue. The next question will be to determine how the new revenue was spent or allocated toward assets. This can be extended to see how cash and assets are produced: is the money coming from operational net income, short-term debt, long-term debt, or increases in current liabilities? These simple questions, along with others, can clarify what is happening to finances, the direction that financial condition in terms of net income and net assets is moving, and where problems are arising.

Key performance indicators (KPIs) are the third component of the baseline data. KPIs are indicators that "describe the functioning of an institution, the way the institution pursues its goals."[25] Two references suggested by this definition are of interest here. The first reference is to the functioning of the institution and suggests that the indicator tracks specific performance in such areas as admissions, ratio of students to faculty, and other processes within the institution. The second reference compares performance to specific goals. A third reference for which performance indicators are used is performance related to some external standard or group, often termed "benchmarking." The performance indicators that are most widely used to track financial condition and the major productive factors that drive financial condition are provided in table 8.5.

Indicators like the previous baseline components usually work best when trend data are used.[26] The references can be to the goals of the institution, to prior performance, or to standards. The standards can include national performance benchmarks (IPEDS data), competitor data (from IPEDS or from state department of higher education reports), or accounting standards such as the current ratio of assets to liabilities. Data analysis is where the hard work lies because the institution has to pierce the stereotypes, platitudes, and glib answers to find the real cause of what is happening, and when a major discrepancy emerges between standards and performance, staff members must do deep drilling to extract the real cause of a variance and in some cases the reason for a continuing decline. In these instances key personnel must collaborate to get to the correct data and to delve into what is putting the institution at risk.

Step 2. Identifying points of financial stress directly follows the analysis completed in step 1. Rigorous analysis means meticulous questioning of every piece of discordant data. Fine points must be extracted that indicate problems because that process is where the construction of a strategic plan starts.

Responsibility-centered analysis (RCA) can substantially enhance financial analysis. Another term for this tool is "responsibility-centered management."[27] This analysis requires a considerable degree of precision of the definition of the variables in the model and the data used to support the model. It is suggested that before the analysis someone review the methodology and data requirements. Simply stated, RCA

Table 8.5. Standard Management Indicators

1. Admission yield rates.
2. Net tuition, gift revenue, or grant revenue ratios.
3. Compensation (arranged by category) ratios.
4. Noncompensation expense ratios, such as utilities, information technology, or advertising).
5. Net income ratios.
6. Cash ratios.
7. Current assets and liabilities ratios.
8. Debt ratios.
9. Net asset ratios.
10. Instructional productivity (class size, faculty loads, or space loads) ratios.
11. Financial health (Composite Financial Index: a measure that taps into major elements in the financial system that shape the financial health of an institution of higher education).

---

involves the allocation of costs to revenue centers such as academic programs, advancement offices, or auxiliaries. The allocation of costs calls for the correct assignment of financial data to academic programs, depreciation to cost centers, administrative expenses to cost centers, and other expenses to their correct centers. Each center will then have either a positive or negative net income, and the sum of the net income should equal the sum of the net incomes for the centers at the end of the year. A separate RCA should be done for at least three years to determine if there is some sort of distortion in any year. RCA is an excellent tool to show where strategies should be targeted. Those strategies could include expansion, management restructuring, cost controls, or even elimination of nonproductive centers, subject to the mission and requirements of the curriculum.

One more highly valuable tool to find stress points within at-risk institutions is the Composite Financial Index (CFI),[28] which measures the financial capacity of ready reserves to cover emergencies and debt service in addition to the capacity to build financial reserves. The CFI is a set of ratios that, when viewed over several years, indicates major weaknesses or strengths in the financial system. Moreover, the overall score generated by the CFI provides a simple indicator of financial health. Before this analysis is conducted, as with the RCA analysis, someone should carefully review the parameters of the computation of the index.[29] The ratios that make up the CFI can be decomposed to locate where the financial system needs to be strengthened to improve the ratio value and the overall CFI score.

There is an orthodox list of stress points that indicate financial risk or a severe deterioration in performance. This does not say that these stress points are the cause of the problems in a particular institution, but they do represent a place to start the exploration. A partial list of stressors is provided in table 8.6.

The conclusion of this step occurs when a catalog of factors is identified around which a strategy will be built that carries the greatest impact on the at-risk financial status of the institution.

Strategic Analysis

Strategic analysis is conducted by employing a financial model, an indicator of financial health, and RCA to evaluate the financial validity of the factors identified in the prior tests. The financial model should generate a forecast for the statements of activities, financial position, cash flow, and critical financial ratios (an example is debt ratios related to potential debt covenants). The model must reflect the operations of the college and should not be abridged to save time. The financial office will need to be diligent in the construction of the revenue and expense factors because they must reflect the dynamics that underlie changes in revenue and expenses. CFI is a fine tool for estimating the impact on financial health. Data from the forecasts can be inserted into the model to estimate the CFI score and to assess whether it is improving or not. By translating the ratios into a set of leverages, specific strategies can be tested to assess how values are improved or if they have deteriorated further.

Finally, data from the forecasts can also be applied to the RCA model to identify the level of contribution that each revenue center is providing. The goal is to have each center achieve a designated rate of return and a positive contribution, subject to its mission. These tests will also shape the final elements of the institution's overall strategic plan.

Conclusion: Triage or Turnaround?

Triage is the only option when the college or university does not have the cash to make payroll, pay bills, or cover its debt payments. When this happens, the institution's fate is shaped by the president's abilities to find resources where there were none before, to make good decisions quickly, and to exercise an innate sense of how to gauge and serve the market. Experience demonstrates that triage too often focuses on cutting expenses through massive amputations, selling land and equipment, and begging board members, alumni, and friends to give

Table 8.6. Standard Warning Signs of Financial Distress

1. Admission yields are falling.
2. Retention rates are low for a particular program or level of instruction, or year of enrollment, or population sector of students.
3. The net tuition rate is declining because enrollment is falling, and financial aid is rising faster than enrollment.
4. The amount of gift or grant income is less than the cost of acquiring the gift or is falling, suggesting problems in operational efficiency.
5. The amount of auxiliary net income or the rate of net income is falling or negative, pointing to management, policy, or strategic problems.
6. Long-term rates of growth of total expenses exceed rates of growth of total revenues, indicating that the institution is not in financial equilibrium.
7. The rate of growth of personnel compensation is outpacing growth of revenues.
8. The rate of growth of instruction compensation is outpacing growth of tuition revenue.
9. Compensation or personnel counts by categories for administration outweigh rate of growth of revenues or of faculty.
10. Advertising or marketing costs are greater than new tuition revenue, or these costs per student are greater than the incremental revenue.
11. With regard to net income, a string of deficits is depleting financial reserves (assets).
12. With regard to cash flow, short-term borrowing or late payments to vendors are growing at a fast pace, or the cash ratio (cash to current liabilities) is shrinking dramatically.
13. The ratio of expendable assets to long-term debt is substantially less than 1:1 and is falling.
14. Revenue centers are not generating positive income after operational expenses are allocated.
15. Debt covenant ratios fail to adhere to the conditions established in the debt covenants.

money. Institutions in these dire circumstances tend to rely on their internal communities to rescue them. Perhaps a savvy president or a generous benefactor or two can start the turnaround process. At least, this is the outcome that many stressed leadership teams dream about. In actuality most triaged universities and colleges continue to stumble from one financial crisis to another. Sometimes luck is with them; in other instances they slip downward to a life of annual deficits within two years.

Successful turnarounds are not based on luck. They happen more realistically because the institution is not destitute and has at least a few resources to devote to tough-minded planning decisions that produce well-designed projects and investments. These strategies are coupled to a monitoring system that tracks performance and are coordinated by a president who insists on flexibility and an entrepreneurial spirit to make midcourse corrections and take advantage of new opportunities.[30] To succeed in this fragile context requires commitment, discipline, and sound decisions that are not easily accomplished in times of vulnerability and within the complex, often-sluggish governance structures of higher education.

Coming shifts in demographics, joined with the heavy debt loads currently carried by many private and public institutions as they try to propel themselves up the rankings ladder, suggest that turnarounds and triage may both become more prevalent in the next decade. Moody's, in particular, believes that the dynamics of those ten years will be harsh for many institutions. To survive and flourish in this period will require a sense of what "at-risk" really means in contemporary higher education and the strategic financial solutions to overcome this persistent challenge.

CHAPTER NINE

Fund-Raising through Fragility: Some Suggestions for Development Officers

W. Stephen Jeffrey

One might think that the last thing an at-risk institution should be doing is fund-raising. There are several reasons, however, that a weakened college or university should fund-raise, especially if the institution's fragility is in large part caused by inadequate funding. Beyond this, one of the most important reasons to fund-raise is more than simply to seek funds; it is, rather, to broaden the institution's base of support by reaching out to old and new constituencies and managing critical dialogues with key alumni, donors, and members of the institutional community. In fact, it may be that one of the principal reasons for the institution's vulnerable circumstances is that these dialogues have broken down, and although it may be appropriate and even necessary for the institution to launch an ambitious fund-raising campaign, the pressure to be successful will be enormous, and there will be an even smaller margin for failure in reaching its financial targets. This chapter attempts addresses two central questions related to this: how can one raise funds for stressed institutions most effectively, and how does fund-raising for these colleges and universities differ from standard higher education advancement activities?

Higher education institutions can be fragile for many reasons besides purely financial ones. In the case of the American University of Beirut (AUB), where this writer has been the vice president for development and external relations since 2002, the institution was fragile as a result of Lebanon's fifteen-year civil war (1975-1990) and continues to be fragile because of the assassination of respected political leaders, the war in the summer of 2006, and the political impasse that has followed. The effects of this conflict—and, indeed, the continuing political uncertainties in the entire region—have made AUB an at-risk university. The impact of the civil war was experienced by AUB long after the war ended in 1990 and was manifested in many ways, including poorly maintained files, "lost" alumni, an unwillingness and even a fear among some staff members to engage in long-term planning, an inadequately staffed advancement office, and a chronic reluctance among many potential donors to give to an institution that they were not convinced was going to survive in spite of its long history.

Most American colleges and universities that are fragile find themselves in this situation for more mundane and structural reasons than a fifteen-year civil war: their tuition discount is too heavy, the ratio between the endowment and the operating budget is less than 1:1, or debt service is 15 percent of the operating budget, as primary examples. Alternatively, strong institutions may experience vulnerable periods due to unforeseen events such as the impact of Hurricane Katrina on Tulane and other New Orleans higher education institutions in 2005 or the multiple student shootings at Virginia Tech in the spring of 2007. Although these particular institutions may not be essentially at risk, the incidents themselves, if not handled skillfully, will weaken the institution to some degree. One of the most common reasons for an institution's vulnerability is weak institutional leadership. Matthew Schuerman notes, "In most cases, a nonprofit on the brink of disaster needs a strategic makeover along with the bailout."[1] Many fragile colleges and universities became fragile because they lacked a strategic plan and the leader necessary to accomplish it. From the perspective of fund-raising, it is critical that the college develop a vision that can be clearly articulated and understood by all constituents and that there be broad support among key members of the college community for it before the development office launches the fund-raising campaign. Without a vision it is far more difficult to raise significant funds, and the money that is raised will carry less impact over the long term.[2]

Malcolm Rogers, director of the Museum of Fine Arts (MFA) in Boston, says that one of the key ingredients in MFA's success in recent years has been convincing those who work at the museum that they must work together for the good of the entire institution. He "has made it very clear that he does not like independent departmental behavior. Our goals will be determined in mutual discussion."[3] It is critical that members of the college or university community not look at fund-raising as a zero-sum exercise but rather appreciate that any gift that benefits a particular department or discipline benefits the institution as a whole. The perception internally must be that everyone is working for the same core vision and that any gift strengthens the institutional mission. Rogers concludes, "People are excited about the vision of a great institution."[4]

In addition to a clear vision for the future, there must also be agreement among the administrative and faculty leadership about the causes of the college or university's fragility before it launches a fund-raising campaign. In the case of the American University of Beirut, there was widespread agreement among the university's leadership team that the fifteen-year civil war had weakened the institution to a dramatic extent academically and financially. At other institutions that are vulnerable, however, this agreement may be much more uncertain and difficult to achieve. Nevertheless, once the best agreement possible is reached on the causes of vulnerability, this information must be communicated openly and sometimes even painfully to the broad institutional community. Ideally a consensus can be developed about these reasons and about the action steps to address them, but if this is not possible, at the very least the president, the cabinet, and the board must lead and speak with one voice from this point with the goal of making the fund-raising campaign a driver of the larger process to strengthen the fragile institution.

Launching a Campaign on a Fragile Campus: Seven Components

Certainly it is appropriate and in many senses easier for an at-risk institution to emphasize a "give-now" approach to fund-raising. If the word is out, so to speak, and the community and region know that the university or college is vulnerable, it is often easier to convince potential donors that their gifts are needed and will be valued highly. The immediacy of this approach cannot be duplicated at other institutions. At AUB the community launched a campaign to rebuild College Hall, the most prominent building on campus, after it was badly damaged by bombing in 1991 after the Lebanese Civil War had ended. There was little question that the bombing of this historic building had shocked and galvanized many individuals. An alumnus who was involved in this campaign offered this reaction to the bombing: "I did not sleep that night after I heard the news while attending a university dinner in New York City. We decided that same evening that we had to do something."[5]

Although this incident demonstrated vividly how weakened AUB was during and immediately after the war, it also prompted a number of friends of the university to make gifts for the first time. A small number of those who contributed to the College Hall Campaign have continued to be regular contributors, and some have increased their giving levels over the following years. Anne Marie Borrego wrote in the *Chronicle of*

Higher Education in 2002 that at wealthier colleges one has the luxury of sometimes taking years to court alumni, but at fragile institutions a "give-now" approach is both necessary and critical.[6] However, fundraising for a once-fragile college or university that has turned the corner in popular perception and is on its way to recovery can be easier because a process and a dynamism are apparent and give key donors confidence that the institution will survive and even prosper.

Higher education institutions do not become fragile overnight. The process usually takes time and includes several noticeable stages. During this period institutional leaders may have adopted some bad administrative habits, whether as a coping mechanism for significant daily anxieties or, in their view, simply to keep the institution operating and moving forward, even to a small degree. For a major new campaign to succeed, institutional leaders will need to reconnect with these administrators, at all levels of the college or university, and keep them engaged in the process of turning the institution around for the campaign to carry its greatest impact.

1. Pragmatic Development Goals

Typically the institutional mission and current strategic plan guide annual priorities and budget allocations. Under normal conditions the development office takes its directions from the president and from the trustees and seeks to raise funds for the priorities that the institution has publicly identified and disseminated. At a fragile institution, however, the development office and the vice president for this area of operations need to become more involved in helping set the institution's strategic goals and priorities. This is appropriate both because the vice president is a member of the senior management team and because he or she knows the donors and their interest areas. Although donors' interests should never dictate a college or university's priorities, they must be considered increasingly carefully. Precisely because an institution is at risk, it is important not to launch a fund-raising campaign that has little or no chance of succeeding.

It is also valuable in these situations for the development team to serve as the pragmatist for the institution as a whole. The development officer needs to be optimistic much of the time—and certainly in public—and to have the ear of the president and key trustees so that she or he can present a realistic view of the situation. However, the development team also needs to think about the short term and reach its goals without ever losing sight of the long term. Even in the midst of fragility it is the development office's responsibility to think and act strategically in achieving current campaign targets and in laying the groundwork so that future campaigns will also be successful. Particularly at a stressed institution there may be a stronger-than-normal tendency to sacrifice the long term for the short term, but it is the development office's challenge to make sure that this does not happen for the long-range health of the institution's mission.

In addition to helping set an institution's priorities, the vice president for development is also the primary source of expertise on campus about what the college or university must do before it launches the fund-raising campaign. Although major campaigns eventually require an increase in the annual development budget, at an at-risk college or university the development office may have to—and should—work with less so that all of the school's priorities can be funded. A perception that the president, board members, and development staff are spending too much on publications and the cultivation of potential, perhaps long-term donors will not serve a fragile institution well. There are well-established norms for fund-raising expenditures, and vulnerable institutions should be guided by those norms while at the same time acknowledging that mature development programs can raise money for less than those that are just beginning the process of building their donor base.

2. Engaged, Informed Trustees

Michael Townsley provides cogent examples in his study *The Small College Guide to Financial Health: Beating the Odds* of colleges that closed because of bad decisions about where to spend their money, including what academic programs to promote or discontinue and what buildings to build or not to build.[7] From an advancement perspective, an institution is more likely to find itself in this situation when the board is not involved and has adopted too much of a hands-off approach. In recent years the expectation of what boards should do has changed. Ideally, trustees should bring a different perspective to key institutional deliberations, should be prepared to educate themselves about emerging problems, and then should play an active role in shaping the decisions and sticking to them.

Although there are many reasons that a campaign might fail, several higher education observers have pointed to trustee fatigue as one critical factor. Also, problems can arise when an institution launches a campaign too soon after the conclusion of the previous one. Additionally, in some communities, many who serve as trustees on university or college boards also serve on the boards of other nonprofit institutions and may find themselves seriously pressured by their external schedules. Senior development officers have come to expect several forms of engagement from higher education trustees: a willingness to give to their fullest capacity; a willingness to help identify potential donors, individual and corporate; and a willingness to make introductions and, when appropriate, to solicit gifts on behalf of the institution. Although this might be the polite way of invoking the familiar descriptor of trustee involvement, "Give, get, or get off," nominating committees nevertheless continue to rate fund-raising experience as one of the most valuable measures of prospective trustee eligibility.

3. Candid Donor Relationships

Most presidents and provosts are now quick to note that over the past twenty years almost all donors, no matter what their net worth is, have become increasingly sophisticated and now are asking more questions about institutional expenditures, strategic plans, returns on endowments, investment managers, and even the salary of the top administrative staff at the institution. Much of this information is readily available, and being forthright and candid in answering questions from donors is absolutely necessary. In this context a weakened college or university needs to reach out—something that may be particularly difficult to do at a time of heightened vulnerability—and look for additional ways, some of which can be low cost or even no cost, to connect with those in its donor group. Many potential funders want to feel and believe that the institutions and its senior leaders are not interested only in their money but also in their ideas and assessments as well. Potential donors may also be seeking assurances that "a new team with a fiscally conservative approach" is now on board and that it will be "completely transparent" with its donors.[8] Another shift is that the decision-making horizon for many givers is lengthening, and although being in regular contact with a donor is always important, it may be even more important at a stressed institution at which the need to reassure the donor is particularly acute.[9]

4. Broad Community Support

At a university or college at risk, it is particularly important that the fund-raising campaign be structured not only to achieve its specific financial targets but also to broaden the school's base of support in the process. Many advancement vice presidents, feeling pressure from many directions, will acknowledge the temptation to focus excessive attention on a small group of key individuals. In the short term it seems much easier to secure ten gifts of $10 million than ten thousand gifts of $10,000. In the long term, however, the college or university will be stronger if it gathers and can depend on the support of tens of thousands rather than dozens of donors. As well, some of those who give at the $10,000 level today will give much larger gifts in the future if they are kept involved and are cultivated by the trustees, the president, and senior development officers.

5. Dependable Academic Quality

Maintaining and even raising the quality of the institution's academic programs is perhaps the most difficult goal to achieve at a fragile college or university. Matthew Schuerman discusses the challenge of keeping the quality of the product high while at the same time scaling back on the costs: "As revenues lag, colleges have no choice but to cut profligate spending."[10] Yet it is extremely difficult to cut many costs because many of them are fixed: facilities and especially technology needs, licenses, insurance, and faculty tenure, as central examples. Nevertheless, even at fragile campuses, preserving and enhancing the quality of academic programs can make the difference in securing a medium-sized gift that might otherwise have been redirected.

6. Expanded Documentation

Donors to fragile colleges need more reassurance and documentation than those at other institutions. Regular reports from the president, the board chair, and the campaign chairs provide opportunities for donor contact and help reassure donors that the college is on the right path to recovery and that fund-raising campaigns are on target to achieve even modest goals. The costs of such communications need to be considered, but electronic communication is gaining wide acceptance, and regular telephone calls to major donors and potential donors from the president and board chair are seen as both increasingly expected and increasingly productive.

7. Adequate Unrestricted Funds

In the context of a capital campaign, unrestricted funds can play a pivotal role. The board and senior leadership team need the flexibility to use money where and when it is needed the most. Even a college or university with a large endowment can be financially fragile because many of the funds that make up that endowment have been restricted for specific programs or purposes by original donors.[11] Building this base of funding support also makes it easier for an institution to survive a period of fragility in the future. Two methods even a fragile campus can implement are a reinvigorated program of alumni reunions, perhaps on commencement weekend to consolidate costs, and an expanded program of alumni volunteers for phone-a-thons that have been precipitated by the school's announcement of a new capital campaign to fund new priorities such as a fresh academic program development agenda or strategic partnerships to leverage institutional strengths.

Closing Thoughts: What Capital Campaigns Cannot Do

Although financial difficulties are often the trigger for fund-raising campaigns, fund-raising cannot and should not be the only way to lead a fragile college back to health. Henry E. Riggs, former president of Harvey Mudd College, argues that fundraising "as a quick fix for budget deficits simply doesn't sell."[12] A 2006 article in the *Hartford Courant* described some of the current difficulties being experienced by Trinity College on its downtown campus. The college decided to trim its administrative staff, "lay-off some part-time professors and even close a faculty lunchroom to fix a financial squeeze caused by years of overspending," according to President James F. Jones Jr. The college was also planning to raise tuition 4.5 percent and was freezing pay increases for faculty and staff. "The new budget is expected to provide financial aid to only about 36 percent of the incoming freshman class, compared with levels of 45 percent to 50 percent at some of Trinity's competitors." The article quoted Tony Pals of the National Association of Independent College and Universities as saying that "it's not unusual for a number of private institutions to be going through budget difficulties" caused by rising costs in health insurance, technology, and building construction.[13] Throughout these difficulties it has been noted that there has been no suggestion that Trinity is planning to mount a major fund-raising campaign to solve its current situation, and that is appropriate. In the view of many observers, with an endowment of almost $400 million, the college needs to get its house in order before initiating such a fund-raising effort.

What happened at Sharp HealthCare in San Diego in 2006 is also relevant for planning teams in higher education.[14] Sharp HealthCare was facing a number of serious challenges: little growth in the number of donors and the number of gifts, significant staff turnover, lack of a clearly defined major gifts process, no prospect research program, and no comprehensive case for support despite the launch of several strategic initiatives. Sharp HealthCare chose to address these problems by engaging all employees "from front-line caregivers to executive management" in the development process so that everyone had a clearer, deeper understanding of the specific role that each individual plays in the institution's development cycle.[15] This type of inclusive reorientation process can help focus a vulnerable college or university by using the development agenda to clarify and even lead the strategic plan.

Launching a Campaign on a Fragile Campus: Seven Components

- Pragmatic development goals
- Engaged, informed trustees
- Candid donor relationships
- Broad community support
- Dependable academic quality
- Expanded documentation
- Adequate unrestricted funds

A key area in which capital-campaign designers often fall short is engaging the main body of the faculty in fund-raising. At some institutions there may be an effort at the level of individual department heads, but rarely is there an effort that effectively targets all faculty members for reasons ranging from logistics to timidity. Even after such transformative events as the attacks in New York and Washington, D.C., on 11 September 2001 and the devastations of Hurricane Katrina in 2005, many faculty members continue to think that getting involved in fund-raising is still not their responsibility. Increasingly this is an attitude that faculties cannot afford because it is in their self-interest to become more involved. As fund-raising expands and succeeds, campus infrastructure and professional development opportunities improve, and their institution attracts both better-prepared students and more credentialed colleagues.

In closing, at-risk colleges and universities should launch a capital campaign only after the causes of the institution's fragility have been identified and discussed and are being addressed. The need for the school to have a current, clearly understood mission and strategic plan complemented by a consistent leadership team that is able and willing to participate in fund-raising is also clear. What may not be as certain is the matter of timing, both with regard to relationships with donors and concerning key public announcements. Vulnerable institutions do not want to be perceived as acting too quickly or desperately, but at the same time they realize that they cannot afford to wait too long for the "perfect" moment. In our experience, although campaigns cannot schedule themselves, this concern turns out to be a minor one because if proper and adequate groundwork has been laid, an effective fund-raising campaign, even in a stressed environment, creates its own timing for those ready to participate.

IV

Strategies That Work:
New Solutions for Key Operations

The leadership of the college did not do enough to differentiate it from its competitors. Rather than trade on its history, they should have stayed fresh with new program choices and a broader mix of programs overall.

> —Patrick O'Leary, former professor of business at Marycrest International University, Iowa, in a telephone interview with James Martin, 9 May 2007

Make sure to stay close to your key student markets and anticipate not simply where your students have been coming from but, even more importantly, where they will need to come from in the future.

> —David Hutchins, former adjunct instructor in engineering and chair of the College Industrial Advisory Committee at Henry Cogswell College, Washington, in a telephone interview with James Martin, 11 May 2007

CHAPTER TEN

Accreditation, Fragility, and Disclosure: Maintaining the Delicate Balance

Sandra Elman

More and more private colleges and universities are now facing insolvency, and this number will increase significantly over the next twenty years. When this happens, the leadership is often confused and frightened about what led to this catastrophe. Trustees wonder and ask who should be held responsible. Presidents, who may have logged endless hours trying to prevent a deteriorating financial situation from hemorrhaging, are left feeling defeated and defenseless. Nevertheless, if past events are a predictor, it is likely that increasing numbers of higher education institutions will face closure, merger, or acquisition in the next two decades.

What goes awry that makes boards and presidents unable to see that their institutions are critically vulnerable? The answer is twofold: (1) failure to recognize that gauging an institution's well-being requires an integral understanding of the complexity of factors that contribute to its vitality; and (2) failure to recognize the warning signs of impending doom.

Interestingly, monitoring specific indicators of one's own health and conditions that portend heart attack or stroke may be more meaningful for assessing a human being's physical vulnerability than monitoring comparable specific indicators of an institution's well-being, in part because the latter usually involves the interaction or interconnectedness of multiple variables that together affect the overall fate of the institution. Whereas an individual's risk of a heart attack may be accurately assessed by measuring discrete indicators such as one's blood pressure, cholesterol levels, and plaque in the arteries, assessing discrete institutional financial indicators such as the size of the endowment, accrued debt, and accumulated deficits may provide necessary

Three Emerging Trends

- Increasing demands for public disclosure and transparency
- Increasing institutional accountability
- Increasing competition from the for-profit sector

but not sufficient information to recognize impending institutional breakdown.

Institutional vulnerability is caused not only by internal financial strife but also by external conditions. At-risk colleges and universities, in particular, are affected by the increasingly turbulent environment in which they operate. Unprecedented external demands for accountability and quality assurance by the public, donors, accreditors, legislative bodies, and the U.S. Department of Education often leave these colleges exasperated and uncertain how best to respond to a range of uncoordinated and burdensome requests for information, data, and reports. Moreover, competition from well-resourced, highly competitive for-profit learning organizations, virtual degree-granting, nonaccredited institutions, and even old-fashioned diploma mills compound pressures to attract new students within the realities of being tuition driven.

What, exactly, is an at-risk institution? From a regional accreditation perspective, an institution that is "at risk" lacks financial stability and needs to be monitored so that conditions will not worsen to the point at which its accreditation is withdrawn. As a college or university's financial well-being becomes more precarious, the institution as a whole typically experiences more widespread destabilization and uncertainty. For some institutions, this is the beginning of a downward spiral that is impossible to reverse.

At-risk institutions tend to fall into two categories: those that are smart and know how to seek and pursue viable venues for changing their circumstances, and those that become insular, focus on discrete rather than holistic components of the problems, and face further decline. Vulnerable institutions in the first category often turn around their circumstances by taking advantage of a unique process of self-appraisal, using the process offered by regional accreditation evaluations. Regional accreditation is a mission-driven, quality-assurance process that allows accredited institutions to engage in a process of self-examination against a set of standards. Regional accreditation, in contrast to specialized or programmatic accreditation, focuses on evaluating the institution as a whole rather than on specific programs. Regional accreditation evaluations are based on the notion of institutional self-appraisal. More often than not, at-risk colleges and universities have avoided engaging in a comprehensive and candid self-appraisal process. If this process is done well, it can be timely and useful for the institution to take its own temperature, assess what its strengths and weaknesses are, and, most important, make careful projections about the future that can drive the institution to improve its overall viability. Accreditation reviews, particularly comprehensive decennial and mid-term evaluations that are conducted in the Northwest region, call for institutions to undertake an in-depth analysis of their financial condition. Institutions accredited by the Northwest Commission on Colleges and Universities, as an example, must assess the totality of their financial circumstances and operations in the context of adequate financial resources, financial management, and fund-raising and development. Institutions are required to "demonstrate that financial planning for the future is a *strategically guided process*" (italics added).[1] At-risk institutions typically discover that financial planning has not been "a strategically guided process" but more likely an ad hoc series of disconnected steps taken in crisis mode. As the college or university begins to address its accreditation standards, the institution needs to provide evidence that "this planning includes a minimum of a three-year projection of major categories of income, specific plans for major categories of expenditures, and plans for the management of capital revenue and expenditures."[2]

Stressed institutions are sometimes pressured into pursuing solutions to their financial problems that appear to offer immediate but short-range access to needed revenues. These attractive and potentially high-risk perceived solutions may include entering into partnerships with third-party entities that will provide venture capital, needed loans, or access to students seeking to earn credits from regionally accredited institutions. Alternatively, they may involve moving to a higher degree level and offering distance-delivered master's degrees in high-demand professional areas, such as business, computer science, or education. More often than not, these options are illusory and may even exacerbate an already-serious financial situation.

Governing boards and presidents are equally responsible for the financial condition of a college. At times these two leadership components may be likened to dance partners where one leads and the other follows, but during troubling times when uncertainty is high and there is no pre-scribed choreography, they need to stay in sync, avoid wrong turns, and calibrate the impact of every step taken. The self-study process that undergirds regional accreditation reviews, if done well, will provide the board with a fresh assessment of the institution's capacity to fulfill its mission, particularly in terms of the fiscal, physical, personnel, and technical resources necessary to support institutional mission and goal fulfillment. Perhaps it is not surprising that there is a high correlation between a governing board's lack of knowledge about the real financial conditions of the institution and the fragility of the institution. In a high-pressure, cost-constrained environment, trustees often do not have sufficient or relevant information to inform their decisions and long-range plans. Board agendas become overloaded, and issues that have potential litigious and public relations consequences often take precedence.

Best Practices; or, How to Write the Self-Study

In a world of shifting dos and don'ts, there is a cardinal sin that presidents and board chairs of fragile institutions simply cannot commit: denial. Although present realities may be tough to acknowledge and finding realistic solutions may be almost unthinkable, a worse act is to deny that the situation is that severe. In one sentence, denial is a precursor to demise. Perhaps most daunting for a president or provost is knowing where to start turning his or her institution around. The following five best practices are for leaders of fragile institutions who are now preparing for a comprehensive decennial accreditation review and between decennial reviews. Beyond these five, it is also valuable to know that a turnaround typically requires a minimum of two and sometimes up to five years, and the path forward is always an arduous one before net gains are realized.

1. Create a vision to sustain institutional identity. Often, vulnerable institutions undergo a period in which they lose sight of their mission and educational objectives in a sometimes-desperate grab to increase enrollments. In these situations they introduce new programs or degree-completion programs without considering either the ramifications of such initiatives for the overall future of the institution or, as important, the effects on the college or university's standing vis-à-vis its peers. A president whose college was on probation for a time with the Northwest Commission on Colleges and Universities forthrightly admitted that in hindsight "we knew we needed to refocus our direction, but we weren't sure what would yield the most effective outcomes. Clearly students are seeking more professionally based programs like computer science and accounting that will better position them in the marketplace. Traditional liberal arts curricula are just a hard sell when you are not a top-tier institution in the East. The fact is we had no vision driving us or guiding us."[3]

Three Best Practices

- Create a vision to sustain institutional identity.
- Establish core values to frame future actions.
- Engage in ongoing self-regulation and self-monitoring, using accreditation mechanisms to enhance stability.

Without a commonly understood vision across its campus, a weakened institution is likely to flounder and make arbitrary decisions that go unchallenged. Strange as it may appear in hindsight, many trustees tend not to question the statements or proposals of outspoken colleagues on the board, particularly when the school is already in crisis mode. For a discerning visiting team member and reader of the self-study, "A vision is a mental perception of the kind of environment . . . an organization aspires to create within a broad time horizon and the underlying conditions for the actualization of this perception."[4] A vision is particularly critical for a financially at-risk institution in order to guide an organization's destiny, to promote cultural changes, and to respond to environmental changes. The vision of an organization will be realized in part on the basis of the institution's sources of competitive strength and capability. It is a description of a new and desirable future reality that can be communicated throughout the organization. In creating a vision, the institution sets in motion a process that will challenge prior assumptions about the institution's persona while simultaneously questioning its future focus. What is critically important for the leadership of the institution is to be able to articulate a vision that presents a credible, attractive future that is distinctly more viable than the one that presently exists. As well, this vision must be distinctive; it cannot sound like one more four-year liberal arts institution approaching extinction.[5] A realistic vision is a necessary but not sufficient condition to position an institution for turnaround. From this starting point, the president and cabinet members then need to redefine the core values that undergird the college or university, the execution of its educational programs, and its relationships with internal and external constituencies.

2. Redefine core values. Core values are the essential, enduring constructs of an institution, and a well-conceived vision must embody them. Presidents must keep in mind that "core values require no external justification"; rather, they have *intrinsic* value and importance to the institution.[6] As an at-risk institution continues to spiral downward, presidents incorrectly assume that there is a magic set of core values that the institution should embrace. This notion is ill founded. To the contrary, there is no universally right set of core values for a particular institution. The leadership must strategically identify with key internal stakeholders what values the institution holds to be at its core apart from competitive requirements or institutional fads. Leaders must be resolute in emphasizing only those values that are truly core and so fundamental that they will endure through periods of even greater adversity as the institution moves forward.[7] Faculty, staff, and administrators must be passionate about these values because institutional survival may hinge on their support. One president explained, "A financially vulnerable institution cannot afford negative energy from cynics or skeptics. They should be encouraged to go elsewhere so they do not distract those who are most invested in having the college succeed in its turnaround."[8] Core values need to be repeatedly articulated by the president and the chief academic officer at every possible opportunity; for example, they should be posted on the institution's website and cited in all institutional publications, such as newsletters, catalogues, and annual reports.

3. *Do not go it alone.* Feeling pressured and isolated in a downward swirl of financial difficulties, some presidents pull away even from close advisors and begin to believe that they have to do everything themselves. Whether well intentioned or not, this kind of strategy is useless. The president and the board chair need to be realistic and acknowledge that neither the administration nor the board can fix all or even most of the institution's problems in isolation. When the college has articulated its vision and reaffirmed its core values, the president's key role is to bring together a small cadre of committed faculty and administrators who will apply their knowledge and expertise to the strategic process of self-examination modeled after the regional accreditation self-study. Presidents who have already invested in and understand the nature of this process often fare well in this regard. Similar to steering committees formed to oversee the self-study process, a "community of practice" needs to come together to lead the institution's turnaround with the emphasis, in the case of fragile institutions, more on function than on structure.[9]

This community of practice should be composed of individuals within the institution who are committed to fulfillment of the vision, who emulate the institution's core values, and who have the energy and determination to turn their college around. The group's primary purpose is to work with the president in formulating and implementing short- and long-term strategies that will achieve needed change. This group ultimately provides the intellectual and political leadership at a grassroots level that is essential on a campus with decentralized structures and autonomous faculty holding greater allegiance to their respective disciplines than to their institution. Effective presidents let the community formulate its own approaches to ensuring that necessary strategic directions are pursued in an environment of open and ongoing communication. In effect, then, the president is responsible for charting the strategic course that will address the financial conditions, while the community of practice sets the rules of the game for deploying its colleagues in repositioning the institution.

4. *Think systematically.* A vulnerable college or university is an amalgam of interdependent units, departments, and services that is suffering weakness or breakdown at various points. Although it may be that one unit initially broke down, typically this failure is the result of a series of related missteps within the system. Specific units have discrete functions, but to understand and address what went wrong overall at the college or university, presidents must analyze the effectiveness of the interrelationships among the parts of its system to discern how best to address the problems. One cannot salvage the whole institution, a president of an Alaskan institution once financially at risk observed, if he or she does not look at the institution holistically and admit that isolating the problem only compounds it.[10] Presidents and boards have the greatest success if they begin from the dual premises that (a) their institution is a collection of interdependent offices and functions that must be appropriately aligned to contribute to the school's overall well-being, and (b) the problems that led to the institution's fragility can only be tackled effectively by determining how each discrete office or function must contribute to the college or university's whole health without placing the burden for rebuilding the entire institution on the back of only one element of the system.

In developing plans to address finance and enrollment conditions, in particular, presidents and provosts should ascertain how the various units of the institution can work together to restore stability and develop a self-regulating enterprise dedicated to ongoing appraisal and continuous improvement. Regional accreditors are continuously working with their member institutions to facilitate the design of models aimed at regeneration and renewal. The self-study process overall is focused on identifying limitations and bottlenecks in the system that thwart these objectives, whether in fragile conditions or not. The more the chief executive officer is able to instill in her or his colleagues the sense

> ## The Single Most Important Piece of Advice for a Leader of an At-Risk Institution
>
> ■ Take firsthand responsibility for understanding and overseeing the institution's financial condition.

that the university's turnaround depends on individuals working toward collective goals, the greater the likelihood that the institution will reinvigorate its mission and attract external support. On the issue of external relations, whether an institution is located in a rural or an urban setting, its malaise cannot be hidden from its surrounding community. Local newspapers and community groups are quick to notice the pulse of a weakened college. The more the campus climate can address this and exude positive energy, the more likely it is that the institution will garner the support of the media.[11] It should be added, however, that mobilizing individuals to think and behave optimistically in at-risk circumstances demands levels of leadership and endurance beyond the reach of even some experienced presidents.

5. Self-regulate for stability. Stressed institutions do not have the luxury of time. Presidents and boards must act quickly and decisively to develop and implement strategic plans that will increase enrollments and achieve financial stability. The extent to which short-term plans and enrollment management strategies are effective will depend in part on the college or university's ability to identify the principal reasons for its current fragile circumstances and then to self-regulate movement forward in order to avoid these pitfalls a second time. Institutions profiled in this book that decided to close their doors and cease operations were also often unable to agree on the specific reasons why the school became at risk originally. To help move fragile institutions back to health, the Northwest Commission on Colleges and Universities has developed an effective tool, the Annual Report on Finance and Enrollment (ARFE), that guides institutions in monitoring their finances and enrollments. When the commission discerns that a college or university is moving closer to at-risk status and is experiencing financial or enrollment challenges, it requests that the institution submit an ARFE. The ARFE process has proved to be valuable for both the commission in its oversight role and, as important, for institutions to verify the specifics of their own negative circumstances. Essentially the ARFE process requires an institution to ask a series of critical questions: Do we have the capacity to generate hard data, to analyze those data, and to use them to inform decisions that will improve our financial and enrollment conditions? Also, are we able to make financial and enrollment projections for the next three to five years on the basis of those data? Financially vulnerable colleges often do not have the institutional research capacity to systematically engage in analytic assessment of financial and enrollment data and to use the findings in determining budgetary and resource allocation.

Even if a regional accrediting commission does not request that the institution submit an ARFE, an at-risk college or university should still consider adopting this tool proactively as a model for self-regulation and increased accountability. In doing so, the institution should hold itself accountable for preparing a report for its board on an annual basis. The task is formidable but not insurmountable and is well worth the investment of time and human resources. A set of guidelines is presented here that the institution should follow in an attempt to "self-correct" and shift its downward slide away from facing possible closure. An ARFE is effective in part because it requires an institution not simply to provide quantitative information but also to explain its significance for the future viability of the college, a helpful exercise for the leadership team of a fragile enterprise. The narrative portion of the report should demonstrate to the board and, as applicable, to the regional accrediting commission the institution's understanding of its fragile circumstances, specifically, its fiscal and enrollment situations, as well as providing evidence that it has developed realistic plans in such areas as budget control and projections, fund-raising capability, and retention progress to address these challenges. The board's and commission's reviews should focus on whether the financial condition of the institution has stabilized or improved and the likelihood of continuous improvement. Essentially the narrative should accomplish the following six objectives:

1. explain and appraise the institution's current financial and enrollment situation in terms of its strengths and concerns (for example, if the institution has debt, an explanation should be provided of how the institution is addressing the issue of that debt);

2. describe the institution's plans and a framework for working through the previously identified challenging issues (for example, how the institution plans to enhance and strengthen available resources);

3. address the board's involvement in financial planning, which includes providing evidence (through minutes of board meetings and board actions) of the board's understanding of the fiscal challenges that are facing the institution and how they are being addressed;

4. explicate the assumptions that underlie the institution's budgetary and enrollment projections;

5. discuss the contents of the audited financial statements, including any data that may require explanation to be understood; and

6. address the nature and results of efforts taken since the last commission review to respond to noted fiscal concerns and the outcomes of those efforts.

The narrative should be accompanied by sufficient detailed information to assure that the board has a comprehensive understanding of the institution's fiscal and enrollment situation. The information provided should include (1) actual budget results for the last three years; (2) budget projections for a minimum of three years; (3) actual enrollments for the last three years; and (4) the institution's most recent audited financial statement. Board chairs of financially vulnerable institutions strongly concur that for enrollment management purposes there are four sets of data elements that are crucial in illuminating real enrollment patterns at the institution and informing future enrollment planning: a schedule of total actual and projected enrollments; a schedule of undergraduate students by head count; a schedule of actual and projected retention for the current year, three previous years, and two years into the future; and information on the numbers of resident students that differentiates between the numbers of current resident students and the institution's normal capacity. Presidents are well aware that achieving financial stability depends on an institution's fund-raising success. Boards need to be apprised of the institution's fund-raising capability. A schedule of fund-raising should be provided to the board that indicates the number of alumni donors versus the number of alumni, unrestricted gifts, restricted gifts, and endowed gifts for three past years and the current year and projections of these numbers for two years. Last, the institution needs to generate data regarding financial management. These data should include information for three past years and the current year and projections for two years with respect to increases or decreases in unrestricted net assets, increases or decreases in restricted net assets, total debt, primary reserve ratios, net operating revenue, return on net assets, and viability.

Presidents who have led turnarounds stress the importance of being able to use these data to determine what factors have had the greatest impact on the overall health of their institutions during the years of difficulty and decline. Fragile colleges and universities do not have the option of choosing whether to engage in a sustained appraisal of their chances for survival. If regional accreditors are not already closely monitoring the condition of the institution, the board needs to implement such an internal process immediately. Put simply, there is no substitute for verifiable data. Trustees of vulnerable colleges from Alaska to Maine are almost uniform in their agreement that the best decisions are made on the basis of hard evidence that accurately assesses the financial conditions and realistically projects enrollment numbers into the foreseeable future.

Critical Decisions for Institutions at Risk

Over the next ten years at-risk institutions will face a number of formidable challenges that will place them in increasingly precarious situations. Unlike most colleges and universities that will be addressing emerging trends and new consumer demands, these stressed institutions will need simply to position themselves for survival. Among the most troublesome challenges these institutions will face will be increasing demands for public disclosure and transparency, increasing competition from the for-profit sector, and the general need to increase their institutional accountability. These challenges are especially distressing for at-risk institutions as they wrestle with balancing their public image against grim realities of financial stability and long-term survival. Over the last decade consumers have witnessed an explosion in the scope and breadth of information available to the public via the Internet. Americans of all ages, particularly those under the age of twenty-five, now use electronic means for educational as well as entertainment purposes. As prospective college-bound students and their family members search for the perfect choice, their expectations of quick and easy access to a broad range of fresh information at websites of institutions in which they are interested will make expectations before 2000 or even 2005 pale in comparison. Things are now moving so quickly that consumer demands for comprehensive profiles of institutions combined with comparative data of peers will require hard-pressed, fragile colleges to maintain much more sophisticated institutional research systems and an information technology infrastructure capable of designing and maintaining user-friendly websites and marketing materials.

As younger consumers become savvier in shopping online, they will expect to ascertain within minutes, if not seconds, the comparative advantages of attending one institution over another with respect to the

---

The One Thing That Should Be Done Differently in Leading an At-Risk Institution

- ■ "Demanding financial discipline is a must."[12]

---

range of majors, degree requirements, scope of cocurricular activities, and the comprehensiveness of athletic facilities. Parents, for their part, will be searching for information that reveals the financial stability of the institution, where graduates are gainfully employed, and the desirability of financial aid package options. The cost of developing and sustaining data bases and information technology structures to support these public relations and marketing efforts will require many fragile institutions to make critical resource-allocation decisions in already-constrained budgetary environments, but the price of not being transparent in providing public information may in the end prove to be even more costly. In an age of sound bites and instantaneous responses, at-risk institutions will increasingly be held accountable for disclosing accurate and thorough information regarding their finances and measures of student achievement via indicators of student learning outcomes. As well, these colleges and universities will need to disclose their status with their respective regional accrediting commission.

In meeting these calls for higher accountability, how will vulnerable institutions avoid portraying themselves as schools that may not be around by the time first-year students are ready to graduate? The balancing act, presidents contend, is in adhering to the principles of truth in advertising without "digging one's own grave." Some presidents of vulnerable institutions in the Northwest report that their websites and publications tell the real story and do not posit any silver linings, while other institutions that are facing similar or even worse financial situations tell only half the story and portray muted realities. The double-edged sword that these institutions already face will be compounded by emerging congressional legislative mandates that will require that regional accreditation commissions publish on their websites the significant findings of regional accrediting commissions following comprehensive and interim evaluative reviews. Fragile colleges and universities will soon have no choice but to be transparent about both their strengths and their weaknesses. One secret to success will lie in the extent to which each institution creates a viable and well-defined niche for itself in a saturated higher education market.

By the year 2010 a growing number of at-risk institutions will most likely go the way of Bradford College in Massachusetts, Henry Cogswell College in Washington, and Notre Dame College in New Hampshire. They will no longer exist. Some will die as a result of the relentless competition from a growing segment of the for-profit higher education sector that lures prospective students with expensive marketing campaigns and promises of flexible degree programs and high-paying jobs upon graduation. Many of these for-profit institutions are not accredited by any national or regional accrediting agency, nevertheless, their glossy brochures and high-powered websites entice recent high-school graduates eager to earn a college degree as quickly and easily as possible.

In the end, the presidents and board chairs of these institutions face two main options: merge or close the college, or aggressively reposition it. There will be times when the first option is more realistic and ultimately better protects the interests of students. Ideally, that option will be initiated by the institution rather than by a regional accrediting commission or the state higher education authority. If circumstances are otherwise, however, and presidents choose the second option, they must be willing to lead the institution forward by following a systematic, clearly articulated, and documented course of action that is supported by the board vigorously and without equivocation. Presidents of vulnerable institutions will need to juggle many strategic and tactical challenges simultaneously. They will need to be able to manage the complexities of the institution's instability while remaining focused and resolute in their decision making. As these leaders display an unwavering commitment to attaining financial stability, any words of optimism will be hollow without adherence to the set of best practices outlined in this chapter.

Board chairs and presidents will also need to be candid in acknowledging that there will be setbacks irrespective of the institution's effectiveness in implementing any best practices. When the college community experiences new difficulties, and it will, it is imperative that the president emphasize the school's vision and core values to sustain momentum and morale. Ultimately, what will sustain the institution are identifiable results: more stable finances, increased enrollments, and measurable indicators of positive student achievement. Leaders of fragile institutions will need to use self-monitoring oversight mechanisms such as the Annual Report on Finance and Enrollment in order to make difficult decisions based on both quantitative and qualitative evidence. Finally, presidents will need to ensure that their college or university provides the human and material resources necessary to support an institution-wide effectiveness plan with multiple methods to assess progress in key areas.

CHAPTER ELEVEN

Keeping the Faith: Leadership Challenges Unique to Religiously Affiliated Colleges and Universities

Robert C. Andringa

In the United States today there are more than sixteen hundred private four-year campuses, of which approximately nine hundred self-define themselves as religiously affiliated. Many of these institutions are fragile and on the brink. This chapter will identify key similarities and differences between faith-based and secular campuses and then offer a set of best practices for the presidents and provosts of all religiously affiliated schools to help them return to strength and stability. Until 2006 I served as president of the Council for Christian Colleges & Universities (CCCU), and this role gave me numerous opportunities to work closely and strategically with a many of the leaders of these nine hundred institutions. Their future can be brighter than that of nonreligious campuses if they leverage their distinctiveness and stay clear of several major pitfalls that confront religious higher education organizations in an increasingly pluralistic and secular society.

It is difficult to generalize about or even to classify this collection of almost one thousand institutions other than to say that they are typically small, with a few notable exceptions, and most have proud histories, along with donors and alumni who will not easily give up the hope that first energized their founders. Nevertheless, with all branches of government generally protecting their existence and treating them essentially like any other institution, religiously affiliated colleges have become as dependent on government support for their existence as their secular counterparts, and this government support is both a blessing and a warning sign for any that intend to keep faith in their distinctive missions.

What Is Religious Higher Learning?

If our research focus were worldwide, we would need to distinguish among several global religions and their roles in various "religious" colleges and universities, but for the purposes of this book, our context is the United States, and, therefore, it is safe to say that our study is overwhelmingly one of "Christian" higher learning. Thus "religiously affiliated" means a sector that is approximately 95 percent Christian. Because our nation is becoming much more pluralistic, however, many have come to use the term "faith-based" to acknowledge the increasing influence of multiple religious histories on American higher education. For institutions to be "religiously affiliated" means that their key elements, including articles of incorporation, bylaws, mission statements, histories, curricula, and personnel, all include a religious purpose and presence. Although not central to this discussion, there are clear distinctions among many faith communities that can be critical to a full appreciation of their missions, for example, the nuances among Wesleyan, Reformed, and Anabaptist institutions or the multiple strains within Catholicism, such as Benedictine, Franciscan, Jesuit, and Sisters of Mercy.

During 2005 I worked with denominational leaders and staff of religiously affiliated higher education organizations to create a national profile of these nine hundred campuses (see table 11.1). In this study the meaning of the phrase "religiously affiliated" ranged on a continuum from full denominational ownership and control to a distant, dormant historical affiliation that few on the campus fully understood. Also to be noted is the significant presence of nondenominational faith-based colleges, for example, Wheaton (Illinois), Taylor (Indiana), Gordon (Massachusetts), Westmont (California), and Azusa Pacific (California), which are clearly faith driven but are not affiliated with a single denomination. Overall, this is a diverse group of campuses in terms of location (45 states), size (100 to 30,000 students), endowment (many at zero up to more than $500 million), scope (associate and baccalaureate degrees only to multiple doctoral programs), and board size (12 to 60).

Are these institutions, or most of them, really sliding toward the brink? The short answer is yes. If finances come first to mind, then we must view them as identical to those among the sixteen hundred independent colleges and universities that have endowments of less than $10 million. Some have more than that, of course, along with sizable student bodies, such as Notre Dame, Brigham Young, and Baylor, three nationally recognized universities whose faith dimension is prominent. Yet although our research reveals that there are approximately one hundred faith-based institutions whose financial foundations should

Table 11.1. Approximate Numbers of Accredited Institutions Participating in Federal Student Aid Programs by Their Primary Religious Affiliation (Best Attempt at Nonduplicative Numbers)

Number	Primary Affiliation (April 2005)
220	Roman Catholic (in Association of Catholic Colleges and Universities)
108	United Methodist (confirmed)
65	Presbyterian (USA) (confirmed)
56	Association of Advanced Rabbinical and Talmudic Schools (confirmed)
55	Association of Southern Baptist Colleges and Schools (confirmed)
36	Evangelical Lutheran Church of America (confirmed, including 8 self-standing seminaries)
21	Churches of Christ (confirmed)
19	Episcopal Church (confirmed)
17	Christian Church/Disciples of Christ (confirmed)
16	American Baptist (confirmed)
16	Christian Churches/Churches of Christ (confirmed by Association for Biblical Higher Education)
14	Assemblies of God (confirmed)
14	Friends (confirmed)
14	Seventh-Day Adventist Church (confirmed)
12	Lutheran Church, Missouri Synod (confirmed)
11	Mennonite denominations (confirmed)
10	Church of the Nazarene (confirmed)
5	Reformed Church in America (confirmed)
5	Free Methodist Church (confirmed)
96	Estimated from 20+ other denominations/organizations with 4 or fewer accredited campuses
810	Subtotal

Estimates of Nondenominational Religious Campuses Not Included Above

26	In the Association for Biblical Higher Education (total 83; confirmed)
20	In the Council for Christian Colleges and Universities (total 129; confirmed)
26	In the Association of Theological Schools (total 150; confirmed)
72	Subtotal
882	Best confirmed Estimate of Separate, Accredited Self-Described Religious Institutions at Which Students Receive Federal Student Aid Benefits

Source: Council for Christian Colleges and Universities.

Three Emerging Trends

- There remains a steady, dependable student market for distinctly Christian institutions.
- Increasing competition is everywhere: public institutions, for-profit institutions, e-learning, international institutions, and private institutions with better locations, programs, and endowments.
- Government student aid appropriations will not keep up with inflation in the long term because of competing priorities.

---

make them competitive for decades to come, this chapter will focus on the remaining eight hundred church-affiliated universities and colleges whose enrollments may not top two hundred students, whose endowments are nonexistent, and who survive, barely, from year to year in deeply fragile environments.

Seven Major Causes of Fragility among Religiously Affiliated Institutions

1. Location, Location, Location

What is true in selling a house today is also true in selling an institution to prospective students. Geography is important, and the majority of religiously affiliated schools are in small, rural towns where their founders believed students would be protected from the sins of the city. Some of these pastoral settings provide an excellent environment in which to build community and allow for focused study. Unfortunately for these institutions, many current undergraduates have demonstrated their preference for urban settings with institutional enrollments of at least five thousand. They seek 24/7 campus life and activities where jobs are more plentiful. Recruiting faculty who often require positions for spouses and good public schools can also be a challenge for a rural campus. Therefore, their bucolic and sometimes-historic locations have become a major negative factor for religious colleges highly dependent on tuition revenue.

2. The Burden of the Liberal Arts

Almost every religious institution we studied prided itself on being rooted in the liberal arts, yet few admissions officers engaged parents, let alone students, in conversations about what a liberal arts education really offers. Perhaps because it does not sound relevant or worth its steep price tag, schools increasingly focus on their more career-oriented programs and slide their liberal arts courses into the core curriculum. Maintaining a prominent commitment to the liberal arts has surprisingly become a risk for many religiously affiliated colleges as they brand themselves among today's career-minded students.

3. The Challenge of Church Relations

As specific denominations play a decreasing role in the lives of many people of faith, it is safe to say that the influence of denominational leaders and their agencies will hold a diminishing role in the life of religious colleges and universities. Our work at the CCCU indicates that the majority of religiously affiliated institutions receive less than 2 to 3 percent of their operating budgets from denominational sources, with Southern Baptist, Nazarene, and Seventh-Day Adventist institutions among the exceptions. Perhaps even more critical is the lack of enthusiastic promotion by pastors of their church's campuses in an age in which national, "elite" colleges garner the majority of respect and resources. As a result, many faith-based campuses today draw less than 20 percent of their student body from their affiliated denomination.

This phenomenon puts institutions that are already at risk in lose-lose situations because if their churches will not put a priority on supporting their own campuses with funding and student applicants, who will? If they brand themselves as primarily denominational, many outside that denomination will understandably be less interested in giving or attending. If they deliberately move away from their denominational roots, the existing church support and the older donors who still have denominational loyalty are likely to dry up even faster. Some of the more conservative religious colleges struggle with a history of denominational authority in appointing trustees when the institution believes that it must gradually bring in a broader representation of the market it actually serves. Denominational loyalists on the governing board are sometimes tempted to interfere in matters of doctrinal purity among the faculty or other initiatives that cause almost instant friction within the institution. Others view themselves as conservators of denominational assets and may be reluctant to take risks to advance the mission. How denominational leaders and leaders on their affiliated campuses collaborate and lead is a dynamic worthy of continued study.

4. Church-Campus Governance Conflicts

Regarding key issues of governance, our research indicates that confusions and conflicts between strong faculty leadership and strong

---

Three Best Practices

- Focus your business model on effective teaching and learning practices, not just the traditional, residential, high-cost model of private higher education.
- Hire and encourage a strong president who is willing to take risks and help the board make bold decisions based on strategic goals that mirror reality.
- Keep seeking new segments of the student market via institutional distinctiveness.

---

governing boards are detrimental to making the adjustments necessary to overcome fragility. Even though many boards understand the significance of their roles and want to be responsive, resistance by faculty and even some administrators may still exist. Presidents can become uncomfortably caught between these forces when difficult questions are raised about phasing out programs with fewer than five students or eliminating tenure for some departments but not the whole faculty, as examples. To move away from the brink requires that an institution determine who is in charge regarding issues such as these on a regular basis.

5. Institutional Independence and Political Decision Making

The "independence" of independent colleges has been eroding since the 1950s and the rise of government aid. In 1965 Title IV of the Higher Education Act set in motion an increasing dependence on federal and, in some places, state student aid, particularly for what we define as vulnerable or at-risk institutions. Thankfully, most politicians have not seen constitutional issues in this form of aid, even for students who are attending a "pervasively" religious institution, but will it stay this way? In recent years some legislators have questioned religious colleges that hire, promote, and terminate some personnel on the basis of religious convictions. Our best estimate is that at least four hundred of the nine hundred religiously affiliated campuses use some faith criteria in hiring a few, many, or even all full-time personnel. To do so is the critical distinction for hundreds of these campuses, and any prohibition by legislatures or the courts would seriously undermine the core values that attract students and donors to these unique schools.

6. The Costs of Residence Life

As we move into the digital age educationally, some are coming to believe that the small residential college has exhausted its usefulness. Because many politicians view higher education primarily as a jobs-creation machine to stay competitive globally, it is more difficult for most state legislatures to invest in small private institutions while their publicly created systems annually call loudly for more funding. Enrollment increases, except in a few states, will soon be over, and students who grew up in and around malls are beginning to shop around for the best higher education deals: an online course from college A, an introductory English course from the local and cheaper community college B, perhaps choosing to live in a dorm at college C to enjoy those benefits of campus life. We have already mentioned many students' bias toward higher-cost urban settings. Add to these the amenities required to stay competitive—single rooms for one's own sound equipment, twenty-four-hour snack bars, the fastest linkages to the Internet, great physical fitness facilities, Division I athletics programs, and comprehensive mental and physical health services—and it is clear that the student consumer now rules. As a result, colleges that defer maintenance, take on added debt, increase their discount rates, and move from full-time to adjunct faculty will eventually be forced to pay a collective price greater than the costs of closure.

7. Faith and Accountability

The federal government is pushing all American higher education institutions and their accrediting bodies to demonstrate models of thorough measurement of learning outcomes. Total quality (TQ) approaches to accreditation can challenge religious campuses in special ways as they fulfill the subtleties and complexities of faith-based missions. A second, related pressure comes from donors who want more engagement in the institutions they designate as religious colleges and universities struggle to upgrade systems and practices developed many decades earlier in different cultural circumstances. The academic and campus model still followed by almost every religiously affiliated college was started by Harvard over 350 years ago and is costly in labor and physical plant. This, combined with the need to hire and compensate a new generation of scholars closer to market rates, is causing many at-risk religious institutions to become, once again, the domains of the white, upper-middle class. Sadly, even for colleges and universities dedicated to diversity and inclusiveness, as one colleague admitted, the path to stability can be a harsh one and can be summed up as "no money, no mission."

Single Most Important Piece of Advice for the President of an At-Risk Institution

- Be honest with the board about trends, brand, and the institution's comparative situation. Be realistic about what can improve quality while reducing costs.

Which Institutions Are Most at Risk and Why?

When James Martin and James E. Samels released their list of twenty indicators of institutional fragility, detailed in the first chapter of this volume, I suggested testing these indicators with member presidents of the CCCU. Using a web-based survey instrument, I asked one hundred presidents to indicate how strongly they agreed or disagreed with each statement as a relevant indicator of a fragile campus.[1] Fifty-four presidents responded, using a scale of 1 (strongly disagree) to 5 (strongly agree). The following five indicators received the highest average agreement:

—Institution is on probation, warning, or financial watch with regional accreditor or a specialty degree licensor (4.35).

—Short-term bridge financing has been required in the final quarter of the last five fiscal years (4.0).

—Deferred maintenance is at least 40 percent unfunded (3.89).

—Majority of faculty do not hold terminal degrees (3.87).

—Debt service is more than 10 percent of annual operating budget (3.76).

These same fifty-four presidents rated the following five as having the least relevance to institutional survival:

—No complete online program has been developed to date (2.57).

—Collectively the leadership team averages more than twelve years or fewer than three years of service at the institution (2.72).

—Less than 10 percent of the operating budget is dedicated to technology (2.79).

—No new degree or certificate program has been developed for at least two years (3.06).

—There is less than a one-to-three ratio between endowment and operating budget (3.13).

Each reader will come to different conclusions about these data. The results demonstrated a wide diversity of opinion among Christian college presidents. Nevertheless, except for three out of twenty indicators, the average rating was above 3.0, and these results give credibility to the list as an overall indicator of at-risk status.

I also asked these same CCCU presidents to think about the list of twenty indicators as a whole and indicate what percentage of campuses in different categories of institutions they believed would be described by half or more of the indicators. They ranked each category provided to them, from most on the brink to least, as follows:

1. All nine hundred religiously affiliated colleges

2. All one hundred or more CCCU campuses

3. All sixteen hundred four-year private colleges

4. All community colleges in your state (tied with all four-year privates)

5. All private four-year institutions in your state

6. All public four-year institutions in your state

These perceptions showed a lower level of confidence in the strength of all religiously affiliated campuses than in that of other types of institutions. I also queried those presidents about whether they believed that intentionally Christian colleges were more or less able to overcome fragility when contrasted with other institutions. Thirty-eight percent believed that their type of campus would be able to address the indicators "about the same," although 42 percent felt more confident about the abilities of faith-focused campuses.

Presidential Leadership at Faith-Based Institutions: Behind the Stereotypes

Recently retired presidents are often best positioned to identify the principal problems that face religious campuses and to articulate solutions. With this in mind, I asked a group of fourteen presidents three strategic questions in the development of new leadership models that close this chapter. These questions and their responses were as follows:

As you have led a vulnerable institution, what were the key strategic decisions, and by whom, that turned the college or university around and toward stability? Several mentioned first that the president will have to learn to help her or his board focus on policy governance rather than on micromanaging. Also mentioned were bringing finances under control through better analysis, more transparency with key players, and more aggressively shifting assets to reflect priorities. Another decision high on the list was to integrate the following activities more systematically under an expanded office of enrollment management: branding, admissions, enrollment, financial aid, retention strategies, and public relations.

What leadership decisions and styles do you consider most important for a president when his or her campus is at risk? More than a few reflected the experience of this president: "I had to change my leadership style from a 'consensus-builder, cheerleader, pastor' to that of a more dynamic individual who leads at the point, takes some risks, and challenges the academic community to get on board and become partners in the future, rather than bemoaning the mistakes of the past."[2] A summary of the responses on this issue included these five priorities: make the difficult decisions in a timely manner, be open about problems, hire the best people you can find, take some risks, and always stay focused on the mission.

Many in American higher education continue to believe that religious colleges are closer to the brink than others. Are they mistaken? The fourteen presidents who responded were divided on this question. They agreed that it is difficult to rally around a clear mission when some trustees, donors, and faculty want more integration of faith and learning and others want less. They also agreed that walking down the middle may carry more risk than choosing one way or the other. Some conservative religious campuses neglect capital campaigns to raise endowments and avoid adopting tough-minded financial policies because their leaders continue to believe that the institution will be "protected" because of its faith-based mission. Other presidents believe that the trend toward secularism and resistance to expressions of faith in government-supported religious campuses may lead politicians to put curbs on tax support for intentionally religious universities and colleges.

One respondent explained, "If you base your assessment on financial statements, endowments, and enrollments, one might conclude that religious colleges are more at risk than others, but being intentional about faith and seeking God's guidance and blessings are factors that are hard to show on paper."[3] During my years at the CCCU, I made close to three hundred campus visits. Numerous times I left a campus thinking that things were going much better there than one would have expected. In this sense the intangible benefits of a faith-based campus community can be more difficult to appreciate and assess, but the demands of external accreditors, high-maintenance donors, faculty stars, and student consumers still remain and must be addressed convincingly through effective leadership and management.

Overcoming Challenges: New Models for Presidents and Trustees

Perhaps the majority of the country's religiously affiliated colleges and universities, even if they are currently defined as fragile or at risk, will survive, but not if they continue many of their present-day business practices. Just as there are many reasons that placed these institutions on the brink, so too are there numerous strategies for them to employ in their recoveries, and we will need the federal government and the courts to continue their generally neutral stance on religious colleges so the playing field remains level.

Although vision and bold leadership are essential for the success of any vulnerable college or university, if a campus wants to position itself as a distinctly religious institution, one key is to hire faculty who see faith not just as a private matter but as one central to development of the whole person. A second is for the leaders of these institutions to take more risks in shaping their futures. American higher education still struggles on many fronts with the realization that external variables, such as the economic and political realities of each state, access to new technologies, and a market of learners with vastly different needs and preferences, can open many new possibilities, but there is no secret solution. Although most religiously affiliated institutions would be strengthened by adopting one of the following models, weaker colleges and universities should immediately consider integrating several into their business practices in order to strengthen themselves in part by attracting key donors who specialize in helping vulnerable institutions make transitions:

Living-Learning Centers

Consider renovating or building a Christian living-learning center close to the campus. These centers can offer the benefits of residential housing accompanied by spiritual formation mentors, a specialized library, and accredited classes from the university's catalogue. By special arrangement, the university can also provide access to its fitness center, performing arts events, and technology laboratories.

Cooperative Education

Create cooperative education programs for eighteen- to twenty-four-year-olds that require students to work and learn in the community and

---

What Should a President of a Fragile Institution Do Differently in Hindsight?

■ Presidents should acknowledge that they cannot fund-raise their way to stability or cut their way to strength.

---

that lead to a résumé with a degree plus enhanced career experience. Even guarantee a job for the first year out of college for those who do not secure one on their own. Engage committed alumni and friends who support the concept to provide those jobs. Build the program around a solid general education core while offering degrees and certificates that reflect the region's economic future and student career interests.

International Partnerships

Since 50 percent of all first-year students today say that they want to study abroad, but fewer than 5 percent actually do, a U.S. campus could grow by partnering with the right international institutions to provide a living-learning experience in another culture. Many Christian campuses have strong international connections with both specific churches and broader organizations with which they can collaborate. They can thus further the theme of globalization that is shaping curricula, as well as cocurricular experiences for increasing numbers of students and their professors.

Work-to-Learn Programs

Reduce the nonteaching payroll on campus and let students learn by building and maintaining campus facilities, managing businesses, and growing food. Working and learning with adults who demonstrate character and ethical decision making while bringing practical experience into their classrooms can make the institution a "destination campus" for those attracted to such a model. Rising percentages of retired professionals can also be attracted to live and work in this kind of environment.

Multicampus Consortia

Many denominationally compatible campuses can now explore merging into multicampus systems that share one expanded board, central administration, cooperative purchasing capacity, streamlined student

Table 11.2. Variables That All Smaller, Residential Private Colleges Must Consider When Planning Their Futures

Impact on Most Campuses	Variables
↓	1. Tendency for colleges to increase tuition price considerably faster than the CPI
↓	2. The uncertain long-term implications of deep tuition discounting (ave. = 47%)
↓	3. The "arms race" to provide more amenities that is deemed necessary to compete for students
↓	4. Threatened government action to hold tuition levels down
↓	5. Outlook for funding of federal student aid programs in an era of competition/deficits
↓	6. Outlook for funding state student aid programs in most states
↓	7. Outlook for increasing numbers of donors willing to invest in private colleges
↓	8. Growth of endowments to contribute to operating expenses
↓	9. Underpaid and overloaded faculty and staff
↓	10. Legal threats to traditional tax-exempt benefits of all nonprofits
↓	11. The protectionist impact of tenure on timely curricular/employment adjustments
↓	12. The inefficiencies of "shared governance" in making timely decisions
↓	13. Declining denominational support (money and students) for their campuses
↓	14. Increasing costs of health care, energy, construction, and technology
↓	15. Threatened denial of government benefits to "pervasively sectarian" campuses

Table 11.2. (*continued*)	
↓	16. Backlog of deferred campus maintenance
↓	17. National decrease in high-school graduates after about 2010
↓	18. Increasing share of eighteen-year-olds who are poor, immigrants, and racial minorities
↓	19. Decreasing numbers of international students coming to the United States to study
↓	20. Increasing competition from for-profit degree-granting institutions
↓	21. Uneven distribution of learners by geographic region
↓	22. Trend of most students wanting larger, urban, and lower-cost campuses
↓	23. Trend of students taking courses from multiple campuses for cost/convenience
↓	24. Lack of trustee comprehension/boldness in making adjustments
↓	25. Decreased parental savings for college and willingness to sacrifice for their children
↑	26. Increasing willingness of small private campuses to meet needs of adult learners
↑	27. The attraction of some students to the distinctive faith characteristics of some private colleges
↑	28. Public's understanding that postsecondary education is key to economic growth

Source: Council for Christian Colleges and Universities.

transfer, faculty exchanges, and shared technologies. Because this model has worked for many public university systems, it can also work for new multicampus, faith-based universities. Some of the stronger Christian campuses have already created satellite campuses in other states and overseas.

Online Programs and Networks

As various denominations grow rapidly in the Southern Hemisphere, the need has emerged for one or more Christian universities to implement a distributed learning system with global reach. Major cities could provide formal "study groups" to bring students together and facilitate their learning experiences, using churches as gathering places, while also offering "course mentors" nationally and even internationally to supervise students via e-mail.

For-Profit Partnerships

Develop a group of investors and educators to provide adult degrees with a Christian worldview in this market. Grand Canyon University in Arizona is attempting to accomplish this. An even stronger model might include an existing nonprofit campus creating or purchasing a subsidiary for-profit so that the profits would go to the parent nonprofit institution rather than to private investors. Many nonprofit colleges court business leaders for board service who have the skills and instincts to create an entrepreneurial model that moves the institution into new markets. Some of them could focus their talents on learners who might not otherwise get a chance at a Christian higher education while also improving a fragile college's business practices.

Community College Partnerships

Half the first-year students in the United States now choose community colleges to start their higher education experiences. Many people, especially those who prefer to work and learn at the same time, have educational goals that could be completed through a certificate or associate's degree program. As the percentage of Americans who claim to be evangelical rises steadily, it would serve many fragile four-year colleges to consider partnering with public community colleges in formal agreements that move beyond traditional articulation arrangements to provide full joint-degree programs in areas supported by the local and regional economies.

Mutual Growth Mergers

Although some higher education mergers have proved to be difficult,[4] many institutions should nevertheless consider consolidating their operations to strengthen their chances for long-term viability. Particularly, campuses owned by the same denomination could merge while designing the smaller, more fragile campus as a satellite of the larger or stronger one. In our view, many schools put off serious discussions about merger, for understandable reasons, until it is almost too late and their balance sheets are negative and their physical plant is run down. Various philanthropic organizations could be helpful in convening and funding a careful process in which interested institutions could discreetly explore this option.

Entrepreneurial Business Ventures

Although many faith-based campuses are calling themselves more entrepreneurial, few take major risks or attempt to go beyond what is accepted by faculty and other prominent community members. This model can take many shapes and might include operating partner Christian schools, assisted-living homes, or a publishing house that could employ students and alumni and make better use of campus buildings. Many religious campuses now own hundreds of acres of unused land that could be deployed in partnership with organizations that will create long-term educational and financial benefits.

Conclusion: The Faith Factor

Will any of these new models save a college or university at risk? The answer depends on many factors. Unfortunately, the gravity pull toward the familiar and traditional is very strong even at fragile institutions. One former Christian college president wrote that he was trying to help another institution explore some of these ideas but that "I am finding a surprising tendency simply to be the best of what is rather than to take up the challenge of setting the pace for what could be."[5] One hopes that the creativity of presidents, provosts, and trustees in the coming decade will not be restricted simply to older, dated models of delivering faith-informed learning.

Some of the institutions discussed in this chapter have let the faith dimension of their heritage fade to the point that it cannot be regained, but they will face the same future academic and economic challenges as their more religiously connected colleague institutions. Having worked directly with several hundred campuses that are unapologetically and intentionally "Christ centered," I have observed the challenges that they have faced and overcome for learners who seek spiritual formation along with academic excellence. These more evangelical institutions still hold under-leveraged advantages in coherence of mission and quality of student life, but the economic realities for them are no less urgent. Today, in fact, most of these colleges and universities are at risk, and their model is aging and under pressure for the reasons discussed earlier. As a path forward, their leaders need to avoid being limited to familiar stereotypes of recovery and, instead, focus on separating and distinguishing the value and uniqueness these institutions offer to new generations of learners.

CHAPTER TWELVE

For-Profit Higher Education and Stressed Colleges: A Strategic Opportunity

Michael Hoyle

In the 1970s and 1980s professors from many state colleges and universities across the nation routinely traveled an hour or more to teach a class at an employer's work site. Today the notion of a teacher from a state university commuting more than an hour to teach students at their places of employment is far less likely, in part because of the emergence of more than one thousand for-profit higher education institutions whose mission is to provide market-relevant programs, convenient locations, flexible scheduling, and instructional delivery platforms that focus on students rather than professors. Michele Howard-Vital, vice chancellor of the North Carolina Higher Education System, describes for-profits as all "about need, speed, and ease."[1] For the purposes of this discussion, for-profit institutions, simply described, return a profit at the end of a fiscal year to an individual or corporation.

As the number of corporate colleges and for-profit universities grows exponentially faster than the traditional higher education sector in America, many traditional colleges and universities are losing their core market share to for-profits and are becoming increasingly at risk financially and academically. In this writer's view, these two sectors have more to learn from each other than they have to fear, but perceptions die hard in higher education, and for-profits are still viewed by many faculty and administrators at traditional institutions as the enemy rather than as a beneficial and lucrative partner. The following discussion will identify the real threats that for-profits pose to fragile traditional universities and colleges, what new opportunities exist, and specifically how the presidents and provosts of traditional institutions can respond to these realities.

185

Before addressing these questions, one needs to understand the current state of the for-profit sector in American higher education. Kevin Kinser and Daniel Levy describe this industry as being composed of two types of institutions: supersystems and enterprise colleges.[2] Supersystems are anchored by the large publicly traded and privately held corporations that have amassed a collection of brick-and-mortar colleges and an online presence nationally, if not globally. These supersystems include such well-known institutions as the University of Phoenix (Apollo), DeVry University, Strayer University, the colleges within the Career Education Corporation network, and those in the Educational Management Corporation network. They benefit from an infrastructure of massive student data bases, extensive curriculum research, bulk purchasing, and access to major capital that would make some of the largest public universities envious. Enterprise colleges tend to be institutions owned by an individual, a family, or a small corporation. Clearly it is the rise and increasing influence of the supersystems that has drawn the close scrutiny of competitor nonprofits and accreditation agencies.

Despite the fear that nonprofits have about the emergence and strength of the for-profit supersystems, their concerns are often unfounded. For-profits account for only 5 percent of total enrollment in the higher education market in the United States.[3] As a testament to their technological innovation, however, for-profits control approximately 35 percent of the online market.[4] Brian Pusser, faculty member at the University of Virginia, notes, "If college and university leaders forthrightly address the concerns shadowing our system of higher education, it becomes less likely that future expansion of for-profit higher education will come at the expense of nonprofit colleges and universities."[5] Pusser's view is correct; if state legislative leaders and policy makers continue to starve their public higher education systems, for-profits will become an even more serious threat to traditional higher education as they become a more financially viable alternative for many prospective students. As market-driven entities, for-profits generally offer programs in fields that have the largest demand by student customers and thus draw large cohorts, resulting in profits. For-profits are also more adaptive and can more quickly seize market trends by offering the most current and in-demand programs. This is where smaller private colleges and universities, who cannot compete with economies of scale, are facing their greatest challenges.

The For-Profit Culture: An Inside View

For-profit higher education generally follows a business model predicated on the following elements:

—Few nonacademic student programs, such as athletics, clubs, or events

—A reliance on adjunct faculty

—Little, if any, emphasis on faculty research or publications

—Small facilities, often located in office parks

—No traditional campus infrastructure

—The ability to introduce, update, or delete programs and curriculum extremely quickly

—Programs that emphasize business, information systems, practical design, culinary arts, health professions, engineering, automotive services, legal services, and education services

For all their recent successes, for-profit higher education leaders still sometimes make the mistake of communicating with accrediting bodies like swashbuckling, Wall Street number-crunchers. Often drawing on training in an M.B.A. program, these chief executive officers lean on terms such as "cost per lead," "cost per start," "revenue per student," "days sales outstanding" (DSO), "bad debt rates," and "profit margins." Traditional accrediting personnel more comfortable with terms like "faculty-student ratio," "faculty research," "faculty load," "faculty office space," and "student achievement" may be dismayed by presidents and cabinets so openly driven by financial indicators of success. Clearly, many in the for-profit sector have not yet mastered speaking to accreditors about the nature and effectiveness of the for-profit sector.

Unlike traditional institutions, for-profit colleges and universities listen very well to their business communities and tailor their curricula accordingly, often updating them on a quarterly basis to ensure that their students learn specifically what industry is demanding. This may mean that new graduates find or develop jobs in classifications that accrediting bodies have not even listed yet as approved placement positions. Often a traditional accrediting body may not have heard of a new position because of the speed of technological changes that are now driving the marketplace, but these new positions are often in high demand, and this demand stimulates the initial curriculum revisions by responsive for-profits. Conversely, because for-profits are for the most part built to be highly regimented, structured, and efficient operating entities, these institutions have not yet figured out how to deal effectively with what some describe as the "Zen" student. Zen students may prefer to take a summer off, skip a class because of a work project, or take leave to plan a wedding; in most cases they simply are not suited to the accelerated pace of the for-profit model for their education. In these instances, for-profits lose out to the advanced counseling and support structures of many public and private nonprofit colleges because they generally do not know how to respond to Zen students and lack the systems to fit the students back into their accelerated schedules or to catch them and counsel them before they drop out. Even more damagingly, some for-profits send unintended signals that they are institutions principally, if not only, for students who can keep up the pace of an accelerated program at the expense of those who require additional support to succeed.

By design, for-profits are built to run operationally. What fall away first in the model are the extras of the traditional "college experience": athletic teams and programming, high-end fitness facilities and gymnasiums, boutique hotel-style residence halls, and Las Vegas–influenced student centers. Although this may be an effective strategy from the financial perspective, it is increasingly questioned as a marketing plus because rising percentages of college-bound students have become accustomed to a world that blends continuous technological advances with the creature comforts of home. With a Starbucks on every fourth corner, wireless connectivity, iPods, and cell phones shrinking to the size of credit cards, many college students now come from high schools that resemble the Mall of America more than a place for reflection and learning. However, these are the students whom both for-profit and traditional higher education institutions are dedicated to recruiting. Even long-established for-profits are acknowledging that a service-oriented approach to mission combined with plentiful, comfortable amenities continues to play a critical role in the college selection process. Sometimes begrudgingly, for-profit CEOs admit that the design purposes and sophistication of student-center spaces are areas in which traditional universities and colleges have learned what their student customers want and how to deliver it.

For-Profit Leadership Lessons for Stressed Institutions

Conversely, traditional higher education institutions are observing and learning from the for-profit sector as well. Although far less mature, this sector has succeeded in developing multiple, competing supersystems through a variety of successful business models. The following nine lessons may have useful applications by traditional college presidents and provosts who are facing at-risk circumstances on their campuses:

> **Emerging Trends for For-Profit Higher Education Organizations**
>
> - Greater transparency in student learning outcomes
> - An expanded presence in the international marketplace
> - A focus on local civic engagement activities and building relationships with local and state leaders, as well as alumni
> - An improved employee turnover via the creation of organizational development departments
> - Growth of mega public universities

1. Update Curriculum Continuously

Perhaps most impressive is the ability that for-profits have to create and update the curriculum almost instantly. The University of Phoenix, founded in 1976, was on version 21 of its M.B.A. program as of this writing. This nimbleness of for-profit colleges and universities to respond to a constantly changing economic landscape by adjusting their curriculum is one of the first and most powerful reasons behind their success.

2. Streamline Admissions

The second area in which the traditional institutions can learn is admissions. Despite a couple of high-profile cases of proprietary schools with admissions practices frowned on by the U.S. Department of Education, for-profits have generally honed their admissions departments to be highly effective and creative sales teams. In this area, in particular, many public institutions nationally can learn valuable lessons about marketing their programs and then closing the deal with savvy student consumers. Many public institutions have relied for too long on stale recruiting formulas to build their first-year classes. For-profits are a case study in effectively using the Internet, direct mail, radio, television, and magazine advertising. More important, for-profits cast a wide net by reaching out to industry and high schools to build a lead base of students whom admissions representatives pursue like any other sales representative in the private sector, but within the parameters of U.S. Department of Education regulations. For-profit admissions managers are trained to use previously mentioned concepts such as cost per lead and cost per start that may only rarely, if ever, cross the desk of an admissions manager at a state college or university. Most tellingly, for-profit colleges and universities are practiced in going directly to potential students rather than waiting for those students to find them.

3. Enhance Management Practices

The third area in which traditional institutions can sharpen their effectiveness is improved management practices. In most for-profits one encounters an intense, entrepreneurial culture focused on goals, benchmarks, accountability, industry awareness, and customer-service training. Even within a rapidly changing higher education culture nationally, these concepts are still not dominant on many traditional campuses because their institutions are not centered on achieving profit margins to specific percentage points, nor are they accountable to a private investor. This lack of focus on the bottom line allows many traditional colleges and universities to maintain a relatively casual business culture—at their peril. These institutions, too, must balance their budgets, and in the future it is likely that even some venerable colleges and universities will acknowledge the value of for-profit commitment to improving managerial practices.

4. Emphasize Academic Excellence

At times in the past, some traditional colleges and universities have used the for-profit model to drive a wedge in the industry and to stress with accreditors that for-profits care only about profit at the expense of academic excellence. It is only fair to note that its accumulated profits have allowed the University of Phoenix to develop its highly successful and widely recognized M.B.A. simulations that have been researched by faculty at MIT, Harvard, and numerous public research universities. With the passing of time, this overall argument is weakening as the public witnesses a growing body of successful for-profit graduates. More traditional colleges are accepting the fact that for-profit enterprises can also produce centers of academic excellence as both types of institutions compete for new niches in an increasingly crowded market.

5. Activate Employer Advisory Boards

Presidents, deans, and department chairs need to ensure that their respective institutions are connected to the employers that hire their graduates, that the curriculum is industry relevant, and that the academic delivery platforms provide an option for most students. This means that each program maintains an advisory board of employers who often are alumni and who meet with program faculty to ensure that new developments in the industry are inserted into the curriculum once, if not twice, per academic year.

6. Diversify Instructional Delivery Models

Instructional delivery platforms need to reflect the variety of learning styles that current students require, including traditional classrooms, online learning, models that blend high touch and high tech, and even weekend programs for those who are time stressed and yet still serious about their educational advancement.

7. Audit Programs Annually

As a complement to assessing programs' academic rigor, provosts should institutionalize a process whereby each of their programs is evaluated at least annually for its income-to-expense ratios. Although some may deplore this exercise, it will effectively begin the debate on campus about which programs are most self-sufficient and whether to support those that are losing money, perhaps a significant amount of money. This model can be created by the chief financial officer and examine the revenue per program against the expense per program with a final tally that represents the contribution of each program to the institution's financial health. Placed against the backdrop of investing in new programs that have the potential to recruit new cohorts of students and also jump-start a local economy, this type of exercise can be pivotal in gaining positive votes from a board of trustees that is seeking nimbleness and entrepreneurial thinking from a traditional university team.

8. Leverage Strategic Partnerships

Understanding how a for-profit college and a traditional public or private university could collaborate in a mutually beneficial partnership is closer than many leaders on both sides realize. Indeed, nonprofits and for-profits already collaborate in many states. For example, Gibbs College in Boston, a for-profit, and Cambridge College, a traditional institution in Cambridge, Massachusetts, entered into a collaborative partnership in 2006. These partnerships also do not have to be limited to the higher education sector. Alliances between colleges and other types of for-profit corporations are increasingly being considered to complement the teaching and learning processes.

9. Instill a Culture of Accountability

Finally, presidents and provosts of fragile institutions might consider the benefits of several for-profit-sector performance models. Although many will continue to argue that both faculty and administrative

---

Best Practices for Presidents of Traditional Higher Education Institutions

- Review all curriculum offerings more often and more aggressively.
- Partner with local for-profits more boldly.
- Reduce internal bureaucracy.

---

productivity in higher education cannot be measured rigidly on a chart or graph, it is the encouragement of a culture of accountability on campus, more than the measurement of an individual's specific performance between October and December of a given year, that is at issue. Developing with an individual professor or a department a set of teaching objectives to be achieved each semester, rather than on the more traditional annual basis, could help a college, particularly one that is at risk, monitor its overall effectiveness. This can be especially useful when the general public or an outside agency has raised a concern about long-term viability.

Conclusion: Mutual Interests, Strategic Partners

Policy makers, presidents, and student consumers concerned about the growing number of fragile colleges and universities that are attempting to survive in the nation's higher education market might consider some of the lessons learned by for-profit higher education leaders over the past twenty years. To move beyond survival and to compete successfully with the for-profit supersystems described earlier, traditional institutions should begin to think creatively about reengineering themselves into more flexible organizational and managerial structures that can take advantage of shifting economies of scale. Additionally, although online education is not for every learner, technological enhancements of online instruction have made it a cost-effective method to deliver those elements of a program that are less hands-on and specialized, such as a general education core, and opportunities continue to emerge for collaboration between for-profit and traditional faculty members in this area, as an example.

To respond to changing student career preferences and their calls for greater mobility within degree programs, traditional institutions might also consider joining with a for-profit college to devise a "learning passport" system that will capture each student's transcripts, recommendations, and financial aid history and allow her or him to move more naturally among multiple institutions in the completion of a life-long learning plan.

Clearly, competition and entrepreneurship continue to grow in American higher education. Traditional colleges and universities have less and less to lose in considering formal partnerships with for-profit learning organizations as they both work to become more nimble and student sensitive. In the process, for-profit enterprises, notoriously known for micromanaging the presidents of their campuses, might consider adopting some of the autonomies and local decision-making models that have been refined by traditional institutions over the past several generations. If tensions persist between the two sides and few alliances are created, the nation's high-school graduates will still have an array of high-quality, cost-effective choices for their degree completions, but a critical opportunity will have been squandered, and there will be fewer institutions, both for-profit and traditional, left to enroll them.

CHAPTER THIRTEEN

Legal Challenges for Fragile Institutions: Survival before Success

James E. Samels and James Martin

One of the presidents interviewed for this book noted that with the exception of a few institutions whose names everyone knows, at one time or another a significant proportion of American colleges and universities could have been considered stressed, at risk, struggling, vulnerable, or fragile. Competition for high-achieving students and accomplished faculty is fierce, and donors are reluctant to part with big money without certain expectations and strings attached. Making institutional ends meet and doing more with less are tough. Yet the rewards for a president or faculty who save an institution are significant. The only way to achieve this is to have a plan in place and benchmarks to guide the way. This chapter will explain the principal ways to minimize legal problems while turning around a college or university. Naturally, most attorneys and accountants will say that nothing is guaranteed in this world, and that even well-planned turnarounds have the potential to run aground. However, these same higher education professionals will also say that the alternative for an at-risk university or college— continuing the patterns that put the institution in the predicament in the first place—is far worse. Knowing where the legal bumps in the road will likely turn up is a key element to achieving success in any institution's turnaround plan.

Further, and importantly, legal issues can often have potentially devastating consequences when institutions declare financial exigency and turn to reductions in force to save money. Whether reductions involve terminating entry-level staff or tenured faculty, careful planning will help officials avoid the pitfalls of reinstatement, back pay, and injunctive constraints. Conversely, understanding the laws that govern revenue enhancements, accessing endowment funds, or floating bonds is just as important as understanding the legal fallout of containing costs. Finally, this chapter offers perspectives on the legal questions that will arise if the leadership team has done everything in its power to save the institution, but circumstances have worked against them, and they must close the institution or effect a forced merger or consolidation.

The Role of Governance in a Turnaround

Turning around an at-risk college or university is seldom a solo effort. It requires hard work by the larger campus community, staff, faculty, administrators, students, and, of course, the board of trustees. Without the careful oversight and full cooperation of the trustees, any efforts on the part of the other constituencies are likely to fail. It follows that any strategic plan that a president might want to put in place to get his or her institution on the road to recovery needs to be fully vetted by the board, and the process should be as transparent as possible.

The board, whether it oversees a public or private institution, has only that power and authority conferred by its charter, bylaws, and enabling legislation. Even though trustees may want to take a particular action to rescue a stressed college or university, they may not be able to act nimbly. For instance, in 2003 a court rejected a decision by the board of trustees of Warren County Community College in New Jersey to approve a property-tax assessment for capital projects. The court said that the county board of freeholders had the authority to block the implementation of the assessment because the citizens of the county had not agreed to be taxed for the projects.[1] Conversely, when Mercer University in Georgia decided to shutter Tift College, it did so despite promises to make a good-faith effort to keep it open. In this instance the court applied pertinent corporate law by holding that the board had the requisite power to close the women's college.[2] That same body of corporate law, however, does not prevent a board from taking the steps necessary to bolster the fortunes of an institution; rather, it applies certain affirmative duties to the board members. Simply stated, trustees have three basic duties when overseeing institutional operations: care, loyalty, and obedience. Essentially these mean that a board member must exercise the degree of care that the "ordinarily prudent person" would exercise; must act in the best interest of the institution, not using information obtained for personal gain; and must be faithful to the mission of the college or university.

When a board delegates authority, it must do so in a measured way. Boards need to consider five principles when balancing oversight of the turnaround with day-to-day operations and execution of the recovery plan to improve the college or university's fiscal position:

—Ensure that any delegation of authority is consistent with the law and the institution's governing documents.

—Give proper guidelines to those to whom the authority is delegated.

—Delegate to legally qualified individuals or committees.

—Delegate authority only to those who will exercise the power consistent with the board's intentions.

—Establish and use procedures to review the actions taken by the people given the authority.[3]

Finally, changes brought about by the Sarbanes-Oxley Act will also need to be taken into consideration as the turnaround proceeds. Although the law was created in the wake of the scandal of the Enron Corporation, politicians at both state and federal levels have been moving toward using Sarbanes-Oxley as a model to create legislation that will also ensure improved oversight of the nation's nonprofits, including its universities and colleges.

Cost Containment and Its Legal Implications

Fragile or at-risk universities and colleges generally know that they fall into this category when they look at their financial statements over a period of time and clear patterns emerge. Of course, one of the most important ways to get back on strong financial footing is to trim expenses. The following sections examine the legal issues within the challenges of containing costs.

Renegotiating Vendor Contracts

Universities contract for a host of goods and services that range from food services to office supplies. All contracts must be examined for potential renegotiation. Golden Gate University in San Francisco was able to save half a million dollars by altering the terms of three of its contracts. A college or university's counsel or contracts administrator should be well versed in the legal intricacies of contract terminations, specific performance, and the interpretation of alternative remedies. Clearly the contract specialists are the ones to determine the provisions of the contract that may allow for flexibility in altering the terms of the deal or ending the contract. Contracts might have special provisions that allow for termination under certain circumstances as long as certain contractually stipulated procedures are followed. Even if the contract terms appear ironclad, and a failure to perform (that is, to pay the vendor for the goods and/or services) on the part of the college or university would amount to breach, there are still ways to restructure the deal without the institution ending up in court as a defendant in a lawsuit.

The first step before the renegotiation process begins is to review the numerous agreements the college has. It is important to determine which contracts are coming up for renewal and therefore can be renegotiated on that basis, and which longer-term ones will require a different strategy to change the terms. Counsel should be acquainted with the applicable state and federal laws that govern contracts (and the risks that are associated with any decision not to fully perform under the terms of the agreement) and should also be intimately familiar with the internal rules and regulations that may be applicable to the way the institution contracts. Public universities and colleges are not the only institutions that have complex regulations governing contractual relations. "Private institutions are not immune to these often Byzantine types of contractual rules and regulations. If it is not the legislature or the department of administration, it's the board of trustees, the president, the faculty or student constitution, or the institution's charter or mission statement."[4]

Although a college could choose, after considering all the factors, to breach an agreement, it is more likely and typically more prudent to approach the vendor, explain the institution's financial situation, and attempt to renegotiate the terms of the contract. In certain instances the contract terms may allow for "mutual rescission" or "accord and satisfaction." These two terms are simply legal language for an agreement by contracting parties to discharge all remaining rights and obligations under an agreement.[5] Mutual rescission, or rescission by agreement, is a discharge of both parties from the obligations of a contract by a new agreement made after the execution of the original contract but before its performance. Recovery is allowed, however, for partial performance. Similarly, accord and satisfaction is an agreement by one party to accept less than is legally due in order to wrap up the matter. The amount paid (even though it is less than owed) means that the debt is wiped out.

Renegotiation with a vendor is fundamentally different from the initial contract negotiation. For one thing, the institution and the vendor now have a track record with each other, for better or worse, that will affect how the sides view each other. Consequently, there are a few tips for renegotiating a contract where the vendor could be disappointed or even angry about the changed circumstances in which its client finds itself and the financial toll a renegotiated contract could take on the vendor:[6]

—Avoid hostility by refraining from belligerent or sarcastic remarks.

—Assess the value of the future relationship to both sides in order to find common ground. Try to convince the vendor that the future relationship, even with revised terms, is more valuable than litigating a breach claim.

—Create a problem-solving atmosphere.

—Consider hiring a mediator (this can be useful for revamping high-value, long-term contracts).

—Think about other forms of alternative dispute resolution, typically arbitration.

When an institution is renegotiating contracts, one route to consider is joining a purchasing consortium or developing other cost-sharing arrangements with other institutions. For instance, Saint Mary's College in Indiana and the University of Notre Dame contracted with a bus company to create a route between the two schools. The move saved Saint Mary's about $50,000 a year while simultaneously allowing faculty and students to ride for free.[7]

Reducing Staff

Personnel costs constitute the largest segment of any college or university's operating budget, but like most decisions made in the employment arena, those that concern reductions in force must be addressed carefully and with the advice of labor counsel to avoid potential legal roadblocks. In order to mitigate the possibility of having to deal with angry employees who feel mistreated by being laid off, administrators should always consider less drastic cost-saving actions first. These options could include staff reduction through natural attrition, early retirement incentives, hiring freezes, travel freezes, furloughs, reducing fringe benefits, and decreasing college-sponsored student aid.[8] The possibilities for creative ways of reducing expenses are limited only by the administrators' imaginations, even though many will likely carry legal implications that will need to be considered before implementation

For our purposes, the focus at this point is on layoffs. The first questions to ask are what, if any, internal policies the institution has that govern how to handle reductions in force, and whether employees are working under a collective-bargaining agreement, are employed under some other type of contract, or are at-will employees. Obviously the least problematic situation is one in which the employees are at will and the employment manual states clearly the institution's layoff policy. Letting employees go in that situation is perhaps less of a legal hassle.

However, chances are pretty good that there is some form of appointment, contract, or collective-bargaining agreements in place for significant segments of the workforce. At the very least, college and university staff members can point to various documents that could be construed by a court as a contract, such as appointment letters, employee handbooks, personnel manuals, and written policies. For instance, in *Mayo v. North Carolina State University* the court found that an employment agreement existed where the documentation consisted of the employee's appointment letter, his annual salary letter, and policies adopted and amended by the university's board of governors and by its board of trustees.[9] Failure to follow the college or university's own internal procedures can result in a potential breach-of-contract suit. Thus it is critical to review with counsel the various institutional personnel policies and procedures before making any layoff decisions.

Another potential way in which laid-off employees can fight an adverse employment decision is by filing a discrimination claim. They might claim that the university or college let them go because of their age, race, religion, sexual orientation, disability, gender, or national origin. Because discrimination claims can be very time consuming and potentially very costly, there are steps that administrators can take before deciding who is let go to avoid this problem. The simplest method of determining who stays and who goes is to use seniority—last in, first out. Various federal laws, such as Title VII of the Civil Rights Act and the Age Discrimination in Employment Act, allow employers to follow a so-called bona fide seniority system as long as seniority is fairly determined.[10] That means that the seniority system has legitimate goals, is not designed to discriminate on the basis of a protected class, and uses the employee's length of service as the primary consideration in selecting the employees.

If, however, an at-risk college or university would rather lay off people on the basis of more quantitative criteria, such as job performance, the administration will have to complete more preparatory work early on. Enlisting the help of human resource professionals, as well as university or college counsel, will be crucial to ensure that any quantitative criteria are neutral and do not create an unfair situation for people in protected classes. "Articulation and even-handed application of reasonable, neutral selection factors is the critical conduct that will allow an employer to defend against charges of discrimination—which are by far the most likely legal action to emerge from a RIF [reduction in force]."[11]

If the staff to be laid off are unionized, the leadership will need to comply with contractual obligations to bargain with the union regarding not only the actual decision to reduce the workforce but also the impact of the decision. Moreover, the federal Worker Adjustment and Retraining Act requires covered employers to notify affected employees or their union sixty days before "mass layoffs."[12] "Mass layoffs" means that fifty or more full-time employees are laid off if they constitute one-third or more of the full-time employees at the site, or five hundred or more full-time employees are laid off. There may also be state laws to consider with regard to notification requirements. Beyond statutory requirements, collective-bargaining agreements are also likely to include provisions addressing the issue of outsourcing that will have to be considered if a college or university wants to shed a particular employment function.

Whatever the particular situation in which a university or college finds itself, there are some basic steps to take if it is going to use layoffs to put the institution back on solid financial ground:

—Develop an appeals process. Create an opportunity for affected employees to "have their day in court." This is especially important for public institutions that have a statutory obligation to have such a process.

—Document and substantiate. This can include the reasons for the reduction in force, the exhaustion of alternatives the college or university has considered and/or implemented, and the reasons specific employees are being let go.

—Communicate. Tell employees the truth and see to it that they fully understand the reasons for the layoffs. Make sure that the supervisors who deliver the bad news have been well prepared on what to say and how to say it.

Restructuring Debt

Retaining a skillful and bold CFO is especially important when a fragile institution is considering how best to manage its debt portfolio. Debt restructuring, at its core, remains a simple idea: a plan to continue business operations without the danger of being overwhelmed by debt. Costs associated with debt restructuring can include the time to negotiate with bankers, creditors, and tax authorities; however, depending on the amount and complexity of an institution's debt, conferring with legal counsel, bond counsel, and other financial advisors is highly recommended.

In the case of Huntingdon College in Montgomery, Alabama, its accrediting agency, the Southern Association of Colleges and Schools, had placed it on two-year probation because of financial difficulties. One of the ways it convinced the agency that it was back on the right track was its plan to restructure its $23 million in long-term debt. By doing so, the college expected to save $600,000 annually in payments.[13]

Before undertaking any kind of debt restructuring, it is important to remember that internal governing documents such as the charter or bylaws or the institution's enabling legislation could constrain the ways in which the endeavor gets handled. But legal and regulatory constraints at the state and federal levels will have the biggest impact on the implementation of this type of strategy.

> For instance, tax-exempt debt management for colleges and universities involves understanding the implications of indirect cost recovery; regulations pertaining to the use of facilities funded with tax-exempt bonds; limitations on arbitrage with proceeds from tax-exempt bonds; possible restrictive covenants, as in loan agreements; and unique opportunities involved in issuing tax-exempt bonds, such as the continuing investor market demand for long-dated maturities.[14]

If this strategy is an option for a given institution, the rewards can be substantial. In 1998, when Stanford University issued new bonds with long maturities to refinance old debt, the institution saved "several million dollars on each refinance."[15] Granted, a vulnerable institution will not have the creditworthiness of Stanford University, but restructuring and refinancing can still be an important tool in turning around a fragile university or college.

Closing a Program

Closing a program is one of the most difficult decisions presidents, provosts, and faculty leaders can make. It may look like a good way to save money, but if it is done improperly, it could provoke very costly litigation. For the purposes of this chapter, the authors will designate the first true step in closing a program that will result in the termination of tenured faculty as the formal declaration of financial exigency.[16] "Financial exigency" is a term of art in the realm of higher education law that is typically deployed where expenditures exceed revenues "without regard to endowment or capital accounts."[17] This declaration must be "bona fide," meaning that courts will consider the trustees' motivation for their action, how adequate the financially stressed college or university's operating funds are, the institution's overall financial situation, what other steps the university or college has taken to cut costs, and any efforts to find alternative work for the affected faculty member or members.

If the institution takes certain precautionary steps, it may never have to defend its financial exigency decision or subsequent layoff actions. The key is to follow the rule of law to the letter. A carefully planned and flawlessly executed program-closure process is critical to undertaking this endeavor successfully. The recommended steps that college and university officials should follow before declaring financial exigency and subsequently moving beyond that include, among other measures, the following illustrative actions:[18]

—Review relevant state and federal statutes.

—Review the institution's bylaws, statutes, and constitution.

—Review existing policies on internal authority relating to closure.

—Review debt instruments.

—Review faculty manuals.

—Review faculty contracts.

—Review practices followed in any prior closure.

Still, process and adherence to it are only part of the picture. Ensuring that the evidence is sufficient to declare financial exigency is equally important. This involves gathering information related to the institution as a whole and to the particular program that will be affected. This kind of objective, measurable evidence will demonstrate whether the actions will mitigate the exigency. The board of trustees will need information such as enrollment patterns, employment trends, availability of qualified faculty, the financial statements of the targeted program and the institution as a whole, and a comparison of that program with other options that might be considered.[19] "Evidence such as precarious cash position, declining enrollments, less drastic measures already taken, and projections of future financial instability are necessary to meet the burden of proof."[20]

If the institution has declared a state of financial exigency, it will then find itself prepared for the next step in the retrenchment process. Ideally an at-risk college or university should have adopted specific retrenchment procedures (such as what constitutes financial exigency and under what circumstances it will close a program) that it will follow in order to avoid potential legal problems. If an institution has not, and internal documents are silent about these issues, it runs the risk that if it is challenged on its decisions, a court "might be tempted to impose faculty oriented (AAUP) standards" for retrenchment, which are likely to be far more restrictive than anything a college or university would impose on itself.[21] However, the American Association of University Professors (AAUP) has stated that an institution has the right to discontinue programs and discontinue tenured faculty from those programs even without a declaration of a state of financial exigency.

When financial exigency has been declared and the college or university has targeted specific programs, the next step is perhaps the most challenging aspect of the entire process: specific faculty reductions. At some institutions the faculty handbook and/or the collective-bargaining agreement will control how this next stage will be accomplished. State and federal laws governing employee benefit plans could also play a role in this very politically and emotionally charged decision. As well, the faculty members will hold certain due process rights that must be honored in a layoff situation. This is particularly true at public institutions. Even at private colleges, however, academic personnel policies may require prior notice and the right to a formal appeal process. The institution may also have a contractual obligation to help the affected faculty member find a job within or outside the institution. As discussed previously with regard to laying off staff members, colleges and universities must pay special attention to the potential for discrimination claims as a result of the terminations. When dealing with faculty, it is critical to avoid firing someone in violation of the academic freedom policy. Generally courts will not substitute their judgment for that of the board of trustees as long as the criteria for termination of particular faculty members are legitimate and rationally applied.[22]

Students also have rights that must be considered in closing a program. Primarily students can expect (and courts have upheld their right to this expectation) that the institution will continue that program for the length of time normally necessary for the students to graduate—so-called teach-out expectations. Bear in mind that if a court finds that a claim of financial exigency is unsupported by the evidence, the court may award compensatory damages to affected students or require that the students be allowed to complete the program, if practicable. On the other side, if a college or university can demonstrate that the circumstances that warrant the program's elimination are legitimate, a program can be closed without requiring continued enrollment to graduation as long as sufficient continuation time is provided to ensure that the students do not suffer any damage. As a general rule, the program should be continued for a sufficient length of time to permit students a reasonable opportunity to transfer to a comparable, convenient, and affordable alternative program elsewhere without suffering a credit loss or a postponement of their graduation date.

Ultimately courts generally agree that a contractual relationship exists between a student and an educational institution upon matriculation. The educational consumer contract is derived from such sources as the catalogue, handbooks, statements of administrators and faculty, other representations made by the institution, and past practice.[23] Courts have, however, placed limits on the lengths that an institution must go to in order to mitigate the damages students might suffer from a program closure.

In addition to contract rights, students may also be able to avail themselves of a state's consumer protection law. It is necessary to understand that it is typically a violation of the state code to deceptively advertise goods and services with the intent not to sell them as advertised. Continuing to enroll students while school officials have knowledge that a particular program might not exist in the near future with no indication to the students could also be considered a "deceptive act or practice" under the consumer protection law.

Increasing Revenues and Opportunities

Containing costs is a key method to stabilize a vulnerable college or university. Finding new ways to boost revenues is another. This section is devoted to ways for colleges to develop new revenue sources and/or implement programs to infuse much-needed cash into the operation.

Bonds

If the leadership at an at-risk college or university has not yet become comfortable with the notion of floating bonds to pay for projects that may have been delayed because the endowment was too small, the capital campaign was not as successful as planned, or tuition revenues are dropping, it may be time to reconsider. Depending on the leadership's appetite for risk, incurring long-term debt could still be a worthwhile strategy for a struggling university or college that knows what it needs in order to attract students and boost tuition revenues, for example. Tax-exempt bonding allows the college to borrow at an interest rate that is much better than it would receive from a bank or other traditional lender. This is generally true even if the institution's bond rating is less than desirable.

Franklin Pierce College, which had been a college in trouble, used a $34 million bond issue in 1999 to restructure its debt, construct student housing, and complete other infrastructure projects. The issuance marked a major step in a turnaround effort that saw an 18 percent increase in enrollment between 1994 and 1999 and the reversal of a nearly $2 million deficit into a positive reserve. But even after the college received the infusion of capital, it was not out of the woods. It still had $39 million in debt, compared with $5.5 million in assets. Obviously the use of bonding authority must be considered carefully, even though it is an important tool available to the administration at a stressed college or university.

Strategic Partnering

Fewer colleges and universities than we anticipated in our first book, *Merging Colleges for Mutual Growth*, have merged as a way to alleviate financial hardship.[24] Instead, it is apparent to us that strategic partnerships are a key method for at-risk colleges and universities to overcome economic downturns. Strategic alliances are a "fluid, temporary, focused set of understandings and covenants between two or more complementary learning institutions or organizations."[25] Yet whatever form the alliances or partnerships take, leaders of the fragile institution must still be wary of the potential legal issues that they raise.

Partnerships with other institutions of higher learning are designed for more effective use of a university or college's finite campus resources.[26] An advantage of these transactional affiliations is that they can exist for a time and be revamped or closed when the demand for them disappears. Additionally, they can easily develop without violating the parameters of the institution's internal governing documents, such as the charter, the bylaws, master plans, personnel policies, and student and faculty handbooks. Also, the partners only assume responsibility for those activities specified in the terms and conditions that memorialize the agreement. In the case of a jointly operated academic program, the vehicle for the agreement is often a memorandum of understanding, which gives the parties a certain amount of flexibility to alter terms, whereas doing so under a more restrictive contract can be more difficult. A memorandum of understanding might, for example, determine who is responsible for marketing a particular program or how tuition differentials will be addressed. Other important issues addressed in it will be the responsibility for faculty hiring, compensation, and professional development.

Academic partnerships can also create opportunities for new funding streams for fragile colleges and universities. These types of entrepreneurial activities can range from transfer articulation to shared library resources. Whenever a nonprofit or public college or university is contemplating a for-profit venture, there are, of course, legal questions to consider. For nonprofits, questions about unrelated business income tax will have to be addressed. Beyond unrelated business income, public institutions will have to determine if their state has laws regarding competition with the private sector and if they are applicable in a particular situation. These types of transactions should not be viewed as a quick solution, because they can take considerable time and effort to negotiate. More important, they could expose the institution to additional financial, legal, or political liability. Consequently, the board of trustees and the administration will need to consider the following factors: [27]

—The institution's appetite for risk

—Consistency with the mission

—Ensuring institutional oversight

—Avoiding disproportionate allocation of institutional resources to business activities

—Avoiding overcommercialization of the institution

Flexible Endowment Management

In the context of weak and fragile institutions, endowment management carries several legal implications. State law, generally based on the Uniform Management of Institutional Funds Act (UMIFA), will govern how endowment monies must be handled. At its most basic, UMIFA, adopted in nearly every state, allows an institution to spend not only the income derived from the investments but some of the increase in value of the principal over its historic dollar value. This idea works well when the markets for investment vehicles are growing; however, problems can occur when endowments are "under water" and their principal shrinks because of outside market downturns. To address this issue, most institutions have adopted an approach that allows them to spend between 4 and 6 percent of the assets based on a rolling multiyear average. Keep in mind too that there are two types of endowment funds: so-called true endowment funds, which are donor restricted, and quasi-endowment funds, which give the institution much more flexibility because they are legally unrestricted.

If the at-risk institution has not already done so, it should make sure that it attempts to get prospective donors to approve purpose clauses in their gift instruments that will allow the school to override restrictive spending limits on the earnings and income from the gift. This will allow for maximum flexibility as the college or university's fiscal situation dictates. Another possible way to build in flexibility is to have an escape clause in the gift instrument. The clause allows the institution to determine if the original purpose of the gift is no longer practicable and to choose a new substitute use for the gift.

What about restricted gifts already in the bank? What avenues can a school pursue to free up that money for uses that could put the institution on sounder financial footing? The most obvious answer is to ask living donors to release the restriction in whole or in part. Another option, if the donor is deceased, is to get a court to agree that the original intent of the gift is no longer possible or has already been satisfied. This kind of approach may be somewhat complex and will require the assistance of competent counsel. The descendants of the donor could conceivably fight the attempt to modify the use of the gift, which could make the attempted action even more difficult and protracted.

Experts suggest some other methods for finding alternative ways to use restricted donor funds.[28] A struggling college or university might, for example, think about consolidating into a single fund all of its small scholarship funds that have essentially identical purposes. If this is done, the principal will generate enough money to endow fully a meaningful scholarship or more. Such an action could potentially help with recruitment. Additionally, at-risk institutions could look into the idea of consolidating funds with similar but not identical purposes. This would require court approval after the institution had proved that administering these funds separately had become impractical. In certain cases the law also will allow institutions to use restricted endowment funds to cover a portion of expenses related to the program a donor supported with a gift. Under UMIFA the donor's intent controls. Consequently, it is arguable that a donor's intent, without language in the gift to the contrary, was to help cover the overhead costs associated with the activities stemming from the gift. Even if a gift comes with narrow restrictions—to endow a specific professorial chair, for instance—there still might be ways to use some of the money for program-related support expenses. Travel expenses for the professor to attend academic conferences are arguably an acceptable use of the gift. Of course, all these alternative ways of reapplying endowment funds will need to be discussed with the institution's CFO and general counsel.

Hood College, a struggling women's college in Maryland, used an unusual legal tactic in 2002–2003 to take $10.5 million of restricted funds and apply them to a loan on which it had defaulted. The college transferred the funds to the college's foundation, which then lent the money back to the college at a rate of 6.25 percent over the next ten years. The court approved the maneuver provided the college continued to award scholarships stipulated by the donors whose gifts the college tapped into. The move, which has been described as "a final option,"[29] was part of a broader plan that included making the school fully coeducational and reducing the workforce.

Legal Responses to Accreditation Decisions

Reputation, ability to attract students, staff, and faculty, and access to federal student aid dollars all hinge on the imprimatur of a regional accrediting agency. Typically colleges and universities maintain careful, cordial relationships with their accrediting agencies, but when circumstances become tough and the institution is at risk, this relationship can become strained and even litigious. In one case the North Central Association of Colleges and Schools withdrew the accreditation of Lewis College of Business, a financially troubled, historically black, two-year college in Michigan. The small school was fighting for its life in mid-2007. A year earlier the college had been placed on "show cause" status "after the accreditor concluded that Lewis was behind in complying with requests to provide information on its financial state and administrative procedures."[30] In addition, the accreditor had expressed serious concerns about the level of involvement of the college's governing board. The college vowed to appeal the 2007 ruling, which is the beginning of a potentially lengthy and expensive process that has a very uncertain outcome.

From a legal perspective, not all decisions of an accrediting agency are considered adverse. When a decision is considered adverse, however, the institution has certain appeal and due process rights as prescribed by federal law.[31] Although it is always advisable when responding to any action taken by an accrediting agency to enlist the help of higher education accreditation experts, it is absolutely essential to consult legal counsel as well when faced with an adverse agency action. As long as the matter is on appeal, the agency cannot implement the adverse decision. If the decision stands, the university or college has the option of moving the challenge into federal court. However, courts are loath to substitute their judgment for that of the agency, even though because of the terrible toll that loss of accreditation can take, some courts have opined that the agency may be entitled to less deference.[32]

The example of St. Andrews Presbyterian College in North Carolina shows how turnaround plans can adversely affect accreditation. The college had had its share of financial and accreditation woes in the past, but in the summer of 2007 it found itself in difficulty again with its accreditor. St. Andrews faced revocation of its accreditation because of the way it had gone about bringing itself back from the brink. Among other actions, the institution had borrowed a large amount of money in the context of its endowment size. With an endowment of $14 million, it was carrying debt of nearly $16 million to pay for projects like the construction of an equestrian center to serve the equine-related majors it offers. The college vowed at the time to fight the revocation, but the lesson is clear that it is necessary for at-risk colleges and universities to consider accreditation factors whenever they are planning ambitious steps to revitalize themselves.

Conclusion: Prepare for the Worst, Hope for the Best

"What's it like to close a college? It is simultaneously awful and exciting,"[33] in the words of Donna Dalton, the last vice president for academic and student affairs at the now-defunct Trinity College of Vermont. She cautions that the emotional trauma that accompanies a closure announcement should not be underestimated.

From a legal point of view, many of the issues are similar to those that have already been discussed with regard to vendor contractual responsibilities, faculty and staff termination, and student teach-out responsibilities. The best way to avoid problems is to plan for them. As an example, when examining internal regulations, contracts, and handbooks, determine whether the university or college has either expressly or implicitly adopted AAUP policies for financial exigency or program closure. If the documents are silent, some institutions may wish to consider using the AAUP guidelines.[34]

Shuttering a college is far more complex than closing one program or terminating faculty and staff in several programs as a result of financial exigency. For example, a nonprofit will have certain obligations by law and in its governing documents that will limit how it must dispose of its assets. The IRS generally requires that assets of a tax-exempt organization must be permanently dedicated to an exempt purpose. This means that should an organization dissolve, its assets must be distributed for an exempt purpose or to the federal government or to a state or local government for a public purpose. What specifically can be done with assets, such as selling them to pay bills, will depend on state law, as well as the charter and bylaws of the college or university. Other than real estate, one of the main assets that a college has is its library collection. Dalton stated that readying the collection at Trinity College of Vermont for disposition was "like preparing a corpse for burial."[35]

The board should also develop goals, a budget, and procedures for the closure in order to ensure that the process goes as smoothly as possible. The trustees also must pass a formal dissolution resolution, which the institution's attorney can help draft. The board should, in cooperation with counsel, determine whether the courts or the state attorney general must approve the decision to dissolve.[36] Checking with the state board of higher education and accrediting associations is also a prudent course of action. Before the fall semester is considered the optimal time to announce the closure because it gives faculty, staff, and students the most flexibility in making alternative arrangements.[37] It may be possible for a college or university to get permission from the state to grant degrees even after it has closed if the students who started their programs at the closing institution take the remaining comparable courses at another institution. Although federal law prohibits students from receiving student financial aid if they are not enrolled in an eligible program, there are creative ways to address this problem, such as using state funds to replace the federal aid or finding other cash reserves the college or university might have to put toward this purpose.

No matter how much preventive legal planning and preparation the board and the administration do, some people may be angry and hurt. As a result, parties may still wind up in court. The more carefully planned and the more detailed the documentation for various processes, the better the opportunity to prevail if litigation does result.

As higher education leaders in an age of accountability, presidents, provosts, and trustees have the obligation to ensure that whatever course they chart, they have done their best to avoid its obstacles. They must ask if a contract exists, remembering that a contract does not necessarily have to be a formal document. They must ask if a certain activity is allowed by the university or college's governing documents, and if state or federal law might apply. They must even go so far as to ask what statutory or regulatory issues the course of action might present. Even if the answers are not readily apparent, engaging in this type of analysis will provide these leaders and college or university counsel with a starting point for discussion and the outline of an effective plan to lead the way from survival to success.

CHAPTER FOURTEEN

The Institutional Research Option: Transforming Data, Information, and Decision Making for Institutions at Risk

Kevin W. Sayers and John F. Ryan

For higher education leaders today, decision making is increasingly constrained by a confluence of high-cost planning issues and accountability demands. These issues and demands, and the challenges they create, are simultaneously influenced by external and internal forces. As a result, although many presidents and provosts are able to recognize emerging crises, their management teams fail to implement long-lasting solutions because the velocity of change creates a disorganized, frenetic approach to decision making. Furthermore, the information that supports decision making is typically fragmented, and ongoing, effective evaluation of those decisions is rare.

Successful leadership and decision-making outcomes on fragile campuses depend heavily on who participates and to what degree. An institutional infrastructure specifically designed to mine information, produce knowledge, and cultivate academic intelligence enables a more effective leadership paradigm. Such an approach to decision making involves the creation of a "decision-support network"—a resource composed of an engaged community with established working relationships and knowledge of each other's expertise that can be tapped in periods of crisis and fragility, whether academic, economic, legal, or all of these.

A more sophisticated understanding of decision making and knowledge management can better inform the leadership of at-risk institutions about where and how to initiate strategic, systematic change for long-term stability. Improved understanding and deployment can also address decision making that is short term and reactionary and often produces marginal results. By identifying and critically reviewing existing information management practices and implementing decision-support

---

Three Emerging Trends

■ The redefinition of traditional office roles and working relationships to reflect the interdependence of one area on another in information sharing
■ The integration of academic and administrative expertise (e.g., practice and theory)
■ A shared community focus and common understanding of the factors and variables that most closely influence the success of the institution

---

networks (DSNs), leaders will be able to implement influential reform that directly addresses the intensifying threats to their campuses.

In this chapter we will explore the concept of decision-support networks and their usefulness at fragile colleges and universities. A defining characteristic of a DSN is the transformation of information beyond simple warehousing and reporting into an integral component of the living mission of the college or university: enhancing knowledge to realize institutional and student success. In what follows, we propose strategies for institutionalizing these characteristics, and we conclude by outlining the next evolutionary step for institutional research and planning offices on fragile campuses in order for those institutions to become more nimble, future focused, and able to anticipate change.

Current challenges and recent professional literature related to institutional research and planning point to the need to redesign the role of institutional research (IR) offices. It is important to point out that one common response is to call on institutional leaders to place more importance and give greater stature to IR offices and those who lead them. Although this is necessary, it is also not sufficient. Simply stated, an effective strategy is now needed to create a more prominent role for institutional research—a strategy based on the argument that greater use of the kinds of management strategies that IR resources and products support is correlated with increases in academic excellence and institutional effectiveness.[1] Stressed institutions, in particular, need to develop the capacity and expertise to design and carry out strategic research beyond the familiar data-repository and reporting functions that continue to monopolize the time and expertise of institutional researchers.

Key IR Factors That Contribute to At-Risk Environments

A number of key factors contribute to ineffective approaches to institutional research and the inability of institutions to respond to at-risk circumstances. The evolution of IR as a means to facilitate decision-support networks can be a force that converts fragility into stability. However, the following challenges and deep-rooted conceptions of IR must be addressed in order to create an effective environment in which the decision-support network can emerge and thrive as an integral part of the college or university community:

1. *IR is commonly isolated and introspective.* The physical location of IR operations, whether centralized or decentralized, is usually an afterthought. Offices and personnel commonly find themselves physically removed from the vital decision-making and leadership areas within the university. Institutional research functions also tend to be peripheral to the core academic life and culture of the campus. Both of these phenomena reflect the "add-on" mentality behind the evolution and initial purpose of these offices that persists today: data collection and data storage to satisfy external and regulatory reporting requirements.

2. *IR personnel are known as the "data" people, not the "institutional knowledge" people.* This view by others in the institution may be perpetuated by institutional researchers themselves and the tendency to interpret service to the college as being only responsive or reactive rather than proactive in engaging the institution on key issues that emerge from the IR office's own insights and expertise.

3. *IR suffers from insufficient resources.* Partly because of many institutions' traditional tendencies to underestimate the return on investment from the IR function, many colleges, especially resource-poor ones, devote insufficient resources to move beyond a focus on simple external reporting requirements. Unfortunately, the ability to leverage more timely and forward-thinking institutional analyses that cultivate knowledge across traditional institutional boundaries remains a challenge at many institutions.

4. *IR is perceived as theoretical and is separated from its natural academic roots in leadership, policy, organization, and higher education programs.* This view unnecessarily perpetuates a problematic divide within the college culture, to the serious detriment of vulnerable institutions. In fact, theories of knowledge creation, dissemination, innovation, and organizational change offer new opportunities to unite institutional research more closely to the academic core of the institution.

5. IR often lacks a strategic and forward-thinking perspective. There is an urgent demand for strategic, forward-thinking perspectives in higher education, and traditional IR arrangements no longer address those demands as they once did. Recent calls by the federal government in the Spellings Commission's report on higher education in the United States to change the status quo to enhance access, improve economic competitiveness, and increase educational attainment via improved learning and degree completion reflect some of these demands.[2]

6. Traditional IR and planning practices and structures have failed to cultivate a contextual approach to converting data and information into knowledge. These practices and structures must be created by all campus users and must emerge from ongoing interaction and reflection within the decision-support system, not solely by those in the IR office. Leaders must construct knowledge via use of information and apply that knowledge over time, and the IR team must be an integral part of this process.

7. IR must more effectively anticipate trends and patterns of internal and external stakeholders. This anticipation can emerge from a strategically focused, research-driven exchange over time that leads to action and collaboration. Current divisions on many campuses contribute to their fragile infrastructures, as well as diminishing their capacities to emerge from fragility. It will not be enough for institutional leaders, faculty, staff, students, and external constituents to work collaboratively within their own domains as if they exist in nonintersecting universes.

How Decision-Support Networks Can Help Transform At-Risk Institutions

Information and stakeholders combined are key components in the success of crisis management on contemporary campuses. Nevertheless, these two areas and the knowledge resources they can independently provide are too often treated as separate entities and are only rarely linked. Specifically, in our observation, this linkage fails to occur in the organizational and bureaucratic structure of many at-risk universities and colleges. Within this context, which is commonly characterized by tensions based on perception and competing values or interests, institutional research and planning offices traditionally play only a tacit role in decision making. Evidence of this can be seen in the professional IR literature, which historically casts the IR function purely as data collection, data storage, and data reporting. Informa-

---

Three Best Practices

- The DSN provides the reliable, accessible, and evolving technological means to share and facilitate data use across units.
- Identifying and tracking of key performance indicators facilitates effective institutional planning and strategic management before and during times of fragility.
- A DSN provides the capability to envision multiple futures and consider the most strategic choices in light of likely outcomes and what may emerge as strategic themes across different scenarios.

---

tion is not only quantitative data or numbers but can also include public forum discussions, office memoranda, meeting minutes, or committee reports. Information is any mechanism that is created or used to reduce uncertainty within an organization.[3] Excellent information is a prerequisite to making sound strategic choices.

In turn, a key factor that must be taken into account in studying the nature of fragile institutions is the broader relationship that exists between information and decision making. Some contend that an organization systematically gathers more data than it can use in rational decision making because organizational expectations of process require it.[4] The role of information is pivotal not only in framing issues and problems but also in the identification of the political, social, and economic ramifications of eventual outcomes. Because institutions of higher education are highly accountable organizations through their accreditation requirements, they are often required to produce information in support of decision making that will be used as a measuring stick against assessment indicators for many years to come.

Presidents, provosts, and the faculty leadership must learn more sophisticated filtering of information and knowledge to identify those critical relationships and predictors of a variety of potential outcomes if their institutions are to negotiate a path to stability, much less excellence. An effective DSN creates a knowledge- and information-support system that pushes the institution beyond considerations of what it presently is to a more systematic, integrated, and future-focused view of itself. The DSN helps develop a more nimble infrastructure that is better positioned to anticipate, avoid, and address key institutional weaknesses and areas of vulnerability.

Table 14.1. Comparison of Traditional Institutional Research Roles with Decision-Support Network Functions

Traditional Model	Decision-Support Network Model
Centralized data collection and analysis	Decentralized data gathering and analysis supported by interpersonal relationships
Centralized data reporting on established schedules	Interdepartmental knowledge sharing and cultivation of intelligence on an ongoing basis
Archival data repository that is input focused and reactionary	Evolving information clearinghouse that is process oriented and focused on outcomes
Isolated from institutional leadership	Tightly coupled to institutional leadership

As a cultural resource, a DSN is heavily grounded in institutional values, and the paramount guiding principle of a DSN is the ongoing assessment of institutional strengths and weaknesses in light of mission, shared goals, and the shifting external environment. This principle is integral to designing initiatives and actions that maximize performance, quality, and institutional impact. Another key guiding principle of a DSN is the concept of institutional improvement and outcomes assessment. Localized assessment of outcomes, often all the way down to the departmental or individual level, is a key factor that can identify and help address sources of fragility and keep them from reoccurring. Decision-support networks operate under the premise that critical levers appear at all levels of the college or university (see table 14.1).

In addition to building awareness and interest across the institutional community in the DSN concept, several other cultural enhancements often accompany this institutional transition:

—A new approach to leadership that is more collaborative and interdependent

—The redefinition of traditional office roles and working relationships to reflect the interdependence of one area on another for information sharing and collaborative interpretation of results

—The integration of academic and administrative expertise[5]

—A deeper community focus and common understanding of the factors and variables that can cause institutional vulnerability

—The cultivation of meaningful and more easily communicated institutional knowledge and self-awareness

Implementing Decision-Support Networks Effectively

The essential components of a DSN are located within traditionally separate and uncoordinated functional units of the institution: institutional research, student outcomes assessment, program review and evaluation, external accountability (institutional and specialized accreditation and mandatory reporting requirements), and activities associated with planning and decision making for facilities and resources. Highly effective DSNs are characterized by the development and maintenance of robust communication and coordination of resources, initiatives, and activities. For example, if an institution that is fragile wants to implement programs centered on academic quality and shaping its incoming class, long-range enrollment plans are required to ascertain the workload and budgetary impacts that may be experienced. However, long-term models are increasingly susceptible to unknown factors or "shocks" as the time frame expands. This is where the ability of a DSN to consider multiple perspectives and research-based insights can provide the capability to envision numerous futures and strategic choices. The process incorporates operational perspectives, market research, predictive modeling, and study of the dynamics of past performance and leads to the articulation of a variety of potential scenarios.

How might the leaders of a fragile college begin to develop a DSN? A natural starting place is to examine the institution's current capabilities for institutional research and strategic planning. Patrick Terenzini has pointed out that initial definitions and explanations of what institutional research does and its function have been varied and somewhat amorphous.[6] The following steps incorporate the guidelines necessary for the creation and implementation of an effective decision support network:

1. Begin with mission and vision. Mission creep is a common obstacle to effective planning and creates conditions for fiscal fragility, crisis of identity, lack of shared purpose, and an inability to see new opportunities, all of which influence the likelihood that crises will emerge from multiple sources. DSNs can serve as a check on mission confusion and

---

**The Single Most Important Piece of Advice for a Leader
of an At-Risk Institution**

- Institutional leadership should pursue concrete steps to integrate IR,
  information technology, assessment, and strategic planning functions.

---

at the same time build trust with internal and external stakeholders.
The process can also be used more specifically to match students and
faculty with signature programs that fit their interests and leverage institutional strengths.

2. *Identify the key issues, challenges, and questions that face the institution through a collaborative strategic planning and environmental
scanning process.* A comprehensive environmental scanning activity, including a careful, honest appraisal of institutional strengths and weaknesses in light of external opportunities, threats, and trends, will provide a fresh sense of where the college currently stands. Multiple
stakeholders on and off campus should actively participate in the process, including faculty, staff, alumni, trustees, and state policy makers,
where applicable.

3. *Assess current IR capacity.* This is the moment for the institution
to assess candidly current IR and related information management staff
and technological infrastructure. This assessment should include linkages and partnerships with key external constituents, the development
of knowledge-sharing capacity, recognition of issues and ideas that
emerge from the bottom up, and changes in leadership strategies that
can move the college or university beyond top-down, command-and-
control tactics.

4. *Articulate the vision of how decision support will specifically
achieve mission and strategic goals.* Presidents and deans must be willing to advocate for the decision-support network concept and its capacity to strengthen fragile operations across the institutional community.

5. *Align DSN operations with parallel assessment and reward mechanisms.* Assessment not only monitors decision making contemporane-
ously to gauge its usefulness but documents outcomes for years to come.
Therefore, it is important for new decision-making models to integrate

---

The One Thing a Leader Should Do Differently

■ Identify and establish a chief strategy officer at the cabinet level.

---

information, stakeholder knowledge, intelligence, leadership, and accountability and reward criteria effectively. This can be achieved through ongoing assessment of the overall decision-making model. For decisions in times of stress and vulnerability to be of high quality, it will also be important to monitor continuously the attitudes of all stakeholder groups. These assessment tools should keep all constituents up-to-date and involved while testing the strength and adaptability of the decision-support network in the context of real planning priorities for the institution.

6. *Pursue concrete steps to integrate IR, information technology, assessment, and strategic planning functions.* Offices of institutional research, information technology, assessment, institutional effectiveness, and strategic planning should become more coordinated and, to the degree feasible, integrated in order to develop and maintain the campus knowledge base more effectively and transparently, especially during periods of institutional stress and vulnerability.

7. *Establish a champion for the DSN.* Most colleges and universities maintain a common set of cabinet members, including a chief academic officer, a chief fiscal officer, a chief student affairs officer, and a chief information officer. To achieve the longer-term goals of the decision support network, it is appropriate on many campuses to consider the development of a new senior position: chief strategy officer (CSO). The creation of a CSO at the cabinet level will provide the expertise necessary to champion the deployment of a DSN. Currently, among many executive teams no one is responsible for developing and driving strategic thought and action across the institution, or, alternatively, all cabinet members claim it as their area and define it principally for their area. Although the president is ultimately responsible for the setting of strategic goals and institutional benchmarks, a CSO would approach the DSN as a collaborative governance and leadership strategy.

8. *Embrace more action-oriented research and planning cycles.* Action research should be embraced as a tool aimed at probing both for

soft spots and opportunities institutionally. Persistence and even urgency in driving innovation based on knowledge developed via a DSN can gradually replace dated, incremental approaches to change and innovation.

Conclusion: Managing New Risks and New Opportunities

Identifying and building the key components of a DSN, as well as communicating the concept with consistency and clarity, may trick institutional leaders at some universities into thinking that such a knowledge network exists. However, an institution can incorporate all the previously mentioned components and still not have a high-functioning DSN. The network only fulfills its purpose if organizational and cultural barriers are removed across traditional units. Furthermore, in its early stages the key to the success of a DSN lies in the ability of presidents and provosts to accomplish the following objectives, even in stressed environments:

—Encourage more candid and effective working relationships at middle-manager and senior levels of the institution, in particular.

—Accept collaboration, shared responsibility, and common information more clearly as institutional norms.

—Emphasize value and minimize redundancy in services that directly support student success.

This approach to decision support—emphasizing a closer coordination of institutional research, assessment, program review, planning, and accountability processes—represents a new, more effective way for the campus as a whole to address its enduring causes of vulnerability. A DSN builds on and taps into historical strengths of research, inquiry, and shared governance. The extent to which the DSN is pursued and embraced will shape the institution's immediate view of institutional governance and faculty involvement in decision making. If leaders advocate this concept as part of a strategy for renewing shared governance and developing an enhanced institutional infrastructure, they will strengthen the institution against the sources of vulnerability discussed earlier and move it to higher levels of performance and academic quality.

CHAPTER FIFTEEN

Managing Reputation: Public Relations for Vulnerable Institutions

John Ross

Effective public relations should be a top priority for stressed institutions. Fragile colleges and universities often focus so heavily on controlling the techniques of communications—websites, new stories, annual publications—that they lose sight of their most important communications asset: people. Effective communications and public relations in vulnerable circumstances rely most on solid professional and personal relationships built on trust, respect, and appreciation. For the purposes of this discussion, "stressed" is defined as a college or university that relies on tuition and fees for more than 85 percent of its operating budget, for which annual fund receipts are a primary source of non-need scholarships, at which the tuition discount rate exceeds 40 percent, and at which faculty and staff compensation levels are noticeably below those of competitor schools in the same geographic area. More intangibly, the campus experience is one of concern, uneasiness, and month-to-month adjustments.[1]

Before launching a conversation about how effective public relations can turn around this type of institution, the specific duties, responsibilities, and influence of the chief communications officer need to be clarified. The senior communications officer is the staff member who holds overall responsibility for the areas of marketing, public relations, branding, media relations, and publications, both print and electronic. This individual may go by various titles, but whatever the designation, he or she should be a member of the president's cabinet and hold senior rank. The Council for Advancement and Support of Education and the Counselors to Higher Education section of the Public Relations Society of America, the two major professional associations for college and university communicators, are united on the issue that senior staff status should be accorded to the chief communications officer, but many smaller colleges and universities follow an advancement model wherein marketing and communications are aggregated and report to the vice president for advancement. The vice president for advancement, with responsibilities for development and alumni/parent relations, is typically also the institution's chief fund-raiser. In these instances, if the chief communications officer serves at the director level, he or she is likely to be a midlevel staffer with two or three subordinates reporting to her or him. Unfortunately, the greater the distance from the president, the greater the likelihood of misinterpreted instructions and failure to be entrepreneurial in both creating and seizing opportunities before they vanish in today's lightning-paced 24/7 information cycle.

At the same time, the personal and professional relationship between the president and the institution's chief communicator is more important than the reporting relationship. To conceive and discharge responsibilities in communications and marketing effectively, the lead staff member in this area must have access to the president and the deliberations of the institution's senior staff. As noted, the most effective model is to invite the chief communications and marketing person to attend cabinet meetings and to participate in discussions on a consistent basis, whatever her or his title. The benefits of such an arrangement are many. First, the chief communicator develops a personal understanding of the issues, their ramifications, and their nuances to a far deeper and more productive degree than if decisions and rationale are communicated to him or her secondhand by a superior. Second, the chief communicator, as a midlevel staff member, is able to observe and learn from the behavior of senior staff and to inject a marketing and public relations perspective into decision making. Finally, the inclusion in cabinet meetings allows the president to assess the capabilities and needs of the communications director and to provide personal guidance, if needed.

At a conference sponsored by the Council for Advancement and Support of Education (CASE) in 2001, the author chaired a panel of presidents and chief public relations officers. The session was an outgrowth of the 1999 CASE/ACE survey of six hundred college and university presidents and three hundred chief public relations officers, the benchmark study of the role and practice of public relations in higher education.[2] The study confirmed that, most important, presidents wanted their chief public relations officers to think and act more strategically.[3] The subject of the session was setting and managing expectations. Toward the end of the presentation, the author asked the presidents, "What is the president's role in mentoring the public relations staff?" Their response was collectively clear: include the chief communications officer in senior staff meetings in order to mentor, set expectations, and evaluate performance more effectively. Not only does this structure allow the institution to obtain maximum value from its communications leader, but it also sends the message that effective communication is a priority at the university or college. This is particularly useful at fragile institutions at which marketing may be called on to make a significant difference immediately in recruiting the next entering class.

Communications, Branding, and Marketing in Fragile Environments

Brands are not made. They evolve, and they are more the fruit of product than of promotion. Wagner College on Staten Island is a useful example. A fine small liberal arts college from its founding into the 1970s, it lost half its prospective student constituency with the decline of German Lutheran families in the New York City metropolitan area, the same demographic shift that contributed to the closing in 1995 of Upsala College in nearby East Orange, New Jersey. Wagner moved quickly to address its changing admissions market by adopting a patchwork curriculum that, with the exception of a very strong and highly regarded theater program, offered little to distinguish it from other small liberal arts colleges that were competing for the same students. Resources diminished, and only the sheer will of trustees, faculty, and senior leadership kept the school open through the 1990s. In 1997 the college created a curriculum that deeply integrated classroom learning with experiential opportunities presented by the educational, financial, and cultural assets of Manhattan, the other boroughs of the city, and metropolitan New Jersey. It labeled the new curriculum "the Wagner Plan for the Practical Liberal Arts," and the institution began to implement this vision strategically.

The transformation moved slowly, but senior leadership stayed the course, weathered a presidential transition, and gathered momentum over time. Enrollment and annual giving began to increase, along with endowment, as debt declined. The reputation of the college improved.[4] The college eventually hired a full-time director of communications in the fall of 2004 who carried forward the work of President Richard Guarasci, Vice President for Enrollment Angelo Araimo, and the entire admissions team, who were committed to highlighting the benefits of the Wagner Plan and of the college's unusual location on a bucolic wooded knoll overlooking lower Manhattan and within an hour's distance of

---

Five Components of Effective Marketing at Stressed Institutions

- Focus on the product.
- Focus on strategic goals that are well defined and long term in scope.
- Make critical decisions on a sound empirical basis.
- Integrate everything you do.
- Commit for the long haul.[5]

---

all that New York City could offer.[6] Guarasci and his colleagues were well aware that students choose colleges on the basis of academic program, alumni outcomes, and a campus visit.[7]

The branding of Wagner, an at-risk college for more than a decade, resulted from enlightened visioning and decision making in the creation of product and a persuasive commitment to stay on message: the benefits of the Wagner Plan and the college's location. The abilities to stay on message and to communicate it effectively are two ingredients in an effective brand, but many institutional leaders and even some professional consultants still equate branding simply with the consistent use of logo and taglines in a graphically united family of web and print publications. Not only the proclivity to reduce branding to attractive graphics but also frequent changes in the presidency limit branding's power and effectiveness significantly. Institutional brands take years to become firmly implanted in the highly conservative and intensely hierarchical universe of higher education, which many vulnerable universities and colleges never appear to negotiate with any form of lasting success, much less prominence. Consistency of approach and a broader view of what their brand actually is are core components in the accomplishment of long-term goals and objectives by vulnerable institutions.

The Benefits of Market Research

Research is an essential component for creating and sustaining an effective program of marketing communications. Some fragile institutions may tend to eschew marketing research because of the costs involved, but there are ways to conduct very useful research that will not break the budget. Cathee Phillips, the director of public relations at Morningside College, conducts a statistically reliable analysis of the penetration of the college's messaging among residents within one hundred miles of the Sioux City, Iowa, campus. She uses the college's fund-raising telethon system, trains students who conduct telephone interviews with three hundred adults, and then inputs the data into Statistical Package for the Social Sciences (SPSS) and analyzes them to track shifts in perceptions of Morningside and the respondents' reliance on media. The results help her shape the college's marketing strategies at a cost of about $1,000, including refreshments for the student volunteers.[8]

Other successful low-cost strategies involve ongoing use of focus groups and periodic structured debriefings of admissions and development representatives. As well, savvy colleges create a cycle of participation in such national surveys as the Council for Aid to Education's Voluntary Support for Education Survey, the National Survey of Student Engagement, and the freshmen survey done by the Cooperative Institutional Research Program (CIRP) at UCLA. CIRP also conducts national surveys of college seniors, first-year students, and faculty. These data, when compared with data from appropriate cohorts of peers and aspirant institutions, allow an institution to monitor trends that describe market position and also track progress toward strategic objectives. Many institutions stagger their participation in these and similar national benchmarking surveys every other year or every third year. Conducted in this manner and pursued consistently over a decade or more, these surveys provide an extremely useful, low-cost alternative for those fragile colleges and universities that cannot afford more expensive custom-designed studies.

Although many resource-challenged colleges cannot afford pricey research studies, surveys of perceptions held by college-bound high-school students who have not inquired but whose credentials fit an institution's current or aspirant profile, research about alumni perceptions and outcomes, and investigations of the attitudes of business and community leaders are nevertheless valuable tools for a vulnerable school that is strenuously attempting to reverse its decline. The challenge is to design such research so that it is surgical in application and affordable for limited budgets. The second challenge is to use the data creatively in other campus offices, including development, alumni, and public relations.

Institutions that purchase these major research studies often fail to use them fully because of a lack of integration among the functions of admissions, alumni, community relations, development, employee relations, institutional research, and legislative relations. At a fragile school all these offices carry communications responsibilities, and all need to be briefed on research conducted by and for the institution and then must be encouraged to use it in motivating their respective constituencies. This is particularly true in the offices of marketing, communications, and institutional research because data are increasingly demanded by various constituents who are attempting to verify claims made in marketing materials.

Shaping Key Internal Messages during Stress

Effective internal communication lies at the heart of transforming a stressed college or university. Jerry Porras, Stewart Emery, and Mark Thompson write in their introduction to *Success Built to Last* that "great organizations and societies can only be built by human beings who can grow and create meaningful success."[9] Each member of the college's internal audiences has a personal and tangible stake in the institution's success, whether it be salary, self-image, or the perceived economic and social value of the educational experience. Success begets success, and finding ways to celebrate forms of success on a regular basis can uplift a vulnerable institution without costing very much. Sometimes the most effective act is a simple handwritten "thank-you" note from the president or provost, well within the reach of even the most fragile budget.

Far too many presidents and board chairs continue to believe that external communications with prospective students and their parents, with potential donors, with media representatives, and with regional and national leaders who shape public opinion should take precedence over basic, repetitive communications with internal constituencies. Effective and innovative external communications are extremely important, as discussed in the following section, but it is the internal audiences that are the most important, especially in the case of a fragile, underfunded institution with an enrollment of two thousand or fewer that relies for more than 85 percent of its operating budget on student tuition and fees.

If you want to know the inside story about your local university, ask your neighbor who works there. Where do prospective students find their best information about future schools? They follow the blogs of those already enrolled and depend heavily on word of mouth from earlier graduates of their high school now in attendance. A scholar who is being recruited is more apt to believe a former graduate-school classmate who teaches there than a rehearsed search-committee presentation. Whom does a state legislator call about the culture of a public institution? Often it is not the president or the government liaison officer but the staff member who worked for her election.

Even small, vulnerable institutions can buttress their market position rapidly and inexpensively by sharpening internal communications via four action steps:

Key Strategies for Effective Internal Communications during Stress

- Set high expectations and mentor for increased performance.
- Celebrate specifically the roles of students, faculty, staff, and other employees in the accomplishments of the institution.
- Simplify and focus communications tactics.
- Create and follow a crisis communications plan that puts people first.
- Use the strategic plan as a template for communicating progress and challenges.

—Set high but appropriate expectations.

—Find learning in failure.

—Mentor junior faculty and staff.

—Regularly demonstrate that personal relationships make a difference.

There is scarcely a senior institutional communicator who has not blanched when the president has forwarded her or him a copy of a *New York Times* story with a note along these lines: "Why weren't we included?" Such missives from the CEO can generate a sense of failure and a defensive response by the chief public relations officer. More productively, the president might ask, "What can we do to be included in future stories like this?" Effective public relations officers are paid and retained to produce winning ideas about how to make this happen.

Nevertheless, in fragile environments internal communications can sometimes become fraught or fragmented, and the chief public relations officer will need to work closely with the president and vice president for academic affairs to stabilize campus communication systems. To start, create an internal communications users group composed of representatives from the following areas: the business office, student services, and information technology; two faculty; three students representing commuters, residents, and graduate/adult constituencies; the chief of campus security; one member of the clerical staff; and one member from maintenance. The senior communications/marketing officer should chair the group's semiannual meetings with an agenda to determine what works, what does not, and what can be improved.

Although stressed status does not routinely equate with emergency management, for the leaders of many colleges and universities, communication during a crisis remains a concern. Many institutions draft extensive emergency communication plans that are overlooked or hidden on hard drives as administrators scramble to address the situation. Emergency communications plans should be summarized in two pages or less and carry five goals:

—Protect the welfare of those adversely affected.

—Coordinate with involved on-campus/off-campus entities.

—Provide accurate and timely information.

—Avoid conjecture and blame.

—Defer to legal authority.

In any emergency situation the senior communications officer should serve as the spokesperson for the institution and take responsibility for shaping statements and for disseminating them through available channels. This is particularly true for colleges already viewed as vulnerable. How the college or university handles a crisis can say as much about its stability as the fact that the incident happened in the first place.[10]

Creating a positive campus communications culture demonstrates an important, concrete step forward for a fragile community. Providing regular updates of the current or emerging strategic plan is an excellent vehicle to raise awareness of progress while highlighting challenges still to be met. Anxious employees and students, particularly, will expect detailed information about where their institution is headed, and a strategic plan communicates belief in the college's future. The chief communications officer should volunteer to prepare and disseminate the updates, which are useful in managing external communications as well.

Too often institutions, especially those under stress, fail to integrate communication activities to present a consistent set of clear messages. Just as the school's strategic plan provides a vision and goals for internal audiences, the institution also needs to develop a road map for external communications. Aside from increases in enrollment and giving, how do institutional communities actually know if they are making progress? Colleges and universities at risk can begin by holding their communications and marketing departments responsible for developing a strategic communications plan framed by the institution's broader strategic goals and the budget designed to support them. The senior officers responsible for achieving objectives under each strategic goal should also participate in the development of the communications plan and assess its effectiveness on an annual basis.

Conclusion: Feeding the Media What You Choose to Serve

Stressed institutions can still be sources of terrific innovation. They are deeply familiar with doing more and better with less and with sharing the results of these experiments with regional and national media. Among the most effective strategies for reestablishing or improving the reputation of an institution is active participation in the leadership of a national association. Richard Guarasci, first as provost and later as president of Wagner College, served on a number of committees of the Association of American Colleges and Universities (AAC&U). He and his staff were frequent presenters at AAC&U conferences and workshops, and when reporters from *U.S. News & World Report*'s *America's Best Colleges* called AAC&U asking for recommendations on outstanding programs in undergraduate education, Wagner came readily to mind. As a result, the college was listed in five of eight *America's Best Colleges'* "programs to look for."

Presidents are well aware of the importance of developing personal relationships with boards of trustees, major donors, legislators, and leaders of targeted foundations. The most effective path to consistent visibility in news media is also based on such relationships, but the pressure for good press is intense. As much as presidents desire stories that focus solely on their institutions, media are far more interested in how emerging trends and issues in higher education affect their readers, and weakened, fragile universities or colleges are much less likely than better-financed ones to retain a cohort of faculty whose scholarship is of sufficient significance to attract sustained national attention. However, a savvy communications officer well versed in current trends and issues can be an extremely valuable ally to journalists in her or his region. By providing advance notice of important national studies and offering commentary on their significance by the institution's president, provost, or a well-positioned faculty spokesperson, even the smallest communications and marketing shop can achieve surprising visibility in media that matter, and these small beginnings can be leveraged later into greater access to journalists who value dependable stories when they are facing deadlines.

In turn, fragile colleges and universities must concentrate on communications in which they can control the content and timing of their messages. Unfortunately, many budget-conscious but shortsighted administrations scrimp on graphic quality in their web and direct-mail

A Model Strategic Communications Plan

1. Five core communications goals.

    a. Enhance appreciation by internal constituencies of the quality and direction of the college.

    b. Increase efforts to recruit and retain qualified students.

    c. Improve support for development.

    d. Obtain greater awareness and appreciation for the college's role as a leading institution.

    e. Broaden and deepen visibility in news media that make a difference.

2. Three objectives that will enhance the communication/marketing office's capacity to achieve its goals.

    a. Be intentional in the use of the institution's strategic plan in determining content and dissemination.

    b. Increase skills and capabilities of staff to meet communications goals.

    c. Expand use of research as evidence of institutional performance.

3. Under each objective, list two or three shorter-term tasks to be accomplished during the coming planning year. List only major objectives. Remember, less is more.

materials. Good taste need not be expensive. Even though they justifiably cannot allocate major resources for design, they can and should emulate the qualities demonstrated in the publications and websites produced by the nation's strongest institutions. The Council for Advancement and Support of Education continues to serve as an influential resource for the development of effective college and university publications. Generally speaking, it is reasonably easy to track response to direct mailings and advertisements. Special events tend to generate prompt feedback during and immediately thereafter. Although one can count hits on a website, it is more difficult to monitor how a viewer's behavior has changed. In sum, the most difficult communications element to evaluate remains media relations.

How does one monitor success of a key communications marketing campaign when dollars are scarce and relatively rapid results are necessary? The degree to which admissions and development met their quantifiable goals provides only a partial answer. More tellingly, how do the admissions, development, and provost's offices feel about the services they received during the past year? What worked and what did not, and why? How will those services be improved in the next twelve months? These qualitative measures can offer more effective assessments because they come from the leaders whose success defines the institution's bottom line.

Public relations officers have a tendency, perhaps understandably, to lean too much on tactics and technologies as the cure-alls for at-risk circumstances when the most effective solution is a positive culture of communications that engages vital constituencies. Effective communication is not the sole province of the marketing office, and it is not based merely on clever themes and messages contrived to achieve annual goals or temporarily to shape public perception. The greater the degree to which community members broadly participate in the development of a marketing campaign, the more rapidly the college or university can address the deeper reasons for its fragility. The president, senior staff members, and trustees finally create the climate for communication on campus, and communications that are candid, accurate, and proactive—and avoid turf battles and the assignment of personal blame to others—are the best prescription both to address the historic causes of a college's vulnerability and to help prevent new causes from emerging.

V

Synthesis: Achieving the Turnaround

In response to how we know that our institution has turned around, the biggest thing is that all-encompassing anxiety has abated on campus, and there is an attitude of personal responsibility for the future of the institution. People are eager to embrace the mission of the college. We realize that we cannot reach beyond what we are, but what we do, we will do effectively.

> —Gary Dill, president of College of the Southwest, New Mexico, in a telephone interview with James Martin and James E. Samels, 6 June 2007

We should have looked much earlier for the steps that can be taken by the institution before it is too late. Finally, do not be afraid to develop younger personnel to lead the college or university who are willing to take prudent risks and to think more innovatively.

> —M. Lonan Reilly, O.S.F., former professor of history at College of Saint Teresa, Minnesota, in a telephone interview with James Martin, 7 May 2007

CHAPTER SIXTEEN

Achieving the Turnaround: From Strategy to Action

James Martin and James E. Samels

For readers who have followed the themes and arguments of this volume straight through, we offer in its conclusion a synthesis of the key strategies that must be implemented to turn around a stressed college or university, along with a final group of leadership lessons gathered from presidents and others who have managed a turnaround process firsthand. In reviewing summary recommendations from the book's core chapters on board leadership, the presidency, academic strategy, and the work of the cabinet, five areas emerge as central to turnaround success: clarity of mission, financial stability, infrastructure health, accreditation transparency, and engaged board, executive, and faculty leadership.

Each of these areas must be integrated into the overall turnaround plan for the institution finally to achieve and sustain stability, but we caution readers to realize that even in the face of a major enrollment decline or budget deficit, or the sudden defection of the president, there will remain multiple ways to address the institution's most pressing problems. Thus we synthesize key strategies of approach and lessons learned with the understanding that they conclude a practitioner's handbook designed to provide solutions for campus leaders who are contending with a broad scope of overlapping and ingrained weaknesses.

Mission

During the uncertainties of a turnaround, the mission of the college or university is sometimes taken for granted and is left unconsidered with the assumption that there must be dozens, if not hundreds, of issues that need addressing—particularly the hard-core financial challenges—before time can be taken to sit and reflect on this sometimes-overlooked element of community life. Amid many campus anxieties, discussions of mission sometimes seem to be a luxury that the leadership team cannot afford, but in our research we have noted how often it has been necessary to rethink the institution's original vision and goals in order to get underneath the current causes of its fragility and to start addressing them seriously. Instead of beginning with a complex plan to reorganize personnel or an expensive outcomes-assessment system, the leadership team should more wisely use this energy to examine how dangerously dated and off-center the institutional mission has become.

William Weary, consultant to the Association of Governing Boards of Universities and Colleges on trustee leadership issues, advises, "The board's final responsibility is not to its current faculty, staff, alumni, or even students. Rather, it is to the institution's mission. Key members of the leadership team and trustees must keep asking: How well does this university implement that mission? From the perspective of best use of available human, financial, and physical resources, can current institutional sacrifices be justified? And, finally, what would the consequences be of shutting our doors?"[1] Rather than jumping too quickly to a new and expensive degree program or an expanded marketing campaign, experienced campus leaders who are working to mitigate risks learn to gauge early on if mission has been considered in any substantive way because without a commonly understood vision across campus, "a weakened institution is likely to flounder and make arbitrary decisions that go unchallenged."[2] Placing mission ahead of all other considerations in a turnaround process focuses the leadership team on the institution's core principles that should drive new program development, personnel hiring, and strategic marketing.

Finances

Daniel J. Levin, former vice president for publications at the Association of Governing Boards of Universities and Colleges, observes concerning the campus resource crunch, "The public policy debates in the nation's capital should not preoccupy presidents of at-risk institutions. The real action is in their own backyards: fixing the school's finances and establishing a solid relationship with an engaged board."[3]

The chapters of this book collectively confirm that restoring financial stability and confidence, in concert with an authentic reconsideration of the institutional mission, is the most essential element in a higher education turnaround. Debra Townsley, president of Nichols College and one of the nation's few college CEOs to lead an institution back from junk-bond status to a rating of BBB−, has raised Nichols's endowment from $5 million to $14 million and its student enrollments from 610 to 1,030 during her eight years of leadership. Townsley agrees that a turnaround must begin with mission and finances. On turning around her own institution financially, Townsley is blunt about what was required: "The president and CFO must be totally up front with the board and all outside agencies that may be monitoring the institution's progress, or lack thereof. Tell them, 'This is what we are going to do,' explain to them that it will take two years to accomplish, and then go out and do it, and remember always to design a highly conservative business plan that is realistic in the extreme. Then perform above that level."[4]

Townsley cites three classic indicators, in particular, as trigger points for a group of more serious problems: tuition discounting of more than 35 percent, tuition dependency of more than 85 percent, and debt service of more than 10 percent. This group includes the most common at-risk characteristics we studied over the past six to eight years; we found dozens of presidents and CFOs who were wrestling with these three issues in order, as Joseph Short, former president of the now-closed Bradford College, described it, "to make the financials work."[5] Michael Townsley, author of this book's chapter on managing the financial challenges in a turnaround, adds a comment that synthesizes the thoughts of a group of higher education leaders on presidential awareness and response during a crisis: "Most presidents . . . of an at-risk college or university are all too aware of the deteriorating condition of their institution if it has a history of deficits, declining enrollment, costs rising faster than revenues, or ever-increasing levels of short-term debt to cover daily cash requirements. . . . These presidents have learned to cope with decline; whether they are successful at coping is another issue."[6]

Infrastructure

Clearly, after mission and money, the declining condition of the campus and the institution's continuing inability to reverse almost all aspects of that decline form one of the most intractable problems within a turnaround. Considering the horizon of challenges from which to choose on a fragile campus, Dennis P. Jones, president of the National Center for Higher Education Management Systems (NCHEMS) and author of the 1986 study Indicators of the Condition of Higher Education,"[7] told the authors in an interview on the twentieth anniversary in 2006 that the two indicators of institutional vulnerability to which he pays most attention today are deferred maintenance and the technology budget. He put it simply: "Pay attention to buildings and technology."[8] E. K. Fretwell believes that campus leaders need to reduce their budgetary appetites and that many are failing in this regard: "Avoid getting into difficult situations by not purchasing the attractive 'bells and whistles' during new construction. . . . Hold back the appetite of your institution and don't go further than is necessary. Don't pay for 'frills.' "[9]

Focusing on the area of technology, Kevin W. Sayers, assistant provost of Capital University, and John F. Ryan, assistant provost of Ohio State University, co-authors of the chapter in this book on the value of institutional research in a turnaround, comment on the dangers of underspending on technology while simultaneously trying to develop a long-term strategic plan and meet the immediate needs of fussy student consumers: "A key factor that must be taken into account in studying the nature of fragile institutions is the broader relationship that exists between information and decision making. . . . Partly because of many institutions' traditional tendencies to underestimate the return on investment from the IR function, many colleges, especially resource-poor ones, devote insufficient resources to [these concerns]."[10]

Plans for infrastructure improvements and technology expansion are typically met with familiar budgetary rejections from the chief financial officer, but if one remembers the persistent efforts and eventual success of presidents like Debra Townsley at Nichols, it is also clear that leadership teams that do not push forward and find new ways to raise funds even when there is no prior record of success in this area, or who give up trying to fix a dated institutional image after three, four, or even five years of declining enrollments, will eventually lose the courage and strength to turn their institution around. As a result, the college or university will continue to decline and, rather than close, will be merged into another institution that, ironically, may be no larger in size but considerably larger in vision and imagination.

Accreditation

In one sentence, institutions must avoid probation. There is little, if anything, more powerful in conveying institutional weakness and vulnerability across the national higher education community than appearing on a regional accreditation association's probationary watch list. Robert Andringa, in his chapter in this book on the fragility of religiously affiliated colleges and universities, cites institutional probation, warning, or financial watch by a regional or specialty accreditor as the foremost indicator of at-risk status acknowledged by the college and university presidents polled in an exclusive survey designed for this book. A college's accrediting officer typically knows more about the institution's vulnerabilities than any other outside observer and often more than even many internal constituents who may find multiple reasons to deny an institution's declining fortunes during the press of daily business.

Beyond the specter of probation, in fact, Sandra Elman, president of the Northwest Commission on Colleges and Universities, notes that the regional accreditation system in American higher education can play a pivotal, if sometimes-feared, role in turning around its member institutions by causing their systems to be assessed and their standards to be raised. From the perspective of a turnaround, accreditation should be viewed as a mark of quality that institutions must earn without shortcuts: "Regional accreditors are continuously working with their member institutions to facilitate the design of models aimed at regeneration and renewal. The self-study process overall is focused on identifying limitations and bottlenecks in the system that thwart these objectives. . . . Fragile colleges and universities do not have the option of choosing whether to engage in a sustained appraisal of their chances for survival. If regional accreditors are not already closely monitoring the condition of the institution, the board needs to implement such an internal process immediately."[11]

Campus Engagement

The final strategy, campus engagement, can be described as the necessity to develop a group of collaborative, engaged faculty, administrative, and trustee leaders—or the need to manage an unprecedented degree of personnel turnover, depending on one's view. At root, as many contributors have pointed to in previous chapters, the institution must take responsibility *for itself* as a community in danger and in need of new solutions if the turnaround is to succeed. Beyond phrases like "committed leadership team" and "dedicated trustees," the drivers of a successful process are board and employee engagement, courage, and decisiveness. Although these qualities can be enhanced by professional development funds, retreats, and a vigorous, merit-based annual evaluation system, the community should nevertheless prepare for much higher levels of personnel transition than perhaps at any time in its history, coupled with the willingness of those who stay to assume new and expanded responsibilities.

Daniel J. Levin comments on the fact that there is no safety net under an institution's leaders during a turnaround and that trust and candor between the board and the chief executive officer can make a critical difference: "Indeed, no institution that is facing financial and strategic challenges can possibly hope to improve itself if it lacks a strong and engaged leader who has earned board support."[12] Levin also makes the helpful distinction between causes of fragility that are controllable and

Summary Lessons from Turnaround Leaders

1. Be a realist.
2. Define health carefully.
3. Manage the managers more closely.
4. Design a new dashboard.
5. Prepare for a long campaign at high speed.
6. Talk faster to the board.
7. Know the difference between late and too late.
8. Hire the right consultant.
9. Leverage partnerships.
10. Refocus on students.

those that are intractable. Drawing on the results of two surveys of more than thirteen hundred campus leaders that were analyzed by John D. Sellars and published a decade apart in *Trusteeship* magazine, Levin describes reasons for decline that are controllable as the continuing, or eroding, perception of academic quality, the percentage of budget resources dedicated to student aid, student-body size and enrollment trends, and annual revenue from gifts and the endowment.[13]

In closing, W. Stephen Jeffrey, charged with developing the plan for a fund-raising campaign for fragile institutions, observes in his chapter in this book how important it remains for the entire community to step forward and to take responsibility for its own turnaround: "Higher education institutions do not become fragile overnight. The process usually takes time and includes several noticeable stages. During this period institutional leaders may have adopted some bad administrative habits, whether as a coping mechanism for significant daily anxieties or, in their view, simply to keep the institutions operating and moving forward. . . . Institutional leaders will need to reconnect with these administrators, at all levels of the college or university, and keep them engaged in the process of turning the institution around."[14] Whether or not the process outlined by Jeffrey requires an immediate departure of one or more senior members of the institution's faculty or administration, the school should prepare for a changing set of teaching and learning priorities, greatly increased individual accountability, and much hard work in mission review and new student recruitment practices as the turnaround moves from strategy to action.

Summary Lessons from Turnaround Leaders

As readers have noted by this point, institutions arrive at fragile status for many different reasons and with many different combinations of symptoms and weaknesses. Regardless of whether it is most apt to describe them as vulnerable, fragile, at risk, or all three, the fact remains that many American colleges and universities are sliding downward. In speaking with more than 200 presidents, provosts, board chairs, cabinet members, and faculty and student leaders over the course of this study, we have assembled a set of final leadership lessons from decision makers at all levels of institutions that have experienced a turnaround—some successful and some that failed. These lessons implicate everything from classic budget pitfalls to the quality of student life and were designed less as a ten-point agenda than as a summary collection of memorable comments from pertinent conversations over the past six to eight years.

1. Be a Realist

The stereotypical approach to problem solving at stressed colleges that we heard most consistently over the years was to focus attention on the senior leadership team and to charge them collectively to turn the institution around. In fact, in our observation, things often did not follow this plan, and the president not only led the turnaround but also played many of the most important, thankless roles in completing it. Thus presidents, most of all, need to be realists on fragile campuses, and they must learn *not* to take yes for an answer, to reverse a phrase, when working with cabinet members who avoid presenting bad news.

Rather than working as a harmonious team, cabinets under pressure often crack, finger-point, and seek positions elsewhere. Michael Riccards, now executive director of the Hall Institute of Public Policy in New Jersey and formerly president of three colleges, Shepherd, Fitchburg State, and St. John's, has extensive experience with senior leadership teams, and he believes that what the presidents of fragile institutions most need is an experienced chief academic officer to manage key responsibilities with vision and creativity: "In at-risk institutions, presidents rarely are able to hire first-rate provosts. They simply cannot recruit or retain them. Thus, by default, the CFO becomes the strongest person on the team, and he or she is often not interested in institutional reform. The CFO is paid essentially to balance the budget. That's his or her role. In fact, CFOs sometimes don't even relate to the president; they relate more to the institutional auditor and the finance committee of the board. If academic change is to be made—and this is what turning around a fragile institution must be about—the president will have to lead the way in the absence of an experienced provost."[15]

2. Define Health Carefully

The most successful presidents and chief academic officers we interviewed, even while managing a crisis, could readily convey the missions of their institutions with authenticity and define what health meant for their college or university. These individuals were not captives to downward trend lines. Rather, they steadfastly remained focused on what made their institution distinctive and worth considering. Jack Wilson, president of the five-campus University of Massachusetts system, offers one definition of institutional health:

> A college or university is healthy when the community it serves looks to it successfully and consistently for leadership on issues such as workforce and economic development, expanded student access, and new cultural opportunities. Having served as an administrator at both public and independent universities, I am struck by their similarities of purpose. The first American university, Harvard, was founded to serve a need for religious and community leaders; the first technological university, Rensselaer Polytechnic Institute, was founded to educate the sons and daughters of farmers and mechanics in the application of science to the common purposes of life. We have traveled a great distance from the agricultural and religious career paths of several centuries ago to globally-focused research and teaching in biotech, infotech, and nanotech, yet definitions of "health" have remained strikingly basic and clear.[16]

We found that collaboratively developing a shared definition of institutional health was one of the most important steps a college or university leadership team could take to move a fragile institution forward, usually accompanied by a fresh set of dashboard indicators to measure its progress.

3. Manage the Managers More Closely

Michael Townsley is equally direct in his cautions to the leaders of weakened institutions: "Experience has shown that most financial systems are treated as a reporting device for board meetings, audits, and a snapshot used for budgeting. Many institutions work on the cheap and do not hire certified public accountants or other skilled personnel. Too often the financial system barely works, and no one knows how well it works until there is a major problem. Neither a viable institutional strategy nor a rigorous management system will succeed if this is how a financial system is employed."[17] Townsley, Daniel Levin, and many others with whom we spoke over the course of this project agreed that perhaps surprisingly, many leaders beset by financial difficulties and uncertainties viewed their financial system as a nuisance, only to be really studied or used when it was time to develop a report for the board or an outside agency that, whatever its destination, "no one understands."[18]

Although it is relatively easy to claim that poor financial management is the main cause of troubles at most stressed institutions, we found that the financial implications of fragility typically were deeper and more complex than this, and that although poor, shortsighted, or uninformed financial management was usually a large component of fragility, there was a larger point to be made about the styles and skills of what were sometimes several leadership teams over a generation. As Townsley finally explains, "A financial system is not a fire extinguisher for emergencies. It only works if it is used every day over the long term to reduce the possibility of negative events."[19]

4. Design a New Dashboard

Although easy-to-grasp, fact-driven data points, universally termed "dashboard indicators," are sometimes maligned as business-talk stereotype, they were valued by most of the presidents we interviewed as concise and very dependable ways to assess whether their institution was advancing in meaningful ways. However, there was also an understandable reluctance among many presidents to accept fully the indicators of previous generations. In fact, some chief executive officers rejected earlier iterations and challenged the members of their cabinets and faculty governance associations to create new indicators that could more accurately measure and predict the likelihood of a lasting turnaround.

When Laurence Spraggs was appointed president of Broome Community College in 2004, he inherited a turnaround situation. Rather than prolong the levels of tension and conflict that were continuing on the six-thousand-student campus in Binghamton, New York, the president approached the college governance system

with the intent to use dashboard planning as a way to empower the entire community. So much of effective leadership is about effective relationships, not about dos and don'ts. Good dashboard indicators can help the campus identify and change behaviors and encourage engaged faculty and students. For example, at Broome we began by measuring student persistence rates rather than the familiar three-year graduation rates as a truer indication of success in teaching and learning on our campus, and then we looked beyond the more common program-completion benchmark to study specific course-completion rates as a more legitimate building block in our turnaround strategy.[20]

Following this broader view of the benchmarking process, strategic planners at another New York community college, Nassau, with 24,000 students, identified a classic Achilles' heel in the accreditation process, full-time/part-time faculty ratios, for special consideration and rethinking. They determined that they would not let the college be backed into a corner by a perceived imbalance between the numbers of full-time professors and adjuncts; instead, they shifted their focus away from this older dashboard indicator, as Ezra Delaney, Nassau's former vice president for administration and planning, explains:

Nassau has moved beyond some traditional measures such as full-time/part-time ratios to target specific strategic objectives and develop achievable benchmarks. The institution agreed, during its 2006–2008 planning process, to improve the performance of at-risk students through support programs and faculty development. New success indicators were developed utilizing a combination of retention and grade point averages of the students who have tested for remediation. In this way, we plan to move away from static measures to new benchmarks that can contribute directly to future decision-making and resource allocations.[21]

Finally, Northland College, a seven-hundred-student institution in Ashland, Wisconsin, that links new approaches to environmental studies with historic approaches to the liberal arts, learned that benchmarking is now all about aspirants rather than peers. Rather than manage their turnaround by comfortably inhabiting a middle ground among small environmental studies colleges nationally, Northland cofounded the Eco League, a well-timed consortium of six colleges ranging from Alaska to Maine that has, among other priorities, rethought dashboard indicators of sustainability and "green" programming. Rick Fairbanks, Northland's provost, explains:

A key to our survival became owning our niche by articulating our distinctiveness. For this to occur, we had to answer two questions about the institutions we defined as aspirants: "What do they do that we must do, and what do they do that we cannot do?" We needed to define carefully how much like them we wanted to be while still maintaining a distinctive market name. Negotiating the space between those two positions has been risky because of a perception of arbitrariness among those tracking the institution. However, we have had to accept that risk because we cannot compete with our betters wholly on their terms, but we also cannot refuse to play the game.[22]

5. Prepare for a Long Campaign at High Speed

Roosevelt University president Charles R. Middleton, author of the chapter in this book on leading the cabinet on a fragile campus, comments, "Quick fixes are anathema for at-risk institutions. There are no quick fixes. Prepare for the long haul. At-risk colleges and universities that survive do so by returning to a basic principle: academic quality. Whether the president is told this or not upon accepting the position, he or she must prepare for a campaign of ten to twelve *years*, not two or three. Most of the new presidents I have met have had no idea how long it takes to turn around a seriously flawed institution. The informal rule should be that if the president is committed to making changes that will last longer than her or his presidency, the work will take a decade or more."[23] At the same time, Middleton cautions new presidents and their leadership teams not to confuse the length of the campaign with the speed of change on their campuses during this process. In fact, Middleton believes that both senior faculty and administrators are increasingly being challenged to act more quickly in their weekly and monthly decision making. Gone are calendars that divided curriculum and educational policy projects into semesters or years of meetings, and replacing them are much more condensed schedules with measurable action steps. In part, driven by the outcomes expectations of the nation's regional accrediting organizations, deans and department chairs are being asked collaboratively to achieve objectives within weeks and months that might have consumed two or even three years of community effort a decade ago.

Several campus leaders with whom we spoke and who were aiming at their first presidencies expressed similar opinions about the pace of change on campuses today. Some provosts and academic vice presidents acknowledged the need to think pragmatically and accept that their first presidency may be their only presidency and that it may be the best opportunity they will have to make significant changes at any institution, fragile or otherwise. At the moment of their appointment, new presidents should take the proverbial deep breath and accept the fact that they will have to work on more projects simultaneously, and succeed at them, than CEOs of the past. Rather than picking and choosing or placing one or two projects on hold, they may need to begin a new strategic plan immediately or to undertake a major fund-raising campaign while working carefully with the faculty senate to raise the academic quality of the most dated degree programs and strategizing new assessment and retention mechanisms with the dean of students. Middleton wryly concludes, "Ambitious presidents should perhaps not seek employment at at-risk institutions. They should go to public universities where the funding, although decreasing, never stops."[24]

6. Talk Faster to the Board

Some presidents with whom we spoke lived in fear that their board chair would find out how low their actual budget and enrollment numbers were, but all agreed that unfiltered, rapid communication links with the chair and the heads of key trustee committees were vital in addressing fragile circumstances. Jim Rogers, chancellor of the Nevada System of Higher Education, is blunt in his description of the communication model he employs with the seven presidents in that state system:

> As a chancellor, I operate with two time frames in my life: now and right now. Coming from the world of communications, I find in higher education, with its emphasis on process, that it is easy to find a quick consensus on 80 percent of the issues we face, and that we spend almost all of our time trying to resolve the remaining 20 percent. I'll take care of that 20 percent tomorrow. In fact, that is the best place for process, to address the remaining 20 percent. I continue to believe that it is better to have a quick decision than no decision.[25]

Although Rogers's view is still contrary to that of many more traditional higher education decision makers, those who share his view are increasing in number. Presidents and board chairs have consistently lamented to us over the past six to eight years how long it takes to achieve significant change on a consensus-driven campus. However, instead of lowering expectations and settling for flawed compromises, some CEOs and trustees are continuing to adopt new technologies to increase the speed and breadth of communication between them. The mobile office, delivered by a personal digital assistant and incorporating wireless e-mail, schedule, calendar, contacts, and telephone service, has become essential to almost every higher education administrator.[26] Mahesh Sharma, former president of Cambridge College in Massachusetts, offered this simple view:

> In the time it takes to give an assistant instruction for a memorandum, check it, and follow through, I have already sent the memo. BlackBerry is

simply a name; whatever the name of the handheld device, my office—phone, e-mail, calendar, and documents—is on it, because there is no such thing as only a cell phone anymore.[27]

7. Know the Difference between Late and Too Late

Of all the lessoned learned at the end of our research, waiting too long to initiate, much less accomplish, major change was probably the most common characteristic observed on vulnerable campuses. As the comments that follow will partially indicate, it was clear that excellent plans for change and honestly innovative ideas to sustain survival were evident right up to the final day of classes in the final year of existence for some closed institutions. In fact, in some cases the urgency of the situation apparently prompted some of the most courageous thinking by leadership teams and faculty senates. Unfortunately, it remained courageous thinking rather than courageous actions as money and resources finally ran out and closure became inevitable. Summary comments by three administrators and board members of colleges that did not survive confirm this:

Pastor George Freyberger, dean of students and former chaplain at Upsala College when it closed in 1995: "Some maintenance could not be deferred. . . . Student life had to be supported, but we could not catch up and find enough money to operate. The Lutheran Church was supportive, but it could not help enough financially."[28]

Leslie Ferlazzo, trustee and former board chair at Bradford College when it closed in 2000: "A college or university ultimately needs to have a reason to exist, and eventually ours did not. . . . We did what we needed to do, i.e., fund-raising campaign, merger explorations, borrowing funds, but there was a sense that even these creative actions would still lead to closure. . . . We should have started earlier to take actions to address our circumstances."[29]

Sister M. Lonan Reilly, former professor of history and assistant to the president at College of Saint Teresa when it closed in 1989: "We should have looked much earlier for the steps that can be taken by the institution before it is too late . . . [such as developing] younger personnel to lead the college or university who are willing to take prudent risks and to think more innovatively."[30]

Developing and acting on a successful sense of timing about the moment when a bold initiative must be launched are extremely difficult for an untested president, provost, or board chair who has never been through a major institutional crisis. We observed many presidents, now in hindsight, who were aiming in the right direction, so to speak, but who spent an extra year or semester or even month gathering still more important information and believing that that information would help her or his institution do the right thing when, in fact, the process of gathering and studying and weighing extended past the final window of new student interest, bank confidence, or faculty commitment.

8. Hire the Right Consultant

After a new president has led the effort to design the new dashboard indicators, identified that small group of competitor institutions to which his or her school aspires, and focused the campus, rightly, on the central need to preserve and improve academic quality as the core of the turnaround, the moment usually arrives at which the chief executive realizes that he or she does not have the staff, resources, and funds to accomplish all these necessary tasks. At this moment the cost of an outside consulting firm is typically also perceived as beyond the budget, so the president turns to the cabinet and the board and recommends a group of tough, belt-tightening moves and then settles on the one or perhaps two strategies that the community considers essential to survive—while the college moves steadily closer to closure.

In fact, modestly priced outside consultants may be exactly what a vulnerable institution needs to complete a turnaround. Experienced help, particularly from advisors who have both turned around and closed colleges in their careers, can be invaluable to a new president who is facing a reduced set of options and a fatigued board of trustees. Richard Carpenter, formerly president of the Wisconsin technical college system and currently president of the Lone Star College System in Houston, a five-campus organization with approximately forty thousand students, has authorized the hiring of dozens of consultants on multiple campuses over the years in order to secure candid outside advice. He offers three reasons for retaining these professionals, even within a declining budget projection:

> Colleges at risk typically cannot afford *not* to hire at least one or two experienced consultants to help design a turnaround. First, a consultant who verifies a leadership team's instincts about even a single cause of vulnerability has provided something as valuable as new information for a complex decision. Second, many campus crises are politically sensitive, and an experienced team of consultants can provide the president with important political "cover" when it becomes necessary to accept the difficult recommendations of outside advisors. Finally, the reasons for an institution's fragility are usually local ones, yet they can dominate discussions on campus for several

years. Savvy consultants challenge the leadership with a "national looking glass" and broader perspective on how its specific, sometimes-narrow, concerns relate to emerging trends in areas such as student program preferences and financial aid packaging.[31]

In closing, Carpenter advises that at the very least consultants bring a depth of thinking and a team approach that no single president can manage, especially when challenged by continuing enrollment losses and an erosion of institutional reputation.

9. Leverage Partnerships

The literature on the benefits of institutional partnerships continues to grow steadily. From individual-course, team-teaching collaborations to joint grant applications for tens of millions of dollars, colleges and universities are joining forces in innovative ways at an increasing rate. The lesson here for at-risk institutions is to move beyond what can become a paralyzing focus on internal concerns to a broader consideration of the college or university's external context, including colleague institutions with which it might partner to leverage strengths in key areas such as faculty professional development, joint degrees, shared fund-raising and alumni outreach, and common residence halls and teaching spaces.

Charles R. Middleton, president of Roosevelt University since 2002, announced in his 2004 start-of-year address a 51 percent increase in student housing at Roosevelt thanks to a major partnership with Columbia College and DePaul University in downtown Chicago. Through this partnership a superdorm called University Center Chicago was opened that housed more than seventeen hundred students, the largest joint student residence hall in the nation. Middleton, author of the chapter in this book on leading the cabinet of a vulnerable institution, has been a highly visible proponent nationally for multiple forms of partnership in higher education, such as those Roosevelt has implemented with Harold Washington College and Houston Community College in which either students are simultaneously accepted or their A.A., A.S., or A.A.S. degree is entirely credited by Roosevelt.[32]

From Golden Gate University in San Francisco offering an M.B.A. cohort program for employees at Gilead Sciences conducted on-site at Gilead's offices to the University of Maine at Fort Kent collaborating with the state of Maine's Acadian Heritage Council to initiate a new website, "Acadian Culture in Maine," higher education partnerships of some kind can now be found in every state, and they are not confined simply to traditional, not-for-profit institutions.[33] In sum, colleges are not islands, as a community college president advised us, and fragile colleges will benefit from continuing to develop strategic alliances with partner organizations that leverage the strengths of both while keeping the emphasis, finally, on students as central.[34]

10. Refocus on Students

As much as attention to mission must come first when addressing stressed conditions, refocusing on students and incorporating their voice into all major decisions is the final lesson for turnaround leaders. Rae Perry was associate dean for student life at Bradford College when it closed in 2000 during its 197th year of operation. The scope of Bradford's history and mission over nearly two centuries made its closure all the more difficult and poignant. As one of its final senior student affairs officers, Perry remembers,

> The College closing was devastating for the entire, extended campus community. For a good number of students, this was their first experience with significant loss, a loss that was unanticipated, beyond their control, and which changed their lives. The closing instantly derailed their inner senses of how their college years were supposed to progress. Student life professionals had to address all of this—fears, transitions, opportunities—while dealing with our own uncertain futures. In retrospect, the most important decision we made was to engage students in the discussions about what they needed. We used existing forums such as community meetings and existing connections between faculty members and students as much as possible, but even with them, we did not anticipate the volume of students who surfaced in crisis.[35]

In closing this narrative, we return to one of its key starting points: the impact of at-risk conditions on students and the capacity of those students to contribute fresh and valuable viewpoints to a turnaround plan. In fact, students have been portrayed in several chapters here as definers of new identities, and we end this conversation in the belief that students are most often among the first to identify a mission and infrastructure that are moving toward risk, and that institutions thus identified will become stronger sooner if they engage students in the process and value their thinking equally with that of the faculty, the president, and the board.

Notes

Preface

1. Telephone interview with Daniel J. Levin, 15 June 2006.

Chapter 1. Defining Stressed Institutions and Leading Them Effectively

1. George Keller, *Academic Strategy: The Management Revolution in American Higher Education* (Baltimore: Johns Hopkins University Press, 1983).

2. George Keller, telephone interview with James Martin, 20 January 2005.

3. Ibid.

4. George Boggs, telephone interview with James Martin and James E. Samels, 1 February 2004.

5. Erica Kelly, "The Changing of the Guard," *Community College Week*, 27 May 2002, 7. The title "The Leadership Gap: Crisis or Opportunity" was uncredited and appeared on the front page of the same issue of the paper.

6. Jamilah Evelyn, "The Outsider: A Community College Hires a President from the Corporate World with Mixed Success," *Chronicle of Higher Education*, 31 March 2006; "The Outsider Solution" appeared as the title of the article on the front page of section 1 of the newspaper; Joann S. Lublin, "The Serial CEO," *Wall Street Journal*, 19 September 2005.

7. National Center for Public Policy and Higher Education, *Losing Ground: A National Status Report on the Affordability of American Higher Education* (San Jose, CA: National Center for Public Policy and Higher Education, 2002), www.highereducation.org/reports/losing_ground/ar.shtml; "Financing Higher Education: A Crisis in State Funding," National Education Association, 2003, www2.nea.org/he/fiscalcrisis/index.html; Philip Trostel, "The Long-Term Economic Effects of Declining State Support for Higher Education: Are States Shooting Themselves in the Foot?" 2003, www.wisconsin.edu/pk16/reference/trostelpaper .pdf; Dennis Jones, "State Shortfalls Projected to Continue despite Economic Gains; Long-Term Prospects for Higher Education No Brighter," issue paper, Secretary of Education's Commission on the Future of Higher Education, www.ed .gov/about/bdscomm/list/hiedfuture/reports.html.

8. Charles Miller and Cheryl Oldham, "Setting the Context," issue paper, Secretary of Education's Commission on the Future of Higher Education, www.ed .gov/about/bdscomm/list/hiedfuture/reports.html.

9. Jones, "State Shortfalls Projected to Continue despite Economic Gains."

10. Trostel, "Long-Term Economic Effects of Declining State Support for Higher Education."

11. Jandhyala B. G. Tilak, "Global Trends in Funding Higher Education," *International Higher Education*, no. 42 (winter 2006): 5.

12. Olin L. Adams III and David M. Shannon, "Cost Control in Higher Education," *University Business*, September 2006, www.universitybusiness.com.

13. Jeanne C. Meister, "Learning Trends to Watch in 2006," *Chief Learning Officer*, January 2006, 58.

14. M. J. Zuckerman, "Email Catches Up to Snail Mail," *USA Today*, 15 May 2001, 30.

15. Robert Sevier, "A New Definition of Marketing: The AMA's Update Can Mean Enormous Opportunities in Higher Education," *University Business*, March 2005, www.universitybusiness.com.

16. Scott Jaschik, "Crisis of Confidence," *Inside Higher Education*, 13 February 2006; Alvin P. Sanoff, "Mud on the Ivory Towers: Colleges Turn to 'Crisis Consultants' for Image Repair," *USA Today*, 29 August 2005; Philip Altbach, "Knowledge and Education as International Commodities: The Collapse of the Common Good," *International Higher Education*, summer 2002, www.bc.edu/ bc_org/avp/soe/cihe/newsletter/News28/text001.htm.

17. Jaschik, "Crisis of Confidence."

18. Altbach, "Knowledge and Education as International Commodities."

19. D. W. Leslie and E. K. Fretwell Jr., *Wise Moves in Hard Times: Creating and Managing Resilient Colleges and Universities* (San Francisco: Jossey-Bass, 1996), xvi.

20. Ibid., xvii.

21. Dennis P. Jones, "Indicators of the Condition of Higher Education" (Washington, D.C.: National Center for Education Statistics, 1985).

22. Dennis P. Jones, telephone interview with James Martin, 8 August 2006.

23. Brian Bissell, telephone interview with James Martin, 10 August 2006.

24. Gordon Winston, "Peer Wages, Tuition, and Price Discounts," *Williams Alumni Review*, summer 2005, 31.

25. Brian Bissell, telephone interview with James Martin, 10 August 2006.

26. A version of this comment was shared with the authors by several presidents in the course of conversations about tuition dependence and tuition discounting between 2003 and 2006.

27. U.S. Department of Education, www.ed.gov/offices/OSFAP/defaultman agement/defaultrates.html.

28. Brian Bissell, telephone interview with James Martin, 10 August 2006.

29. Jeffrey J. Williams, "Debt Education: Bad for the Young, Bad for America," *Dissent*, summer 2006, www.dissentmagazine.org.

30. Standard and Poor's, "Fiscal 2005 Ratios for U.S. Private Colleges and Universities," http://www.standardandpoors.com, 5 July 2006.

31. Charles R. Middleton, telephone interview with James Martin and James E. Samels, 9 September 2006.

32. *Trends in College Pricing—2005* (New York: College Board Publications, 2005), 10–11, www.collegeboard.com/prod_downloads/press/cost05/trends_college _pricing_05.pdf.

33. See www.finaid.org.

34. Marjorie Simmons and Anthony Duce, "Maintenance Crunch," *University Business*, online edition, November 2005, www.universitybusiness.com/view-article.aspx?articleid=137.

35. Dennis P. Jones, interview with James Martin, 8 August 2006.

36. E. K. Fretwell, telephone interview with James Martin, 9 August 2006.

37. Standard and Poor's, "Fiscal 2005 Ratios."

38. Debra Townsley, interview with James Martin, 5 August 2006.

39. See http://mba.tuck.dartmouth.edu/pecenter/.

40. Weymouth Spence, interview with James Martin, 24 August 2006.

41. Society for College and University Planning, "Trends in Higher Education," February 2006, 10, www.scup.org/knowledge/pdfs/SCUP_Trends_2-2006.pdf.

42. W. Stephen Jeffrey, telephone interview with James Martin, 1 August 2006.

43. Charles Goldman, "Mind Your Ps and Rs," *Case Currents*, January 2002, 62.

44. Ibid., 63.

45. George Wolfe, "Corporate Universities: Transforming Learning, Accelerating Results," *Chief Learning Officer*, February 2005, 24.

46. Louisiana Board of Regents, Academic Affairs policy, http://asa.regents .state.la.us/PP/Policies/2.13.

47. Oregon State University, *Accreditation Handbook*, 1999 ed., glossary entry for "probation," http://oregonstate.edu/accreditation/handbook/glossary.html.

48. "Malone College President Announces Retirement," press release, no date, www.malone.edu/5611.

49. IUSB-NCA Self Study, chap. 10, "General Institutional Requirements," 28 July 2000, www.iusb.edu/~acadaff/nca/chap10.html.

50. College of Charleston, "Planning and Reference Guide," http://ir.cofc .edu/prg/tablecon.htm.

51. Whittier College, "About Whittier College: Facts," www.whittier.edu/ about/facts.html.

52. Jefferson Dodge, "A&S Council: Halt Churchill Review," online report, 17 February 2005, https://www.cu.edu:443/silverandgold/messages/4205.html.

53. Denise K. Magner, "The Graying Professoriate," *Chronicle of Higher Education*, 3 September 1999.

54. American Council on Education, "Rate of Increase for Women and Minorities as College Presidents Slows According to a New Report on the College Presidency from the American Council on Education," press release, 9 December 2002, www.acenet.edu.

55. Magner, "Graying Professoriate."

56. William Rezak, "Leading Colleges and Universities as Business Enterprises," *AAHE Bulletin*, October 2000, 9.

57. Joseph Panettieri, "Inside Tips for Better Online Ed: Don't Just Envy the University of Phoenix, Learn from It," *University Business*, July 2004, www .universitybusiness.com/viewarticle.aspx?articleid=543.

58. Quoted in Linda Anderson, "Clicks and Bricks Work Together in the World of Corporate Teaching," *Financial Times*, business education supplement, 21 March 2005.

59. Panettieri, "Online: Inside Tips."

60. Rezak, "Leading Colleges and Universities as Business Enterprises," 9.

61. Jeffrey B. Cufaude, "Crisis Leadership: Do You Have What It Takes to Lead Your Staff and Colleagues during Difficult Times?" *NACUBO Business Officer*, April 2002, 51.

62. U.S. Department of Education, *A Test of Leadership: Charting the Future of Higher Education*, Washington, DC, 2006, www.ed.gov/about/bdscomm/list/ hiedfuture/reports/final-report.pdf.

63. E. K. Fretwell, telephone interview with James Martin, 9 August 2006.

64. Roy Austensen, telephone interview with James Martin, 10 August 2006.

65. Brian Bissell, telephone interview with James Martin, 10 August 2006.

66. James L. Fisher and Scott D. Miller, "Getting More, Better, or Less," *College Planning and Management*, April 2004, 18.

67. Debra Townsley, telephone interview with James Martin, 4 August 2006.

68. James C. Hearn, *Diversifying Campus Revenue Streams: Opportunities and Risks* (Washington, DC: American Council on Education, 2003), 27–28.

69. James C. Hearn, "Revenue Diversification in Higher Education," *International Higher Education*, no. 35 (spring 2004), 7.

70. Dennis Berkey, telephone interview with James Martin, 17 August 2006.

71. John Steele Gordon, "50/50: The 50 Biggest Changes in the Last 50 Years—Business," *American Heritage*, June/July 2004, 23.

72. Joseph McNabb, telephone interview with James Martin, 10 August 2006.

73. Dennis Berkey, telephone interview with James Martin, 17 August 2006.

74. Rezak, "Leading Colleges and Universities as Business Enterprises," 9.

75. Stephen Trachtenberg, telephone interview with James Martin, 1 September 2006.

76. Roy Austensen, telephone interview with James Martin, 10 August 2006.

77. Joseph McNabb, telephone interview with James Martin, 10 August 2006.

78. Quoted in Bill Breen, "The Hard Life and Restless Mind of America's Education Billionaire," *Fast Company*, March 2003, 84.

79. Stephen Trachtenberg, telephone interview with James Martin, 1 September 2006.

80. Robert M. Rosenzweig, *The Political University* (Baltimore: Johns Hopkins University Press, 1998), 124.

81. Daniel Levin, telephone interview with James Martin, 10 August 2006.

82. Stephen Trachtenberg, telephone interview with James Martin, 1 September 2006.

83. Mark Gilbraith, "Lays the Groundwork for Change," *InfoComm Review* 10, no. 3 (2005): 30.

84. Quoted in Tad Simons, "The Confidence Game," *Presentations*, November 2004, 31.

85. Charles Miller and Geri Malandra, "Accountability/Assessment," issue paper, Secretary of Education's Commission on the Future of Higher Education, www.ed.gov/about/bdscomm/list/hiedfuture/reports/miller-malandra.pdf, 2006.

86. Karine Joly, "License to Recruit?" *University Business*, August 2006, 79.

87. Daniel W. Barwick, "The Blog That Ate a Presidency," *Inside Higher Education*, 1 August 2006.

88. Don Aucoin, "Finding Their Religion: Young People Are Seeking Faith in Nontraditional Ways,"*Boston Globe*, 13 April 2005, C8.

89. Standard and Poor's, "Fiscal 2005 Ratios."

90. Ann McGrath, "A+ Options for 'B' Kids," *U.S. News & World Report*, 29 August 2005, 56.

91. Barbara Kantrowitz and Karen Springer, "25 New Ivies," *Newsweek*, 21–28 August 2006, 68.

92. Roy Austensen, telephone interview with James Martin, 10 August 2006.

93. Ken Smith, "To Blog or Not to Blog," *University Business*, December 2005, 60.

94. Jim Hightower and Phillip Frazer, "The People's Media Reaches More People Than Fox Does,"*Hightower Lowdown* 6, no. 5 (May 2004): 1.

95. Kelly Greene, "Bye-Bye Boomers? Companies May Face Exodus as Workers Hit Retiring Age; Some Bosses Are Afraid to Ask," *Wall Street Journal*, 20 September 2005.

96. Charles M. Vest, "World Class Universities: American Lessons," *International Higher Education*, winter 2005, 6. Reprinted from *Times Education Supplement*, 5 November 2004.

Chapter 2. An International Perspective on the Fragility of Higher
Education Institutions and Systems

1. *Systems* refers to sets of institutions, as in the American public multicampus systems (e.g., the University of California system or the Minnesota State College system) or the collective public institutions of a state or a country that are governed by an agency or a ministry with objectives that transcend the welfare of any single institution (e.g., the need to accommodate more students or to present a particular array of academic programs that a single institution might not necessarily choose).

2. This section is taken mainly from D. Bruce Johnstone, "Financing the American Public Research University: Lessons from an International Perspective," in *The Future of the American Public Research University*, ed. Roger Geiger, Carol L. Colbeck, Roger L. Williams, and Christian K. Anderson (Rotterdam: Sense Publishers, 2007).

3. See D. Bruce Johnstone, Sharing the Costs of *Higher Education: Student Financial Assistance in the United Kingdom, the Federal Republic of Germany, France, Sweden, and the United States* (New York: College Entrance Examination Board, 1986); Johnstone, "Cost-Sharing in Higher Education: Tuition, Financial Assistance, and Accessibility," *Czech Sociological Review* 39, no. 3 (June 2003): 351–74; Johnstone, "The Economics and Politics of Cost Sharing in Higher

Education: Comparative Perspectives," *Economics of Education Review* 20, no. 4 (2004): 403–10.

4. Bruce Chapman and Chris Ryan, "Income Contingent Financing of Student Charges for Higher Education: Assessing the Australian Innovation," in "Paying for Learning: The Debate on Student Fees, Grants and Loans in International Perspective," ed. Maureen Woodhall, special issue, *Welsh Journal of Education* 11, no. 1 (2002): 64–81.

5. See Ken Richards, "Reforming Higher Education Student Finance in the UK: The Impact of Recent Changes and Proposals for the Future," in "Paying for Learning: The Debate on Student Fees, Grants and Loans in International Perspective," ed. Maureen Woodhall, special issue, *Welsh Journal of Education* 11, no. 1 (2002): 18–36. See also D. Bruce Johnstone, "Financing Higher Education in the United States: Current Issues," in *Higher Education in the World 2006: The Financing of Universities*, ed. Joaquim Tres and Francisco López Segrera (Basingstoke: Palgrave Macmillan, 2005).

6. The *units* referred to in *unit costs* are most commonly thought of, at least in the United States, as student credit hours, even though these are clearly not true outputs or products, and furthermore the costs per credit hour will vary enormously by institution, discipline, level, and course. However, student credit hours, unlike higher education's true products, are unambiguously measured, and these measures also correspond closely to the ways that the principal revenue sources of tuition fees and state assistance are dispensed. The real units of higher education output, of course, are units of learning or of scholarly product, but these lack the easy and unambiguous metric of the student credit hour (or its derivative, the full-time-equivalent student). See D. Bruce Johnstone, "Those 'out of Control' Costs," in *In Defense of the American Public University*, ed. Philip G. Altbach, D. Bruce Johnstone, and Patricia J. Gumport (Baltimore: Johns Hopkins University Press, 2001). See also Johnstone, "The Fiscal Future of Higher Education: Austerity, Opportunity, and Accessibility," in *Charting the Course: Earl V. Pullias Lecture Series on the Future of Higher Education* (Los Angeles: University of Southern California Center for Higher Education Policy Analysis, fall 2003), 1–14.

7. William G. Bowen, *The Economics of the Major Private Universities* (Berkeley, CA: Carnegie Commission on the Future of Higher Education, 1968); William J. Baumol and William G. Bowen, *Performing Arts: The Economic Dilemma* (New York: Twentieth Century Fund, 1966).

8. D. Bruce Johnston, "Those 'Out of Control' Costs."

9. A net export balance in higher education means that the country receives many more students from outside the country than it sends abroad. The United States, the United Kingdom, Australia, Canada, and New Zealand are all among the top exporters of higher education in the world.

10. Taxes can be direct, as on personal income or sales or property (and so directly felt by the taxpayer), or indirect, as on business and ultimately passed on to people via higher prices. Either way, the purchasing power passes from the general citizen to the government. In a very similar way a government can effectively acquire purchasing power by the printing of money, which similarly confiscates the purchasing power of the people, but via a deficit-induced inflation rather than a di-

rect or indirect taxation. The cost-sharing construct embraces all these mechanisms under the rubric *government or taxpayer.*

11. Student loan programs exist in some form in more than fifty countries, but most of these are not generally available, that is, available to students without cosignatories or other tests of creditworthiness.

12. See Maureen Woodhall, ed., "Paying for Learning: The Debate on Student Fees, Grants and Loans in International Perspective," special issue, *Welsh Journal of Education* 11, no. 1 (2002); D. Bruce Johnstone, "Higher Education Accessibility and Financial Viability: The Role of Student Loans," in *Higher Education in the World 2006: The Financing of Universities,* ed. Joaquim Tres and Francisco López Segrera (Basingstoke: Palgrave Macmillan, 2005).

13. Pamela N. Marcucci and D. Bruce Johnstone, *Tuition Policies in a Comparative Perspective: Theoretical and Political Rationales* (Buffalo, NY: Center for Comparative and Global Studies in Education, 2003).

14. There are obvious equity problems in a system that provides free higher education to a relatively small number of potential students who score the highest on an entrance examination and requires tuition fees from all the rest, particularly in the absence of means-tested grants and generally available loans.

15. D. Bruce Johnstone, "A Political Culture of Giving and the Philanthropic Support of Public Higher Education in International Perspective," *International Journal of Educational Advancement* 5, no. 3 (2005): 256–64.

16. We are concerned in this section mainly with public colleges and universities because private institutions of higher education, although certainly frequently financially fragile, are so mainly because the demand for their relatively high-priced product is insufficient. In turn, this is mainly because of demographics (the relatively low birthrate of the upper-middle and upper socioeconomic classes), compounded by increasing competition from increasingly upscale public colleges and universities.

Chapter 3. A View from Washington

1. National Academy of Sciences, National Academy of Engineering, and Institute of Medicine of the National Academies, *Rising above the Gathering Storm: Energizing and Employing America for a Brighter Economic Future* (Washington, DC: National Academies Press, 2007), 3.

2. Ibid., 4.

3. Robert Zemsky, "The Rise and Fall of the Spellings Commission," *Chronicle of Higher Education,* 26 January 2007, http://chronicle.com.

4. Ibid.

5. Ibid.

6. Moody's Investors Service, "2007 Higher Education Outlook" (NACUBO, January 2007), www.nacubo.org/documents/07Moodys%202007%20HE%20Outlook%20Jan07.pdf.

7. Ibid.

8. The ten issues are paraphrased from Moody's Investors Service, "2007 Higher Education Outlook."

9. Jeffrey Selingo, "At 'Campus of the Future' Meeting, College Officials Learn How Much Money Will Matter," *Chronicle of Higher Education,* 11 July 2006, http://chronicle.com.

10. Kent John Chabotar, *Strategic Finance: Planning and Budgeting for Boards, Chief Executives, and Finance Officers* (Washington, DC: Association of Governing Boards of Universities and Colleges, 2006).

11. Ibid., 108.

12. John D. Sellars, "The Warning Signs of Institutional Decline," *Trusteeship*, November/December 1994, 11–14; Sellars, "Lessons Learned at the Brink," *Trusteeship*, July/August 2005, 14–18.

13. Robert E Lowdermilk III, "Climbing Out of the Rut of Complacency," *Trusteeship*, May/June 2003, 27.

14. Ibid., 28.

15. Ibid.

16. *The Leadership Imperative: The Report of the AGB Task Force on the State of the Presidency in American Higher Education* (Washington, DC: Association of Governing Boards of Universities and Colleges, 2006), vii.

17. Ibid.

18. This list is paraphrased from Sellars, "Lessons Learned at the Brink," 14–18.

Chapter 4. Leading Stressed Institutions

1. That this is a topic of continuous discussion is hardly surprising these days, given the public's focus on the cost of higher education and accountability, among other issues. Merely to Google the phrase "university presidential leadership" yielded (January 2007) 48,600,000 entries. It is best to begin with James Martin, James E. Samels, and associates, *Presidential Transition in Higher Education: Managing Leadership Change* (Baltimore: Johns Hopkins University Press, 2004).

2. Ben Leubsdorf, "Boomers' Retirement May Create Talent Squeeze," *Chronicle of Higher Education*, 1 September 2006, http://chronicle.com.

3. Suzanne Johnson, "Riders on the Storm," *Tulanian* 77, no. 3 (winter 2006): 4.

4. Ibid., 5.

5. Scott S. Cowen, president of Tulane University, Cynthia Cherrey, chief student affairs officer of Tulane University, and Yvette Jones, senior vice president for external affairs of Tulane University, in an interview with Martin and Samels, 30 May 2006.

6. David McCullough, "Knowing History and Knowing Who We Are," *Imprimis*, April 2005, 1, www.hillsdale.edu/imprimis/2005/04/.

Chapter 5. Fragile Universities and Colleges

1. See, for instance, Karin Fischer, "The Rescuer: A Consummate Politician, Hank Brown Steps into a Minefield at the Beleaguered U. of Colorado," *Chronicle of Higher Education*, 11 November 2005. A remarkable concluding section of a work on the interim presidency lists the kinds of reasons their predecessors were dismissed and, often, a definition of "scandal": E. K. Fretwell Jr., *The Interim Presidency: Guidelines for University and College Governing Boards* (Washington, DC: AGB, 1996).

2. Two seminal articles on the subject appeared many years ago and still are worth considering: John D. Sellars, "The Warning Signs of Institutional Decline," *Trusteeship*, November/December 1994; and Ruth B. Cowan, "A Prescription for Vitality for Small Private Colleges," *Trusteeship*, November/December 1994. See also David W. Leslie and E. K. Fretwell Jr., *Wise Moves in Hard Times: Creating and Managing Resilient Colleges and Universities* (San Francisco: Jossey-Bass, 1996).

3. Many sample codes exist. Consider Merrill P. Schwartz, *Board Basics: Assessing Individual Trustee Performance* (Washington, DC: AGB, 2001), 7–9. See also Bruce M. Flohr, "Mirror, Mirror on the Wall," *Trusteeship*, September/October 2004, which describes the way one liberal arts college has used assessments of individual members.

4. See, for instance, Jeffrey Selingo, "Tulane U. Struggles to Enroll Freshmen because of Misperceptions about the Condition of New Orleans," *Chronicle of Higher Education*, August 14, 2006. See also the Tulane website, www2.tulane.edu.

5. Richard T. Ingram, *Board Basics: A Guide to Conflict of Interest and Disclosure* (Washington, DC: AGB, 2006).

6. The essential work is Robert H. Atwell and Jane V. Atwell, *Presidential Compensation in Higher Education: Policies and Best Practices* (Washington, DC: AGB, 2000). See also Raymond D. Cotton, "Avoiding Trouble with the IRS," *Chronicle of Higher Education*, 8 October 2004.

7. Richard T. Ingram and William A. Weary, *Presidential and Board Assessment in Higher Education: Purposes, Policies, and Strategies* (Washington, DC: AGB, 2000). The Association of Governing Boards of Colleges and Universities (AGB) offers a workshop on the subject at its National Conference on Trusteeship.

8. For an analogous example of the difficulties possible here, see "Fisk U. Argues for the Right to Sell Art Gifts," *Chronicle of Higher Education*, Daily News Blog, 16 August 2006, http://chronicle.com/news. AGB and the National Association of College and University Business Officials (NACUBO) publish many guides to endowment management.

9. The website of AGB (www.agb.org) is the best starting point. That for the Corporate Library (www.thecorporatelibrary.com) provides insights into the charges that can, rightly or wrongly, be leveled against boards. See also Richard P. Chait, "Why Boards Go Bad," *Trusteeship*, May/June 2006. A useful study of church conflict carries over well to the world of higher education: Kenneth C. Haugk, *Antagonists in the Church: How to Identify and Deal with Destructive Conflict* (Minneapolis: Augsburg Fortress Publishers, 1988).

10. Edwin H. Friedman, *Generation to Generation: Family Process in Church and Synagogue* (New York: Guilford Press, 1985). Excellent summary overviews may be found in Patricia A. Comella, J. Bader, J. S. Ball, K. K. Wiseman, and R. R. Sagar, *The Emotional Side of Organizations: Applications of Bowen Theory* (Washington, DC: Georgetown Family Center, 1996).

11. Robert C. Dickeson, Prioritizing Academic Programs and Services: Reallocating Resources to Achieve Strategic Balance (San Francisco: Jossey-Bass,

1999). See also Richard Morrill, *Strategic Leadership in Academic Affairs: Clarifying the Board's Responsibilities* (Washington, DC: AGB, 2002).

12. Jeffrey Selingo, "Tulane Slashes Departments and Lays Off Professors: 233 Professors Will Lose Jobs and 14 Doctoral Programs Will Be Eliminated," *Chronicle of Higher Education*, 16 December 2005, http://chronicle.com.

13. Charlotte Allen, "How the Small Survive: Small Catholic Women's Colleges Have Saved Themselves by Adapting to New Markets," *University Business*, October 2000.

14. The publications offered at www.nacubo.org and at www.agb.org are the starting points.

15. See the very helpful article by Holly Hall, "Planning Successful Successions: Preparing for a Leader's Departure Can Prevent Problems," *Chronicle of Philanthropy*, 12 January 2006. See also Ben Leubsdorf, "Boomers' Retirement May Create Talent Squeeze," *Chronicle of Higher Education*, 1 September 2006.

16. For comprehensive literature on the advancement office, see the publications available from the Council for Advancement and Support of Education (CASE) at www.case.org.

17. See the later section on presidential assessment.

18. Schwartz, *Board Basics*.

19. See sample policies in Ingram and Weary, *Presidential and Board Assessment*. On annual reviews, see Merrill P. Schwartz, *Board Basics: Annual Presidential Performance Reviews* (Washington, DC: AGB, 2001).

20. William A. Weary, *Board Basics: Essentials of Presidential Search* (Washington, DC: AGB, 1998), and Weary, "The Role of the Board in Presidential Transition," in James Martin, James E. Samels, and associates, *Presidential Transition in Higher Education* (Baltimore: Johns Hopkins University Press, 2004).

21. AGB offers numerous works on planning, such as *The Board's Role in Strategic Planning* by Lawrence Butler (2006), and *Strategic Responses to Financial Challenges* by Arthur M. Hauptman (1998).

Chapter 6. Preserving and Extending the Academic Mission
of Vulnerable Institutions

1. In *Student Success in College: Creating Conditions That Matter* by George D. Kuh, Jillian Kinzie, John H. Schuh, Elizabeth J. Whitt, and associates (Washington, DC: American Education for Higher Education, 2005), as part of the Documenting Effective Educational Practice (DEEP) project, examined twenty colleges and universities that shared six features that foster student engagement and persistence, which included having "a 'living' mission and 'lived' educational philosophy, an unshakeable focus on student learning, environments adapted for educational enrichment, clearly marked pathways to student success, an improvement oriented ethos, and shared responsibility for educational quality and student success" (Kuh et al., 24). The authors' final recommendations included the following:

—Featuring student success as a key part of an institution's vision

—Clearly defining the mission and implementing it

—Having high expectations for all members of the campus community

—Recognizing the types of students the university accepts and setting performance standards that are high but still attainable

—Providing constructive feedback for students through student-faculty interactions

—Cultivating "an ethic of positive restlessness" where administration and faculty are continuously assessing and feel free to make suggestions that would improve the institution

—Attracting and highlighting diversity

—Attracting faculty members who are compatible with and fully socialized for the campus culture

—Encouraging collaboration throughout the campus and into the community

—Focusing always on student success (Kuh et al., 295–317)

The highlighted institutions in *Presidential Essays: "Success Stories"; Strategies That Make a Difference at Thirteen Independent Colleges and Universities*, edited by Allen P. Splete (Indianapolis: USAGroup, 2000), all give evidence that supports the categories discussed in this chapter. Some examples follow. Park College (Missouri) made a conscious decision to increase minority enrollment, and to facilitate that growth, the board of trustees and the faculty/staff were diversified, minority recruiters were hired, faculty were given sensitivity training, and the curriculum was developed to reflect these changes. Georgetown College (Kentucky) focused on forming creative alliances with external communities like a local high school, a local professional football team, and an auto company with factories nearby, as well as establishing Georgetown College Partners, which connects alumni businesses with big business. Georgetown also encourages internal collaboration between academic departments. The leadership team of the College of Mount St. Joseph (Ohio) decided to avoid waiting until a crisis forced change. The college community assessed its situation by sharing information freely, established a new change-friendly governance structure, and agreed to examine programs and procedures, as well as the surrounding environment, on an ongoing basis. It also discouraged lack of communication among operational departments by meeting in a retreat-like gathering with an independent moderator. The University of the Incarnate Word (Texas) developed a new mission statement through open-ended workshops and ultimately formed partnerships with local companies to exchange billing for employee scholarships; advertised to recruit Hispanics; created an adult degree completion program; and "globalized" its student population by building an International Conference Center, encouraging more international study, and making sister-school agreements. All of the colleges mentioned in this publication focused on collaboration under the umbrella of their mission and took risks in order to establish a more academically supportive environment.

In *Work and Peace in Academe: Leveraging Time, Money, and Intellectual Energy through Managing Conflict* (Boston: Anker Publishing, 2005), James R. Coffman, while focusing on dealing with and preempting conflicts, discusses many of the skills necessary to encourage positive academic interactions on a higher level. He emphasizes the importance of communication and even specifically discusses sharing financial information: "[Faculty] believe that the more transparent the institutional priorities and fiscal conditions are to the faculty and staff, the better. They are right. There are times when maximum, intensive efforts must be made to communicate as much information as feasible to as many people as possible" (Coffman, xvii–xviii). He encourages face-to-face or phone conversations, asserting that "memo exchange as a tool for conflict resolution is counterproductive in almost every instance, especially at the level of the CEO, university executives, and deans. Communication is a good example of how the administrative style of the institution's leadership creates an atmosphere that favors the prevention and resolution of conflict. A feedback loop and exchange of information is essential, but writing should be used only to document facts and to finalize outcomes, not for exchanging opinions or initial exploration of options" (Coffman, p. 65). An academically supportive environment can be created only when the faculty themselves feel supported. Coffman feels that it is "essential that the moving institution-wide parts . . . know each other personally. . . . Each individual must understand what each of the others does and, to some extent, how they do it. They must have a sense of the individual personalities as well as the collective personality of the group" (Coffman, 116).

The most helpful resource is *Wise Moves in Hard Times: Creating and Managing Resilient Colleges and Universities* (San Francisco: Jossey-Bass, 1996) by David W. Leslie and E. K. Fretwell Jr. They suggest that universities become more "student centered" and add that this is, ironically, one of the hardest changes to implement. They recognize the importance of mission and continuous self-examination, as well as the importance of having an inviting campus and the dangerous but tempting quick fix of deferring maintenance in order to "save" money. The authors suggest a path that they call "enlightened change," which "includes generating good information, sharing it widely, and cooperating responsibly in framing new directions. Above all, it urges that institutions make honest self-assessments and hold accountable those with a real interest in the future of the college or university for helping to secure it" (Lesley and Fretwell, 25). Leslie and Fretwell discuss the possible outcomes, positive and negative, of having input from many different constituents and the necessity of working with the community that the institution serves.

2. Edward M. Penson, *Presidential Review in Colleges and Universities*, www.pensonassociates.com/protocol/fiveclusters.html.

3. James Martin, James E. Samels, and associates, *First among Equals: The Role of the Chief Academic Officer* (Baltimore: Johns Hopkins University Press, 1997).

4. Leslie and Fretwell, *Wise Moves in Hard Times*, 78.

5. Paula Wasley, "Underrepresented Students Benefit Most from 'Engagement,'" *Chronicle of Higher Education*, 17 November 2006, A39–A40.

6. Leslie and Fretwell, *Wise Moves in Hard Times*, 227.

7. Information for this section was provided by Mary J. Meehan, president of Alverno College, and Sister Kathleen O'Brien, senior vice president of academic affairs of Alverno College, in a telephone interview with the author, 7 September 2006.

8. Information for this section was provided by the Reverend Dr. Floyd H. Flake, president of Wilberforce University, in a telephone interview with the author, 12 September 2006.

9. Information for this section was provided by William Merwin, former president of Florida Gulf Coast University, in a telephone interview with the author, 5 September 2006.

10. Information for this section was provided by Jim Votruba, president of Northern Kentucky University, in a telephone interview with the author, 7 September 2006.

11. Information for this section was provided by the Honorable Paul Trible, president of Christopher Newport University, in a telephone interview with the author, 19 September 2006.

12. Information for this section was provided by Lorna Edmundson, president of Wilson College, and Mary Hendrickson, associate dean of Wilson College, in a telephone interview with the author, 3 October 2006.

13. Information for this section was provided by Diana Natalicio, president of the University of Texas at El Paso, in a telephone interview with the author, 3 October 2006.

14. Information for this section was provided by Pamela Fox, president of Mary Baldwin College, in a telephone interview with the author, 5 October 2006.

Chapter 7. The Challenge for Student Affairs in Stressed Institutions

1. J. D. Thompson, *Organizations in Action* (New York: McGraw-Hill, 1967).

2. J. S. Green, A. Levine, and associates, *Opportunity in Adversity: How Colleges Can Succeed in Hard Times* (San Francisco: Jossey-Bass, 1985).

3. A. Sandeen and M. J. Barr, *Critical Issues for Student Affairs* (San Francisco: Jossey-Bass, 2006).

4. All interviews were conducted in confidentiality, and the names of interviewees are withheld by mutual agreement.

5. D. W. Leslie and E. K. Fretwell Jr., *Wise Moves in Hard Times: Creating and Managing Resilient Colleges and Universities* (San Francisco: Jossey-Bass, 1996).

6. Ibid.

7. Interview with a senior student affairs officer, 23 May 2006.

8. Sandeen and Barr, Critical Issues for Student Affairs.

9. Interview with a student affairs director, 24 May 2006.

10. Sandeen and Barr, Critical Issues for Student Affairs.

11. Interview with a senior student affairs officer, 30 May 2006.

12. Interview with a student affairs director, 17 May 2006.

13. Interview with a senior student affairs administrator, 23 May 2006.

14. Interview with a senior student affairs administrator, 19 April 2006.

15. Interview with a student affairs director, 17 May 2006.

16. Interview with a student affairs director, 16 May 2006.

17. Interview with a student affairs director, 24 May 2006.

18. Ibid.

19. Ibid.

20. Interview with a senior student affairs officer, 30 May 2006.

21. Interview with a senior student affairs officer, 19 April 2006.

22. Ibid.

23. R. H. Ackerman and P. Maslin-Ostrowski, *The Wounded Leader: How Real Leadership Emerges in Times of Crisis* (San Francisco: Jossey-Bass, 2002).

24. Leslie and Fretwell, *Wise Moves in Hard Times*.

25. Interview with a student affairs director, 16 May 2006.

26. Interview with a senior student affairs officer, 23 May 2006.

Chapter 8. Effective Financial Leadership of Stressed Colleges and Universities

1. Table 245, "Degree-Granting Institutions That Have Closed Their Doors, by Control and Type of Institution: 1960–61 through 2004–05," *Digest of Education Statistics Tables and Figures 2005*, http://nces.ed.gov/programs/digest/d05/tables/dt05_245.asp.

2. Data provided by the Austen Group, Eagle, Colorado, 2006.

3. Michael Townsley, "Recognizing the Unrealized," *Business Officer*, March 2005, www.nacubo.org/x5632.xml.

4. Martin Van Der Werf, "Moody's Says Financial and Governance Issues Could Spell Trouble for Some Colleges," *Chronicle of Higher Education*, 1 January 2007, http://chronicle.com/daily/2007/01/2007010901n.htm.

5. Quoted in ibid.

6. Moody's Investors Service, "2007 Higher Education Outlook" (NACUBO, January 2007), www.nacubo.org/documents/07Moodys%202007%20HE%20Outlook%20Jan07.pdf.

7. Gordon C. Winston, "Subsidies, Hierarchy, and Peers: The Awkward Economics of Higher Education," *Journal of Economic Perspectives* 13, no. 1 (1999): 17.

8. David S. Hopkins and William F. Massey, *Planning Models for Colleges and Universities* (Stanford: Stanford University Press, 1981).

9. Quoted in Nathan Dickmeyer, "Financial Management and Strategic Planning," in *Successful Responses to Financial Difficulty*, ed. Carol Frances (San Francisco: Jossey-Bass, 1982), 53.

10. Hans Jenny, "Specifying Financial Indicators: Cash Flows in the Short and Long Run," in *Assessing Financial Health*, ed. Carol Frances and Sharon L. Coldren (San Francisco: Jossey-Bass, 1979), 18.

11. Dickmeyer, "Financial Management," 53–54.

12. Raymond Zammuto, "Growth, Stability, and Decline in American College and University Enrollments," *Educational Administration Quarterly* 19, no. 1 (1983): 84.

13. Ibid.

14. David Whetten, "Organizational Responses to Scarcity: Exploring the Obstacles to Innovative Approaches to Retrenchment in Education," *Educational Administrative Quarterly* 17, no. 3 (1981): 80.

15. Ibid., 83–89.

16. George Keller, *Academic Strategy: The Management Revolution in American Higher Education* (Baltimore: Johns Hopkins University Press, 1983), 61, 125.

17. Dickmeyer, "Financial Management," 41.

18. Ibid., 55–56.

19. See Sean Rush, "Benchmarking—How Good Is Good?" in *Measuring Institutional Performance in Higher Education*, ed. William F. Massey and Joel W. Meyerson (Princeton, NJ: Petersons, 1994), 89–90. See also Kim S. Cameron, "Critical Questions in Assessing Organizational Effectiveness," *Organizational Dynamics* 9 (autumn 1980): 78.

20. J. Fred Weston and Eugene F. Brigham, *Managerial Finance*, 7th ed. (Hinsdale, IL: Dryden Press, 1981), 405–6.

21. David W. Leslie and E. K. Fretwell Jr., *Wise Moves in Hard Times: Creating and Managing Resilient Colleges and Universities* (San Francisco: Jossey-Bass, 1996).

22. D. Francis Finn, "Developing and Applying Useful Financial Indicators," in *Assessing Financial Health*, ed. Carol Frances and Sharon L. Coldren (San Francisco: Jossey-Bass, 1979), 81–83.

23. William M. Wilkinson, "Implications of Accounting Practice for Financial Analysis," in *Assessing Financial Health*, ed. Carol Frances and Sharon L. Coldren (San Francisco: Jossey-Bass, 1979), 40.

24. Martin Kramer, "What the New Indicators Cannot Tell Us," in *Successful Responses to Financial Difficulty*, ed. Carol Frances (San Francisco: Jossey-Bass, 1982), 101.

25. F. J. R. C. Dochy, M. S. R. Segars, and W. H. E. W. Wijnen, eds., *Management Information and Performance Indicators in Higher Education: An International Issue* (Assen and Maastricht: Van Gorcum, 1990), 72.

26. Martin Cave, Stephen Hanney, Mary Henkel, and Maurice Kogan, *The Use of Performance Indicators in Higher Education*, 3rd ed. (London: Jessica Kingsley Publishers, 1996), 212–15.

27. Jon Strauss and John R. Curry, *Responsibility Center Management: Lessons from 25 Years of Decentralized Management* (Annapolis, MD: NACUBO, 2002), 1–3.

28. Ronald E. Salluzzo, Philip Tahey, Frederic J. Prager, and Christopher J. Cowen, *Ratio Analysis in Higher Education*, 9th ed. (Washington, DC: KPMG LLP and Prager, McCarthy and Sealy, LLC, 1999).

29. Ibid.

30. Leslie and Fretwell, *Wise Moves in Hard Times*.

Chapter 9. Fund-Raising through Fragility

1. Matthew Schuerman, "Best Practices: Philanthropy, Saving a Spendthrift," *Worth*, August 2005, 98–100, www.worth.com/Editorial/Money-Meaning/Philanthropy/Best-Practices-Philanthropy-Saving-a-Spendthrift-2.asp.

2. As Schuerman eloquently puts it, "To get backers to believe in a failing venture, it was not enough to rattle a tin cup—that had been done before, too many times, and it is exactly that sort of stopgap fund-raising that had led to ACT's serial deficits in the past." Ibid., 99.

3. Deborah Weisgall, "The Miracle Worker," *Town and Country*, 1 February 1996.

4. Ibid.

5. "Making an AUB Education Accessible," *MainGate* 3, no. 4 (summer 2005): 36.

6. Anne Marie Borrego, "When You Can't Wait for Money," *Chronicle of Higher Education*, 2 August 2002, http://chronicle.com.

7. Michael K. Townsley, *The Small College Guide to Financial Health: Beating the Odds* (Annapolis, MD: National Association of College and University Business Officials, 2002).

8. Schuerman, "Best Practices," 98.

9. Bruce W. Flessner, "Where Do We Go from Here?" *Bentz Whaley Flessner Occasional Papers* 13 (spring 2003): 1.

10. Quoted in Shawn Tully, "Finally, Colleges Start to Cut Their Crazy Costs," *Fortune*, 1 May 1995, 112.

11. Ibid.

12. These are all points that Henry E. Riggs makes in "The Limits of Fund Raising," *Chronicle of Higher Education*, 3 May 1996, B1–B2. The quote is on page B2.

13. Robert A. Frahm, "Trinity Forced to Cut Back: Overspending, Rising Costs Fuel Financial Crunch," *Hartford Courant*, 21 April 2006, http://www.hartfordinfo.org/issues/documents/education/htfd_courant_042106.asp.

14. Bill Littlejohn, "Creating a Culture of Philanthropy," *Association of Healthcare Professionals Journal*, spring 2006, 8–15.

15. Ibid.

Chapter 10. Accreditation, Fragility, and Disclosure

This chapter represents the views of the author and not necessarily those of the Northwest Commission on Colleges and Universities.

1. Northwest Commission on Colleges and Universities, *Accreditation Handbook*, 2003 ed. (Washington, DC: Redmond, 2003), 77.

2. Ibid.

3. Anonymous president, in a telephone conversation with the author, 23 June 2007.

4. M. S. S. El-Namaki, "Creating a Corporate Vision," *Long Range Planning* 25, no. 6 (1992): 25.

5. Ibid.

6. James C. Collins and Jerry I. Porras, "Building Your Company's Vision," *Harvard Business Review*, September–October 1996, 66.

7. Ibid., 67.

8. Dr. John M. B. Craig, former interim president of Unity College, in an interview with the author, 28 June 2007.

9. Etienne C. Wegner and William H. Snyder, "Communities of Practice: The Organizational Frontier," *Harvard Business Review*, January–February 2000, 139.

10. Anonymous president, in a telephone interview with the author, 22 June 2007.

11. James D. Thompson, *Organizations in Action* (New Brunswick, NJ: Transaction Press, 1967).

12. David Dobler, president of Sheldon Jackson College, in a telephone conversation with the author, 13 August 2007.

Chapter 11. Keeping the Faith

1. SurveyMonkey.com was the survey instrument used, and the input came mostly in November 2006.

2. Jay Barber, president of Werner Pacific University, in an e-mail message to the author, 15 December 2006.

3. Don Jeanes, president of Milligan College, in an e-mail message to the author, 12 December 2006.

4. James Martin, James E. Samels, and associates, *Merging Colleges for Mutual Growth: A New Strategy for Academic Managers* (Baltimore: Johns Hopkins University Press, 1994), 4–5, 35–37, 142–45, 155–56.

5. Dr. David Gyertson, e-mail message to the author, 1 January 2007.

Chapter 12. For-Profit Higher Education and Stressed Colleges

This chapter is dedicated to my late father, Edward Lou Hoyle, for his devotion to my education and constant love, and to my partner, Mark Taggart, for his love and patience.

1. Michele Howard-Vital, "The Appeal of For-Profit Institutions," *Change* 28, no. 1 (January/February 2006).

2. Kevin Kinser and Daniel C. Levy, *The For-Profit Sector: U.S. Patterns and International Echoes in Higher Education*, Program for Research on Private Higher Education Working Papers (Albany: State University of New York, 2005), www.albany.edu/dept/eaps/prophe/publication/paper/PROPHEWP05_files/PROPHEWP05.pdf.

3. Ibid.

4. Brian Pusser, "New Competition from For-Profit Education Providers," *AGB Priorities*, no. 27 (winter 2006).

5. Ibid.

Chapter 13. Legal Challenges for Fragile Institutions

1. *Warren County Community College v. Warren County Board of Chosen Freeholders*, 824 A.2d 1073 (N.J. 2003).

2. *Mercer University v. Smith*, 371 S.E.2d 858 (Ga. 1988).

3. James F. Shekleton, "Delegation of Board Decision-Making Authority to Administrative Officers" (presentation, NACUA meeting, 29 June 2002), www.nacua.org (by subscription).

4. Matt Walton, "An Introduction to Contracting in the Higher Education Environment: From Animal Cage Washers to International Consortiums" (presentation, NACUA conference for lawyers new to higher education, 13 October 2001), www.nacua.org.

5. Bryan A. Garner, ed., *Black's Law Dictionary*, 8th ed. (St. Paul, MN: West Group, 2004), 17, 1332.

6. Jeswald W. Salacuse, "You Cut a Bad Deal. Now What?" *Negotiation* 8, no. 8 (August 2005), Harvard Business School Working Knowledge for Business Leaders website, http://hbswk.hbs.edu/archive/5015.html.

7. Laurie Stickelmaier and Susan Vance, "How to Prevent a Financial Fiasco: Saint Mary's College Turned a Budgetary Blip into a Wake-up Call to Ready the

Campus for Any Monetary Emergency," *Business Officer Magazine*, January 2007, http://www.nacubo.org/x8675.xml.

8. Thomas P. Hustoles and Ellen M. Babbitt, "Planning and Implementing Institutional Reductions in Force and Other Personnel Cost-Saving Measures Involving Administrators and Staff" (presentation, NACUA conference, 3–5 March 2004), www.nacua.org (by subscription).

9. *Mayo v. North Carolina State University*, 168 N.C.App. 503, 608 S.E.2d 116, 195 Ed. Law Rep. 366 (2005).

10. Martin Michaelson and Lawrence White, "Effectively Managing Legal Risks Associated with Layoffs and Terminations of College and University Staff," www.nacua.org (by subscription).

11. Hustoles and Babbitt, "Planning and Implementing."

12. 29 USC § 2101 et seq.

13. Burton Bollag, "Update on Accreditation Actions Taken by Regional Organizations," *Chronicle of Higher Education*, 5 January 2007, A27.

14. John H. Augustine, "Take a Strategic Direction with Debt," *Business Officer Magazine*, September 2002, 19.

15. "How Stanford Pays for Capital Plan," *Stanford Online Report*, 10 June 1998, www.news-service.stanford.edu.

16. "In order to discuss the focus of retrenchment decisions, it is necessary to recognize that there are in fact at least three levels of decisions: 1) the initial decision or declaration of financial exigency, 2) the intermediate decision to eliminate certain departments, programs, or positions and 3) the ultimate decision to terminate specific faculty or staff members." Annette B. Johnson, "The Problems of Contraction: Legal Considerations in University Retrenchment," *Journal of Law and Education* 10, no. 3 (July 1981): 281.

17. Steven G. Olswang, Ellen M. Babbitt, Cheryl A. Cameron, and Edmund K. Kamai, "Retrenchment," *Journal of College and University Law* 30 (2003): 60.

18. Ellen M. Babbitt, "Closing an Academic Program without Litigation: Process, Planning, and Pragmatism," in *Academic Program Closures: A Legal Compendium*, ed. Ellen M. Babbitt (Washington, DC: NACUA, 2002), 30–31.

19. Ibid.

20. Edward A. Johnson and Kent M. Weeks, "To Save a College: Independent College Trustees and Decisions on Financial Exigency, Endowment Use and Closure," *Journal of College and University Law* 12, no. 4 (spring 1986): 469.

21. Olswang et al., "Retrenchment," 40.

22. *Levitt v. Board of Trustees*, 376 F. Supp. 945 (D. Neb. 1974).

23. See *Peretti v. Montana*, 464 F. Supp. 784 (D. Mont. 1979), *rev'd on jurisdictional grounds*, 661 F.2d 756 (9th Cir. 1981), and *Zumbrun v. University of S. Cal.*, 25 Cal. App. 3d 1, 10 (1972).

24. James Martin, James E. Samels, and associates, *Merging Colleges for Mutual Growth: A New Strategy for Academic Managers* (Baltimore: Johns Hopkins University Press, 1994).

25. James Martin, James E. Samels, and associates, "We Were Wrong: Try Partnerships, Not Mergers," *Chronicle of Higher Education*, 17 May 2002, B10.

26. Martin, Samels, and associates, *Merging Colleges for Mutual Growth*, 30.

27. Robert J. Haverkamp, "The Entrepreneurial Institution: Guiding Entrepreneurial Decision Making" (presentation, NACUA meeting, 20 June 2001), www.nacua.org (by subscription).

28. The following suggestions come from Robert E. Harding, "Endowments: The Basics" (presentation, NACUA conference, 26–29 June 2005), www.nacua .org (by subscription).

29. John L. Pulley, "Unorthodox Strategy Saves Financially Strapped College, for Now," *Chronicle of Higher Education*, 19 September 2003, A29, www.chronicle .com.

30. Burton Bollag, "Update on Actions of Regional Accrediting Groups," *Chronicle of Higher Education*, 18 May 2007, A25.

31. 34 CFR pt. 602.

32. Peter S. Leyton, "Accreditation and Program Licensing" (presentation, NACUA Annual Conference, 2000), www.nacua.org.

33. Donna Dalton, "Closing a College," *Chronicle of Higher Education*, 28 February 2003, www.chronicle.com/jobs/news/2003/02/2003022801c/printable .html.

34. William A. Kaplan and Barbara A. Lee, *The Law of Higher Education*, 4th ed. (San Francisco: Jossey-Bass, 2006), 596.

35. Dalton, "Closing a College."

36. Joseph O'Neill and Samuel Barnett, "Closing a College: Trustees' Decisions and Administrative Policies," in *Academic Program Closures: A Legal Compendium*, ed. Ellen M. Babbitt (Washington, DC: NACUA, 2002).

37. Ibid., 56.

Chapter 14. The Institutional Research Option

1. K. S. Cameron, "A Study of Organizational Effectiveness and Its Predictors," *Management Science* 32, no. 5 (May 1986): 87–112.

2. U.S. Department of Education, *A Test of Leadership: Charting the Future of U.S. Higher Education* (Washington, DC, 2006). For the final report, see www .ed.gov/about/bdscomm/list/hiedfuture/reports/final-report.pdf.

3. Arthur Stinchcombe, *Information and Organizations* (Berkeley: University of California Press, 1990).

4. Martha S. Feldman and James G. March, "Information in Organizations as Signal and Symbol," *Administrative Science Quarterly* 26, no. 2 (June 1981): 171–86.

5. Peter Drucker, *The Effective Executive* (New York: HarperCollins, 2005).

6. Patrick Terenzini, "On the Nature of Institutional Research and the Knowledge and Skills It Requires," in *What Is Institutional Research All About? A Critical and Comprehensive Assessment of the Profession*, ed. J. F. Volkwein (San Francisco: Jossey-Bass, 1999).

Chapter 15. Managing Reputation

1. Key sources of data on higher education trends and issues include National Association of College and University Business Officers, *National Endowment Study*, www.nacubo.org; National Association for College Admission Counseling, *State of College Admission*, www.nacac.com; Council for Aid to Education,

Voluntary Support of Education survey, www.cae.org; American Association of University Professors, *Annual Report on the Economic Status of the Profession,* www.aaup.org; *U.S. News & World Report, America's Best Colleges,* www .usnews.com; ACT and SAT score trends, www.act.org/news and www.college board.com; College Board, *Trends in College Pricing* and *Trends in Student Aid,* www.collegeboard.com; Institute for International Education, *Open Doors Report on International Educational Exchange,* www.iie.org; National Association of Colleges and Employers, *Job Outlook,* www.naceweb.org; National Survey of Student Engagement, *College Student Report,* www.indiana.edu/~nsse; *Chronicle of Higher Education,* annual presidential salary survey, www.chronicle.com; National Science Foundation, Office of Science Resource Statistics, www.nsf.gov/sbe/ srs; National Center for Education Statistics, *Condition of Education,* annual survey, nces.ed.gov/programs/coe; *Postsecondary Education Opportunity,* www .postsecondary.org; and Pew Research Center for People and the Press, www.people -press.org. See also John Ross, "Finders Keepers, Users Reapers," *Currents,* January 2004, 31–35.

2. John Ross and Carol Halstead, *Public Relations and the Presidency: Strategies and Tactics for Effective Communications* (Washington, DC: Council for Advancement and Support of Education Books, 2001).

3. Ibid.

4. Richard Guarasci, "On the Challenge of Becoming the Good College," *Liberal Education* 92, no. 1 (winter 2006): 16.

5. Richard Hesel, "Know Thyself: 5 Strategies for Marketing a College," *Chronicle of Higher Education,* 30 April 2004.

6. Richard Guarasci, president of Wagner College, and Angelo Araimo, vice president for planning and enrollment of Wagner College, in discussion with the author, August 2004.

7. Higher Education Research Institute, *The American Freshman National Norms, 2006* (Los Angeles: UCLA, January 2007).

8. John Ross, "Spend It Wisely," *Currents,* January 2004, 31–35.

9. Jerry Porras, Stewart Emery, and Mark Thompson, *Success Built to Last* (Upper Saddle River, NJ: Wharton School Publishing, 2006), 3.

10. Ross and Halstead, *Public Relations and the Presidency.*

Chapter 16. Achieving the Turnaround

1. William Weary, e-mail to James Martin, 19 July 2007.

2. This point is made by Sandra Elman in chapter 10 of this book.

3. Daniel Levin, e-mail to James Martin, 19 July 2007.

4. Debra Townsley, in a telephone conversation with the authors, 15 November 2007.

5. Joseph Short, former president of Bradford College, in a telephone interview with James Martin, 27 April 2007.

6. Michael Townsley makes this point in chapter 8 of this book.

7. Dennis P. Jones, "Indicators of the Condition of Higher Education" (Washington, DC: National Center for Education Statistics, 1985).

8. Dennis P. Jones, telephone interview with James Martin, 8 August 2006.

9. E. K. Fretwell, telephone interview with James Martin, 9 August 2006.

10. Kevin W. Sayers and John F. Ryan make these points in chapter 14 of this book.

11. Sandra Elman makes these points in chapter 10 of this book.

12. Daniel J. Levin makes this point in chapter 3 of this book.

13. John Sellars, "Lessons Learned at the Brink," *Trusteeship*, July/August 2005, 14–18.

14. Steven Jeffrey makes this point in chapter 9 of this book.

15. Michael Riccards, telephone conversation with James Martin, 30 July 2007.

16. Jack Wilson, e-mail to James Martin, 30 July 2007.

17. Michael Townsley, e-mail to James Martin, 24 July 2007.

18. Ibid.

19. Ibid.

20. Laurence Spraggs, conversation with James Martin, 31 July 2007.

21. Ezra Delaney, e-mail to James Martin, 2 August 2007.

22. Rick Fairbanks, e-mail to James Martin, 3 August 2007.

23. Charles R. Middleton, conversation with the authors, 18 July 2007.

24. Ibid.

25. Jim Rogers, telephone conversation with James Martin, 27 July 2007.

26. Matthew Conlon, conversation with James Martin, 2 August 2007.

27. Mahesh Sharma, conversation with James Martin, 2 August 2007.

28. George Freyberger, telephone conversation with James Martin, 10 May 2007.

29. Leslie Ferlazzo, telephone conversation with James Martin, 27 April 2007.

30. M. Lonan Reilly, O.S.F., telephone conversation with James Martin, 7 May 2007.

31. Richard Carpenter, telephone conversation with James Martin, 6 August 2007.

32. Charles R. Middleton, conversation with the authors, 18 July 2007.

33. Dan Angel, president of Golden Gate University, in an interview with the authors, 19 June 2007. For the Acadian Heritage Council website, see www.umfk .maine.edu/archives/.

34. William Austin, president of Warren County Community College, in a telephone interview with the authors, 18 July 2007.

35. Rae Perry, e-mails to James Martin, 25 and 27 July 2007.

Bibliography

Ackerman, R. H., and P. Maslin-Ostrowski. *The Wounded Leader: How Real Leadership Emerges in Times of Crisis.* San Francisco: Jossey-Bass, 2002.

Adams, Olin L., III, and David M. Shannon. "Cost Control in Higher Education." *University Business*, September 2006. www.universitybusiness.com/viewarticle.aspx?articleid=459.

Allen, Charlotte. "How the Small Survive: Small Catholic Women's Colleges Have Saved Themselves by Adapting to New Markets." *University Business*, October 2000, 42–46, 53, 77–80.

Allen, I. Elaine, and Jeff Seaman. *Making the Grade: Online Education in the United States, 2006.* Sloan Consortium, November 2006. www.sloan-c.org/publications/survey/pdf/making_the_grade.pdf.

Altbach, Philip T. "Academic Salaries, Academic Corruption, and the Academic Career." *International Higher Education*, no. 44 (summer 2006): 2–3.

Anderson, Linda. "Clicks and Bricks Work Together in the World of Corporate Teaching." *Financial Times*, business education supplement, 21 March 2005.

Association of Governing Boards of Universities and Colleges. *Board Basics: AGB Statement on Institutional Governance and Governing in the Public Trust.* Washington, DC: AGB, 2001.

Astin, Alexander W. *Assessment for Excellence: The Philosophy and Practice of Assessment and Evaluation in Higher Education.* Phoenix, AZ: Oryx Press, 1993.

———. *What Matters in College? Four Critical Years Revisited.* San Francisco: Jossey-Bass, 1993.

Atwell, Robert H., and Jane V. Atwell. *Presidential Compensation in Higher Education: Policies and Best Practices.* Washington, DC: AGB, 2000.

Aucoin, Don. "Finding Their Religion: Young People Are Seeking Faith in Nontraditional Ways." *Boston Globe*, 13 April 2005.

Augustine, John H. "Take a Strategic Direction with Debt." *Business Officer Magazine*, September 2002, 16–26.

Babbitt, Ellen M., ed. *Academic Program Closures: A Legal Compendium.* Washington, DC: NACUA, 2002.

————. "Closing an Academic Program without Litigation: Process, Planning, and Pragmatism." In *Academic Program Closures: A Legal Compendium*, ed. Ellen M. Babbitt. Washington, DC: NACUA, 2002.

Banta, Trudy. *Assessment Update: The First Ten Years.* San Francisco: Jossey-Bass, 1999.

Barak, Robert J., and Barbara E. Breier. *Successful Program Review: A Practical Guide to Evaluating Programs in Academic Settings.* San Francisco: Jossey-Bass, 1990.

Barwick, Daniel W. "The Blog That Ate a Presidency." *Inside Higher Education*, 1 August 2006.

Baumol, William J., and William G. Bowen. *Performing Arts: The Economic Dilemma.* New York: Twentieth Century Fund, 1966.

Bazerman, Max H., and Michael D. Watkins. *Predictable Surprises: The Disasters You Should Have Seen Coming and How to Prevent Them.* Boston: Harvard Business School Press, 2004.

Benne, Robert. *Quality with Soul: How Six Religious College and Universities Keep Faith with Their Religious Traditions.* Grand Rapids, MI: Eerdmans, 2001.

Birnbaum, Robert. *Management Fads in Higher Education: Where They Come From, What They Do, Why They Fail.* San Francisco: Jossey-Bass, 2000.

Bollag, Burton. "Update on Accreditation Actions Taken By Regional Organizations." *Chronicle of Higher Education*, 5 January 2007, A27.

————. "Update on Actions of Regional Accrediting Groups." *Chronicle of Higher Education*, 18 May 2007, A25.

Borden, Victor M. H., and Trudy W. Banta. *Using Performance Indicators to Guide Strategic Decision Making.* San Francisco: Jossey-Bass, 1994.

Borrego, Anne Marie. "When You Can't Wait for Money." *Chronicle of Higher Education*, 2 August 2002. http://chronicle.com.

Bowen, William G. *The Economics of the Major Private Universities.* Berkeley, CA: Carnegie Commission on the Future of Higher Education, 1968.

Breen, Bill. "The Hard Life and Restless Mind of America's Education Billionaire." *Fast Company*, March 2003, 80–87.

Brinkley, Douglas. *The Great Deluge: Hurricane Katrina, New Orleans, and the Mississippi Gulf Coast.* New York: Harper Perennial, 2007.

Burke, Joseph. *Achieving Accountability in Higher Education: Balancing Public, Academic, and Market Demands.* San Francisco: Jossey-Bass, 2005.

Burtchaell, James. *The Dying of the Light: The Disengagement of Colleges and Universities from Their Christian Churches.* Grand Rapids, MI: Eerdmans, 1998.

Butler, Lawrence. *The Board's Role in Strategic Planning.* Washington, DC: Association of Governing Boards, 2006.

Cameron, Kim S. "Assessing Institutional Effectiveness: A Strategy for Improvement." In *Determining the Effectiveness of Campus Services*, ed. Robert A. Scott. San Francisco: Jossey-Bass, 1984.

————. "Critical Questions in Assessing Organizational Effectiveness." *Organizational Dynamics* 9 (autumn 1980): 66–80.

————. "Measuring Organizational Effectiveness in Institutions of Higher Education." *Administrative Science Quarterly* 23, no. 4 (December 1978): 604–32.

———. "Organization Adaptation in Higher Education." In *Organization and Governance in Higher Education*, ed. M. W. Peterson. Needham Heights, MA: Simon & Schuster Custom Publishing, 1991.

———. "Strategic Responses to Conditions of Decline: Higher Education and the Private Sector." *Journal of Higher Education* 54 (1983): 359–80.

———. "A Study of Organizational Effectiveness and Its Predictors." *Management Science* 32, no. 5 (May 1986): 87–112.

Cameron, Kim S., and Raymond Zammuto. "Matching Managerial Strategies to Conditions of Decline." *Human Resource Management* 22, no. 4 (winter 1983): 359–75.

Carroll, William J. "A Discordant Melody of Sameness." *Trusteeship*, March/April 2003, 13–17.

Cave, Martin, Stephen Hanney, Mary Henkel, and Maurice Kogan. *The Use of Performance Indicators in Higher Education*. London: Jessica Kingsley Publishers, 2006.

Chabotar, Kent John. *Strategic Finance: Planning and Budgeting for Boards, Chief Executives, and Finance Officers*. Washington, DC: Association of Governing Boards of Universities and Colleges, 2006.

Chaffee, Ellen Earle. *After Decline, What? Survival Strategies at Eight Private Colleges*. Boulder, CO: NCHEMS Publications, 1984.

Chait, Richard P. "Why Boards Go Bad." *Trusteeship*, May/June 2006, 8–12.

Chait, Richard P., Thomas P. Holland, and Barbara E. Taylor. *The Effective Board of Trustees*. Phoenix, AZ: Oryx Press, 1993.

———. *Improving the Performance of Governing Boards*. Phoenix, AZ: Oryx Press, 1996.

Chait, Richard P., William P. Ryan, and Barbara E. Taylor. *Governance as Leadership: Reframing the Work of Nonprofit Boards*. Hoboken, NJ: Wiley, 2005.

Chapman, Bruce, and Chris Ryan, "Income Contingent Financing of Student Charges for Higher Education: Assessing the Australian Innovation." In "Paying for Learning: The Debate on Student Fees, Grants and Loans in International Perspective," ed. Maureen Woodhall. Special issue, *Welsh Journal of Education* 11, no. 1 (2002): 64–81.

Coffman, James R. *Work and Peace in Academe: Leveraging Time, Money, and Intellectual Energy through Managing Conflict*. Boston: Anker Publishing, 2005.

Cohen, A. M., and J. March. *Leadership and Ambiguity*. New York: McGraw-Hill, 1974.

College Board. *Trends in Student Aid, 2004*. New York: College Board, 2004. www.collegeboard.org.

Collins, James C., and Jerry I. Porras. "Building Your Company's Vision." *Harvard Business Review*, September–October 1996, 65–67.

Comella, Patricia A., J. Bader, J. S. Ball, K. K. Wiseman, and R. R. Sagar. *The Emotional Side of Organizations: Applications of Bowen Theory*. Washington, DC: Georgetown Family Center, 1996.

Cotton, Raymond D. "Avoiding Trouble with the IRS." *Chronicle of Higher Education*, 8 October 2004.

————. "Firing the President: The Price of the Generous Compensation Being Offered to New Presidents Is Tougher Governing Boards." *Chronicle of Higher Education*, 11 March 2005, sec. C.

Cowan, Ruth B. "A Prescription for Vitality for Small Private Colleges." *Trusteeship*, November/December 1994, 15–19.

Cufaude, Jeffrey B. "Crisis Leadership: Do You Have What It Takes to Lead Your Staff and Colleagues during Difficult Times?" *NACUBO Business Officer*, April 2002, 51–56.

Dalton, Donna. "Closing a College." *Chronicle of Higher Education*, 28 February 2003. http://chronicle.com.

Deem, Rosemary. "'New Managerialism' and Higher Education: The Management of Performances and Cultures in Universities in the United Kingdom." *International Studies in Sociology of Education* 8, no. 1 (1998): 47–70.

Dickeson, Robert C. *Prioritizing Academic Programs and Services: Reallocating Resources to Achieve Strategic Balance*. San Francisco: Jossey-Bass, 1999.

Dickmeyer, Nathan. "Financial Management and Strategic Planning." In *Successful Responses to Financial Difficulty*, ed. Carol Frances. San Francisco: Jossey-Bass, 1982.

Dochy, F. J. R. C., M. S. R. Segars, and W. H. E. W. Wijnen, eds. *Management Information and Performance Indicators in Higher Education: An International Issue*. Assen and Maastricht: Van Gorcum, 1990.

Dockery, David, ed. *Shaping a Christian Worldview: The Foundation of Christian Higher Education*. Nashville, TN: Broadman & Holman, 2002.

Drucker, Peter. *The Effective Executive*. New York: HarperCollins, 2005.

Dyer, Jeffrey H., and Kentaro Nobeoka. "Creating and Managing a High-Performance Knowledge-Sharing Network: The Toyota Case." *Strategic Management Journal* 21, no. 3 (March 2000): 345–67.

Ehrenberg, Ronald G. *Tuition Rising: Why College Costs So Much*. Cambridge, MA: Harvard University Press, 2000.

El-Namaki, M. S. S. "Creating a Corporate Vision." *Long Range Planning* 25, no. 6 (1992): 25–29.

European Higher Education Area. *Joint Declaration of the European Ministers of Education* (the Bologna Declaration). 19 June 1999. www.bologna-bergen2005 .no/Docs/00-ain_doc/990719BOLOGNA_DECLARATION.PDF.

Evelyn, Jamilah. "The Outsider: A Community College Hires a President from the Corporate World with Mixed Success." *Chronicle of Higher Education*, 31 March 2006, 30–32.

Ewell, Peter T., and Dennis P. Jones. *Indicators of "Good Practice" in Undergraduate Education: A Handbook for Development and Implementation*. Boulder, CO: National Center for Higher Education Management Systems, 1996.

Fain, Paul. "Is Less More at Small Colleges? Earlham College, for One, Is Resisting Increasing Pressure to Grow and Compete." *Chronicle of Higher Education*, 9 September 2005.

————. "Thanks, Enron: Auditors Gain Clout at Colleges." *Chronicle of Higher Education*, 10 June 2005.

Feldman, Martha S. *Order without Design: Information Production and Policy Making*. Stanford: Stanford University Press, 1989.

Feldman, Martha S., and James G. March. "Information in Organizations as Signal and Symbol." *Administrative Science Quarterly* 26, no. 2 (June 1981): 171–86.

Finkelstein, Martin, Carol Frances, Frank Jewett, and Bernhard Scholz, eds. *Dollars, Distance, and On-Line Education: The New Economics of College Teaching and Learning.* Phoenix, AZ: Oryx Press, 2000.

Finn, D. Francis. "Developing and Applying Useful Financial Indicators." In *Assessing Financial Health,* ed. Carol Frances and Sharon L. Coldren. San Francisco: Jossey-Bass, 1979.

Fischer, Karin. "The Rescuer: A Consummate Politician, Hank Brown Steps into a Minefield at the Beleaguered U. of Colorado." *Chronicle of Higher Education,* 11 November 2005.

Fisher, James L., and Scott D. Miller. "Getting More, Better, or Less." *College Planning and Management,* April 2004, 18–24.

Flessner, Bruce W. "Where Do We Go from Here?" *Bentz Whaley Flessner Occasional Papers* 13 (spring 2003): 1–3.

Flohr, Bruce M. "Mirror, Mirror on the Wall." *Trusteeship,* September/October 2004, 24–28.

Fretwell, E. K., Jr. *The Interim Presidency: Guidelines for University and College Governing Boards.* Washington, DC: AGB, 1996.

Friedman, Edwin H. *Generation to Generation: Family Process in Church and Synagogue.* New York: Guilford Press, 1985.

Garber, Steve. *The Fabric of Faithfulness: Weaving Together Belief and Behavior during the University Years.* Downers Grove, IL: InterVarsity Press, 1996.

Gilbraith, Mark. "Lays the Groundwork for Change." *InfoComm Review* 10, no. 3 (2005): 28–33.

Goldman, Charles. "Mind your Ps and Rs." *Case Currents,* January 2002, 62–63.

Gordon, John Steele. "50/50: The 50 Biggest Changes in the Last 50 Years—Business." *American Heritage,* June/July 2004, 22–24.

Green, J. S., A. Levine, and associates. *Opportunity in Adversity: How Colleges Can Succeed in Hard Times.* San Francisco: Jossey-Bass, 1985.

Greene, Kelly. "Bye-Bye Boomers? Companies May Face Exodus as Workers Hit Retiring Age; Some Bosses Are Afraid to Ask." *Wall Street Journal,* 20 September 2005.

Guarasci, Richard. "On the Challenge of Becoming the Good College." *Liberal Education* 92, no. 1 (winter 2006): 14–21.

Hall, Holly. "Planning Successful Successions: Preparing for a Leader's Departure Can Prevent Problems." *Chronicle of Philanthropy,* 12 January 2006.

Haugk, Kenneth C. *Antagonists in the Church: How to Identify and Deal with Destructive Conflict.* Minneapolis: Augsburg Fortress Publishers, 1988.

Hauptman, Arthur M. *Strategic Responses to Financial Challenges.* Washington, DC: Association of Governing Boards, 1998.

Hearn, James C. *Diversifying Campus Revenue Streams: Opportunities and Risks.* Washington, DC: American Council on Education, 2003.

———. "Revenue Diversification in Higher Education." *International Higher Education,* no. 35 (spring 2004): 6–8.

Henry, Douglas V., and Bob R. Agee. *Faithful Learning and the Christian Scholarly Vocation.* Grand Rapids, MI: Eerdmans, 2003.

Henry, Douglas V., and Michael D. Beaty. *Christianity and the Soul of the University.* Grand Rapids, MI: Baker Academic, 2006.

Hesel, Richard. "Know Thyself: 5 Strategies for Marketing a College." *Chronicle of Higher Education,* 30 April 2004.

Higher Education Research Institute. *The American Freshman National Norms, 2006.* Los Angeles: UCLA, January 2007.

Hightower, Jim, and Phillip Frazer. "The People's Media Reaches More People Than Fox Does." *Hightower Lowdown* 6, no. 5 (May 2004): 1–4.

Holmes, Arthur. *The Idea of a Christian College.* Grand Rapids, MI: Eerdmans, 1987.

Hopkins, David S., and William F. Massey. *Planning Models for Colleges and Universities.* Stanford: Stanford University Press, 1981.

Howard-Vital, Michele. "The Appeal of For-Profit Institutions." *Change: The Magazine of Higher Learning* 38, no. 1 (January/February 2006): 68–71.

Hudack, Lawrence R., Larry L. Orsini, and Brenda M. Snow. "How to Assess and Enhance Financial Health." *NACUBO Business Officer,* April 2003, 31–39.

Ingram, Richard T. *Board Basics: A Guide to Conflict of Interest and Disclosure.* Washington, DC: AGB, 2006.

———. "A Test of an Effective Board." *Trusteeship* 11, no. 3 (May–June 2003): 30–32.

Ingram, Richard T., and William A. Weary. *Presidential and Board Assessment in Higher Education: Purposes, Policies, and Strategies.* Washington, DC: AGB, 2000.

Jacobsen, Douglas, and Rhonda Hustedt Jacobsen, eds. *Scholarship and Christian Faith: Enlarging the Conversation.* New York: Oxford University Press, 2004.

Jenny, Hans. "Specifying Financial Indicators: Cash Flows in the Short and Long Run." In *Assessing Financial Health,* ed. Carol Frances and Sharon L. Coldren. San Francisco: Jossey-Bass, 1979.

Johnson, Annette B. "The Problems of Contraction: Legal Considerations in University Retrenchment." *Journal of Law and Education* 10, no. 3 (July 1981): 269–324.

Johnson, Edward A., and Kent M. Weeks. "To Save a College: Independent College Trustees and Decisions on Financial Exigency, Endowment Use and Closure." *Journal of College and University Law* 12, no. 4 (spring 1986): 455–88.

Johnson, Suzanne. "Riders on the Storm." *Tulanian* 77, no. 3 (winter 2006). http://tulane.edu/news/tulanian/riders-on-the-storm.cfm.

Johnstone, D. Bruce. "The Challenge of Planning in Public." *Planning for Higher Education* 28 (winter 1999–2000): 57–64.

———. "Cost-Sharing in Higher Education: Tuition, Financial Assistance, and Accessibility." *Czech Sociological Review* 39, no. 3 (June 2003): 351–74.

———. "The Economics and Politics of Cost Sharing in Higher Education: Comparative Perspectives." *Economics of Education Review* 20, no. 4 (2004): 403–10.

———. "Fear and Loathing of Tuition Fees: An American Perspective on Higher Education Finance in the UK." *Perspectives* 9, no. 1 (January 2005): 12–16.

———. "Financing Higher Education in the United States: Current Issues." In *Higher Education in the World, 2006: The Financing of Universities*, ed. Joaquim Tres and Francisco López Segrera. Basingstoke: Palgrave Macmillan, 2005.

———. "Financing Higher Education: Who Should Pay?" In *American Higher Education in the Twenty-first Century: Social, Political, and Economic Challenges*, ed. Philip G. Altbach, Robert O. Berdahl, and Patricia J. Gumport. Baltimore: Johns Hopkins University Press, 1999.

———. "Financing the American Public Research University: Lessons from an International Perspective." In *The Future of the American Public Research University*, ed. Roger Geiger, Carol L. Colbeck, Roger L. Williams, and Christian K. Anderson. Rotterdam: Sense Publishers, 2007.

———. "The Fiscal Future of Higher Education: Austerity, Opportunity, and Accessibility." In *Charting the Course: Earl V. Pullias Lecture Series on the Future of Higher Education*. Los Angeles: University of Southern California Center for Higher Education Policy Analysis, fall 2003, 1–14.

———. "Higher Education Accessibility and Financial Viability: The Role of Student Loans." In *Higher Education in the World, 2006: The Financing of Universities*, ed. Joaquim Tres and Francisco López Segrera. Basingstoke: Palgrave Macmillan, 2005.

———. "Patterns of Finance: Revolution, Evolution, or More of the Same?" *Review of Higher Education* 21, no. 3 (spring 1998): 254–55.

———. "A Political Culture of Giving and the Philanthropic Support of Public Higher Education in International Perspective." *International Journal of Educational Advancement* 5, no. 3 (2005): 256–64.

———. *Sharing the Costs of Higher Education: Student Financial Assistance in the United Kingdom, the Federal Republic of Germany, France, Sweden, and the United States*. New York: College Entrance Examination Board, 1986.

———. "Those 'Out of Control' Costs." In *In Defense of the American Public University*, ed. Philip G. Altbach, D. Bruce Johnstone, and Patricia J. Gumport. Baltimore: Johns Hopkins University Press, 2001.

Joly, Karine. "License to Recruit?" *University Business*, August 2006, 79–80.

Jones, Dennis P. "Indicators of the Condition of Higher Education." Washington, DC: National Center for Education Statistics, 1985.

June, Audrey Williams. "Colleges Add Anonymous Tip Lines to Root Out Fraud." *Chronicle of Higher Education*, 4 August 2006.

Kantrowitz, Barbara, and Karen Springer. "25 New Ivies." *Newsweek*, 21–28 August 2006, 66–74.

Kaplan, William A., and Barbara A. Lee. *The Law of Higher Education*. 4th ed. San Francisco: Jossey-Bass, 2006.

Keller, George. *Academic Strategy: The Management Revolution in American Higher Education*. Baltimore: Johns Hopkins University Press, 1983.

Kelly, Erica. "The Changing of the Guard." *Community College Week*, 27 May 2002, 6.

Kelly, Kathleen. *The Rise of For-Profit Degree Granting Institutions: Policy Considerations for States*. Denver, CO: Education Commission of the States, 2001. www.ecs.org/clearinghouse/28/37/2837.htm.

Kinser, Kevin, and Daniel C. Levy. *The For-Profit Sector: U.S. Patterns and International Echoes in Higher Education*. Program for Research on Private Higher Education Working Papers. Albany: State University of New York, 2005. www.albany.edu/dept/eaps/prophe/publication/paper/PROPHEWP05_files/PROPHEWP05.pdf.

Kirp, David L. *Shakespeare, Einstein, and the Bottom Line: The Marketing of Higher Education*. Cambridge, MA: Harvard University Press, 2003.

Klassen, Norman, and Jens Zimmerman. *The Passionate Intellect: Incarnational Humanism and the Future of University Education*. Grand Rapids, MI: Baker Academic, 2007.

Kramer, Martin. "What the New Indicators Cannot Tell Us." In *Successful Responses to Financial Difficulty*, ed. Carol Frances. San Francisco: Jossey-Bass, 1982.

Kuh, George D., Jillian Kinzie, John H. Schuh, Elizabeth J. Whitt, and associates. *Student Success in College: Creating Conditions That Matter*. Washington, DC: American Education for Higher Education, 2005.

The Leadership Imperative: The Report of the AGB Task Force on the State of the Presidency in American Higher Education. Washington, DC: Association of Governing Boards of Universities and Colleges, 2006.

Leslie, David W., and E. K. Fretwell Jr. *Wise Moves in Hard Times: Creating and Managing Resilient Colleges and Universities*. San Francisco: Jossey-Bass, 1996.

Leubsdorf, Ben. "Boomers' Retirement May Create Talent Squeeze." *Chronicle of Higher Education*, 1 September 2006. http://chronicle.com.

Levine, Arthur. "Higher Education's New Status as a Mature Industry." *Chronicle of Higher Education*, 31 January 1997, A48.

———. *Why Innovation Fails*. Albany: State University of New York Press, 1980.

Litfin, Duane. *Conceiving the Christian College*. Grand Rapids, MI: Eerdmans, 2004.

Littlejohn, Bill. "Creating a Culture of Philanthropy." *Association of Healthcare Professionals Journal*, spring 2006, 8–15.

Lowdermilk, Robert E., III. "Climbing out of the Rut of Complacency." *Trusteeship*, May/June 2003, 26–29.

Lublin, Joann S. "The Serial CEO." *Wall Street Journal*, 19 September 2005.

Magner, Denise K. "The Graying Professoriate." *Chronicle of Higher Education*, 3 September 1999.

"Making an AUB Education Accessible." *MainGate* 3, no. 4 (summer 2005): 36–37.

Mannoia, V. James. *Christian Liberal Arts: An Education That Goes Beyond*. Lanham, MD: Rowman & Littlefield, 2000.

Marcucci, Pamela N., and D. Bruce Johnstone. *Tuition Policies in a Comparative Perspective: Theoretical and Political Rationales*. Buffalo, NY: Center for Comparative and Global Studies in Education, 2003.

Marsden, George. *The Outrageous Idea of Christian Scholarship*. New York: Oxford University Press, 1998.

Martin, James, and James E. Samels. "We Were Wrong: Try Partnerships, Not Mergers." *Chronicle of Higher Education*, 17 May 2002, B10.

Martin, James, James E. Samels, and associates. *First among Equals: The Role of the Chief Academic Officer*. Baltimore: Johns Hopkins University Press, 1997.

————. *Merging Colleges for Mutual Growth: A New Strategy for Academic Managers*. Baltimore: Johns Hopkins University Press, 1994.

————. *Presidential Transition in Higher Education: Managing Leadership Change*. Baltimore: Johns Hopkins University Press, 2004.

Massey, William F. "Remarks on Restructuring Higher Education." In *Straight Talk about College Costs and Prices: Report of the National Commission on the Cost of Higher Education*. Phoenix, AZ: Oryx Press, 1998.

McCullough, David. "Knowing History and Knowing Who We Are." *Imprimis*, April 2005. www.hillsdale.edu/imprimis/2005/04/.

McGrath, Ann. "A+ Options for 'B' Kids." *U.S. News & World Report*, 29 August 2005, 54–68.

Meister, Jeanne C. "Learning Trends to Watch in 2006." *Chief Learning Officer*, January 2006, 58.

Migliazzo, Arlin, ed. *Teaching as an Act of Faith: Theory and Practice in Church-Related Higher Education*. New York: Fordham University Press, 2002.

Morley, Jay, and Doug Eadie. "To Leader." *NACUBO Business Officer*, June 2001, 23–25.

Morrill, Richard. *Strategic Leadership in Academic Affairs: Clarifying the Board's Responsibilities*. Washington, DC: AGB, 2002.

Morris, Betsy. "Tearing Up the Jack Welch Playbook." *Fortune*, July 2006. http://money.cnn.com/2006/07/10/magazine/fortune/rules.fortune/index.htm.

Nadler, David A., Beverly A. Behan, and Mark B. Nadler, eds. *Building Better Boards: A Blueprint for Effective Governance*. San Francisco: Jossey-Bass, 2006.

National Academy of Sciences, National Academy of Engineering, and Institute of Medicine of the National Academies. *Rising above the Gathering Storm: Energizing and Employing America for a Brighter Economic Future*. Washington, DC: National Academies Press, 2007.

National Center for Public Policy and Higher Education. *Losing Ground: A National Status Report on the Affordability of American Higher Education*. San Jose, CA: National Center for Public Policy and Higher Education, 2002.

Northwest Commission on Colleges and Universities. *Accreditation Handbook*. 2003 ed. Washington, DC: Redmond, 2003.

Olswang, Steven G., Ellen M. Babbitt, Cheryl A. Cameron, and Edmund K. Kamai. "Retrenchment." *Journal of College and University Law* 30 (2003): 47–74.

O'Neill, Joseph, and Samuel Barnett. "Closing a College: Trustees' Decisions and Administrative Policies." In *Academic Program Closures: A Legal Compendium*, ed. Ellen M. Babbitt. Washington, DC: NACUA, 2002.

Panettieri, Joseph. "Inside Tips for Better Online Ed: Don't Just Envy the University of Phoenix, Learn from It." *University Business*, July 2004. www.universitybusiness.com/viewarticle.aspx?articleid=543.

Peterson, Michael. *With All Your Mind: A Christian Philosophy of Education*. Notre Dame, IN: University of Notre Dame Press, 2001.

Porras, Jerry, Stewart Emery, and Mark Thompson. *Success Built to Last*. Upper Saddle River, NJ: Wharton School Publishing, 2006.

Pulley, John L. "Unorthodox Strategy Saves Financially Strapped College, for Now." *Chronicle of Higher Education*, 19 September 2003, A29.

Pusser, Brian. "New Competition from For-Profit Education Providers." *AGB Priorities*, no. 27 (winter 2006): 1–16.

Rezak, William. "Leading Colleges and Universities as Business Enterprises." *AAHE Bulletin*, October 2000, 6–9.

Richards, Ken. "Reforming Higher Education Student Finance in the UK: The Impact of Recent Changes and Proposals for the Future." In "Paying for Learning: The Debate on Student Fees, Grants and Loans in International Perspective," ed. Maureen Woodhall. Special issue, *Welsh Journal of Education* 11, no. 1 (2002): 18–36.

Riggs, Henry E. "The Limits of Fund Raising." *Chronicle of Higher Education*, 3 May 1996.

Rosenbaum, Lee. "At the New York Public Library, It's Sell First, Raise Money Later." *Wall Street Journal*, 1 November 2005.

Rosenzweig, Robert M. *The Political University*. Baltimore: Johns Hopkins University Press, 1998.

Ross, John. "Finders Keepers, Users Reapers." *Currents*, January 2004, 31–35.

———. "Spend It Wisely." *Currents*, January 2004, 31–35.

Ross, John, and Carol Halstead. *Public Relations and the Presidency: Strategies and Tactics for Effective Communications*. Washington, DC: Council for Advancement and Support of Education Books, 2001.

Rush, Sean C. "Benchmarking—How Good Is Good?" In *Measuring Institutional Performance in Higher Education*, ed. William F. Massey and Joel W. Meyerson. Princeton, NJ: Petersons, 1994.

Rutherford, Gregory. "Academics and Economics: The Yin and Yang of For-Profit Higher Education; A Case Study of the University of Phoenix." Ph.D. diss., University of Texas at Austin, 2002.

Salacuse, Jeswald W. "You Cut a Bad Deal. Now What?" *Negotiation* 8, no. 8 (August 2005). http://hbwk.hbs.edu/archive/5015.html.

Salluzzo, Ronald E., Philip Tahey, Frederic J. Prager, and Christopher J. Cowen. *Ratio Analysis in Higher Education*. 9th ed. Washington, DC: KPMG LLP and Prager, McCarthy and Sealy, LLC, 1999.

Sandeen, A., and M. J. Barr. *Critical Issues for Student Affairs*. San Francisco: Jossey-Bass, 2006.

Saupe, Joseph L. *The Functions of Institutional Research*. Tallahassee, FL: Association for Institutional Research, 1981.

Schuerman, Matthew. "Best Practices: Philanthropy, Saving a Spendthrift." *Worth*, August 2005. www.worth.com/Editorial/Money-Meaning/Philanthropy/Best-Practices-Philanthropy-Saving-a-Spendthrift-2.asp.

Schwartz, Merrill P. *Board Basics: Annual Presidential Performance Reviews*. Washington, DC: AGB, 2001.

———. *Board Basics: Assessing Individual Trustee Performance*. Washington, DC: AGB, 2001.

Selingo, Jeffrey. "At 'Campus of the Future' Meeting, College Officials Learn How Much Money Will Matter." *Chronicle of Higher Education*, 11 July 2006. http://chronicle.com.

———. "Tulane Slashes Departments and Lays Off Professors: 233 Professors Will Lose Jobs and 14 Doctoral Programs Will Be Eliminated," *Chronicle of Higher Education*, 16 December 2005. http://chronicle.com.

———. "Tulane U. Struggles to Enroll Freshmen Because of Misperceptions about the Condition of New Orleans." *Chronicle of Higher Education*, 14 August 2006.

Sellars, John D. "Lessons Learned at the Brink." *Trusteeship*, July/August 2005, 14–18.

———. "The Warning Signs of Institutional Decline." *Trusteeship*, November/December 1994, 11–14.

Sevier, Robert. "A New Definition of Marketing: The AMA's Update Can Mean Enormous Opportunities in Higher Education." *University Business*, March 2005. www.universitybusiness.com.

Simmons, Marjorie, and Anthony Duce. "Maintenance Crunch." *University Business*, November 2005. www.universitybusiness.com/viewarticle.aspx?articleid=137.

Simons, Tad. "The Confidence Game." *Presentations*, November 2004, 25–31.

Smith, Ken. "To Blog or Not to Blog." *University Business*, December 2005, 59–62.

Society for College and University Planning. "Trends in Higher Education." February 2006. www.scup.org/knowledge/pdfs/SCUP_Trends_2-2006.pdf.

Splete, Allen P., ed. *Presidential Essays: "Success Stories"; Strategies That Make a Difference at Thirteen Independent Colleges and Universities*. Indianapolis: USA-Group, 2000.

Sterk, Andrea, and Nicholas Wolterstorff. *Religion, Scholarship, and Higher Education*. Notre Dame, IN: University of Notre Dame Press, 2002.

Stickelmaier, Laurie, and Susan Vance. "How to Prevent a Financial Fiasco: Saint Mary's College Turned a Budgetary Blip into a Wake-up Call to Ready the Campus for Any Monetary Emergency." *Business Officer Magazine*, January 2007. www:nacubo.org/x8675.xml.

Stinchcombe, Arthur L. *Information and Organizations*. Berkeley: University of California Press, 1990.

Strauss, Jon, and John R. Curry. *Responsibility Center Management: Lessons from 25 Years of Decentralized Management*. Annapolis, MD: NACUBO, 2002.

Strout, Erin, "The Trustees' Tipping Point: When Does a Governing Board Say Enough Is Enough and Fire the President?" *Chronicle of Higher Education*, 6 May 2005.

Terenzini, Patrick. "On the Nature of Institutional Research and the Knowledge and Skills It Requires." In *What Is Institutional Research All About? A Critical and Comprehensive Assessment of the Profession*, ed. J. F. Volkwein. San Francisco: Jossey-Bass, 1999.

———. "On the Nature of Institutional Research and the Knowledge and Skills It Requires." *Research in Higher Education* 34, no. 1 (February 1993): 117–24.

Thompson, J. D. *Organizations in Action: Social Science Bases of Administrative Theory*. New York: McGraw-Hill, 1967.

Tilak, Jandhyala B. G. "Global Trends in Funding Higher Education." *International Higher Education*, no. 42 (winter 2006): 5–6.

Townsley, Michael K. "Recognizing the Unrealized." *Business Officer*, March 2005. www.nacubo.org/x5632.xml.

———. *The Small College Guide to Financial Health: Beating the Odds*. Annapolis, MD: National Association of College and University Business Officials, 2002.

Trends in College Pricing—2005. New York: College Board Publications, 2005.

Trostel, Philip. "The Long-Term Economic Effects of Declining State Support for Higher Education: Are States Shooting Themselves in the Foot?" www.wisconsin.edu/pk16/reference/trostelpaper.pdf.

Tully, Shawn. "Finally, Colleges Start to Cut Their Crazy Costs." *Fortune*, 1 May 1995, 110–12, 114.

United States Department of Education. "A Test of Leadership: Charting the Future of U.S. Higher Education." Washington, DC, 2006. www.ed.gov/about/bdscomm/list/hiedfuture/reports/final-report.pdf.

Van Der Werf, Martin. "Moody's Says Financial and Governance Issues Could Spell Trouble for Some Colleges." *Chronicle of Higher Education*, 1 January 2007. http://chronicle.com/daily/2007/01/2007010901n.htm.

Vest, Charles M. "World Class Universities: American Lessons." *International Higher Education*, winter 2005, 6–7.

Volkwein, J. Fredericks, ed. 1999. *What Is Institutional Research All About? A Critical and Comprehensive Assessment of the Profession.* San Francisco: Jossey-Bass, 1999.

Wasley, Paula. "Underrepresented Students Benefit Most from 'Engagement.'" *Chronicle of Higher Education*, 17 November 2006, A39–A40.

Weary, William A. *Board Basics: Essentials of Presidential Search.* Washington, DC: AGB, 1998.

———. "The Role of the Board in Presidential Transition." In James Martin, James E. Samels, and associates, *Presidential Transition in Higher Education: Managing Leadership Change.* Baltimore: Johns Hopkins University Press, 2004.

Wegner, Etienne C., and William H. Snyder. "Communities of Practice: The Organizational Frontier." *Harvard Business Review*, January–February 2000, 139–45.

Weick, Karl. "Educational Organizations as Loosely Coupled Systems." *Administrative Science Quarterly* 21 (March 1976): 1–9.

Wergin, Jon F. *Departments That Work: Building and Sustaining Cultures of Excellence in Academic Departments.* Boston: Anker Publishing, 2003.

Weston, J. Fred, and Eugene F. Brigham. *Managerial Finance.* 7th ed. Hinsdale, IL: Dryden Press, 1981.

Whetten, David. "Organizational Responses to Scarcity: Exploring the Obstacles to Innovative Approaches to Retrenchment in Education." *Educational Administrative Quarterly* 17, no. 3 (1981): 80–97.

———. "Sources, Responses, and Effects of Organizational Decline." Chap. 10 in *The Organizational Life Cycle.* San Francisco: Jossey-Bass, 1980.

Wilkinson, William M. "Implications of Accounting Practice for Financial Analysis." In *Assessing Financial Health*, ed. Carol Frances and Sharon L. Coldren. San Francisco: Jossey-Bass, 1979.

Williams, Jeffrey J. "Debt Education: Bad for the Young, Bad for America." *Dissent*, summer 2006. www.dissentmagazine.org.

Winston, Gordon C. "Peer Wages, Tuition, and Price Discounts." *Williams Alumni Review*, summer 2005, 29–32.

———. "Subsidies, Hierarchy and Peers: The Awkward Economics of Higher Education." *Journal of Economic Perspectives* 13, no. 1 (1999): 13–36.

Wolfe, George. "Corporate Universities: Transforming Learning, Accelerating Results." *Chief Learning Officer*, February 2005, 21–25.

Wolterstorff, Nicholas. *Education for Shalom: Essays on Christian Higher Education*. Grand Rapids, MI: Eerdmans, 2004.

Woodhall, Maureen, ed. *Financial Support for Students: Grants, Loans or Graduate Tax?* London: Kogan Page, 1989.

———, ed. "Paying for Learning: The Debate on Student Fees, Grants and Loans in International Perspective." Special issue, *Welsh Journal of Education* 11, no. 1 (2002).

Zammuto, Raymond F. "Growth, Stability, and Decline in American College and University Enrollments." *Educational Administration Quarterly* 19, no. 1 (winter 1983): 83–99.

Zemsky, Robert. "The Rise and Fall of the Spellings Commission." *Chronicle of Higher Education*, 26 January 2007. http://chronicle.com.

Ziderman, Adrian, and Douglas Albrecht. "Alternative Objectives of National Student Loan Schemes." In "Paying for Learning: The Debate on Student Fees, Grants and Loans in International Perspective," ed. Maureen Woodhall. Special issue, *Welsh Journal of Education* 11, no. 1 (2002): 37–47.

———. *Financing Universities in Developing Countries*. Washington, DC: Falmer Press, 1995.

Zuckerman, M. J. "Email Catches up to Snail Mail." *USA Today*, 15 May 2001.

Contributors

JAMES MARTIN has been a member of the Mount Ida College faculty since 1979. Now a professor of English, he served for over fifteen years as the college's vice president for academic affairs and provost. An ordained United Methodist minister, he was awarded a Fulbright Fellowship to study mergers in the University of London system.

With his writing and consulting partner, James E. Samels, Martin has coauthored three previous books available from the Johns Hopkins University Press: *Merging Colleges for Mutual Growth* (1994), *First among Equals: The Role of the Chief Academic Officer* (1997), and *Presidential Transition in Higher Education: Managing Leadership Change* (2005). He cowrites a column on college and university issues, "Future Shock," for *University Business*. Martin and Samels also cohosted the nation's first television talk program on higher education issues, *Future Shock in Higher Education,* from 1994 to 1999 on the Massachusetts Corporation for Educational Telecommunications (MCET) satellite learning network. A graduate of Colby College (A.B.) and Boston University (M.Div. and Ph.D.), Martin has written articles for the *Chronicle of Higher Education*, the London *Times*, the *Christian Science Monitor*, the *Boston Globe*, *Trusteeship*, *CASE Currents*, and *Planning for Higher Education*.

JAMES E. SAMELS is the founder and CEO of both the Education Alliance and the Samels Group, a full-service higher education consulting firm. He is also the founding partner of Samels Associates, a law firm that serves independent and public colleges, universities, and nonprofit and for-profit higher education organizations. Samels has served on the faculties of the University of Massachusetts and Bentley College and as a guest lecturer at Boston University and Harvard University. Before his appointment at the University of Massachusetts, Samels served as the deputy and acting state comptroller in Massachusetts, special assistant attorney general, Massachusetts Community College counsel, and general counsel to the Massachusetts Board of Regents.

Samels holds a bachelor's degree in political science, a master's degree in public administration, a juris doctor degree, and a doctor of education degree. He has written or cowritten a number of scholarly articles, monographs, and opinion editorials that have appeared in the *Chronicle of Higher Education*, *AGB Trusteeship*, the *Christian Science Monitor*, the *London Guardian*, the *Boston Globe*, the *Boston Herald*, the *Boston Business Journal*, the *Journal of Higher Education Management*, and *Planning for Higher Education*. He is the coauthor, with James Martin, of *Merging Colleges for Mutual Growth* (1994), *First among Equals: The Role of the Chief Academic Officer* (1997), and *Presidential Transition in Higher Education: Managing Leadership Change* (2005), all from Johns Hopkins University Press. Samels has previously consulted on projects and presented research papers at universities, colleges, schools, and ministries of education in China, Canada, Great Britain, France, Korea, Sweden, Thailand, and Turkey.

ROBERT C. ANDRINGA left Michigan State University in 1967 with three degrees, including a Ph.D. in higher education. During his last two years there, he was assistant director of the Honors College. After service in the army, Andringa was the minority staff director of the Education Committee in the U.S. House of Representatives, focusing on higher education. After managing a successful gubernatorial campaign for Congressman Al Quie, Bob served the Minnesota governor as director of policy research. From 1980 to 1985 Andringa lived in Denver and served as CEO of the Education Commission of the States.

Andringa is now president emeritus of the Council for Christian Colleges and Universities after another twelve years in Washington, D.C., this time serving 170 intentionally Christian campuses in twenty-four nations. When he retired in 2006, Andringa had logged more than three hundred campus visits over the twelve years. Andringa, recipient of four honorary degrees, is now a Phoenix-based higher education consultant and writer.

CYNTHIA CHERREY is the vice president for student affairs and dean of students at Tulane University. She also holds an appointment as a clinical professor in the A. B. Freeman School of Business. Cherrey's research interests are in leadership and change theory. She has published chapters and professional articles in the areas of leadership, organizational development, and higher education. Her books include *Systemic Leadership: Enriching the Meaning of Our Work* and a co-edited series titled *Building Leadership Bridges*. She consults and speaks for profit and nonprofit organizations and was a select delegate to France to meet with Centre National des Oeuvres Universitaires et Scolaires university rectors and presidents. Cherrey is the president and chair of the board of the International Leadership Association, a global network for those who study, practice, and teach leadership, and a recipient of a Fulbright Scholarship.

PATRICIA CORMIER is currently president of Longwood University in Virginia, where she has served as chief executive officer since 1996. Longwood is a public comprehensive university with forty-five hundred students. Cormier has been in higher education teaching and administration for over forty years, in both public and private institutions, and has served as a chief academic officer for almost half that period. Beginning her career in academic health care at Tufts University, she remained in health-care administration at both the University of Virginia and the University of Pennsylvania.

Cormier was both dean and vice president for academic affairs at Wilson College in Chambersburg, Pennsylvania, and at Winthrop University in Rock Hill, South Carolina. She was an American Council on Education fellow from 1982 to 1983 and has played leadership roles at the American Association of State Colleges and Universities, the Southern Association of Colleges and Schools, the Commission on Colleges, the American Council on Education, and the National Collegiate Athletic Association. Cormier completed her undergraduate degree at Boston University and earned master's and doctoral degrees at the University of Virginia.

SCOTT S. COWEN is Tulane University's fourteenth president. He also holds joint appointments as the Seymour S. Goodman Memorial Professor of Business in Tulane's A. B. Freeman School of Business and professor of economics in the Faculty of Liberal Arts and Sciences. Cowen came to Tulane in 1998 from Case Western Reserve University, where he was a member of the faculty for twenty-three years and dean and Albert J. Weatherhead III Professor of Management at its Weatherhead School of Management for fourteen years. He is the author of four books and over one hundred academic and professional articles, essays, and reviews and is the recipient of several national awards and honors.

In June 2003 Cowen invited his fellow university leaders to join together in a national effort to reform intercollegiate athletics and ensure that their sports programs are consistent with the values, missions, and aspirations of their institutions. This effort included working to alter the Bowl Championship Series arrangement to minimize, if not eliminate, its adverse impact on Division I-A intercollegiate athletics. Cowen has also held several leadership positions in national academic and professional associations. He is a past board member of the American Council on Education, a former board member of the National Association of Independent Colleges and Universities, and past president of the American Assembly of Collegiate Schools of Business. Cowen also has extensive experience in business as a corporate director and consultant. He is a member of the boards of directors of Newell Rubbermaid, American Greetings Corporation, Jo-Ann Stores, and Forest City Enterprises.

In August 2005 Hurricane Katrina devastated the city of New Orleans, flooded half of Tulane's uptown campus and all of its downtown Health Sciences Center, and dispersed its faculty and staff around the country for an entire semester. Under Cowen's leadership the campus was repaired, and a remarkable 87 percent of its students returned for classes in January 2006. On December 8, 2005, the board of Tulane approved Cowen's renewal plan, a sweeping effort that strengthens and focuses the university's academic mission while strategically addressing its current and future operations in the post-Katrina era.

SANDRA ELMAN is the president of the Northwest Commission on Colleges and Universities in Redmond, Washington. She is the immediate past chair of the Council of Regional Accrediting Commissions (CRAC), which is composed of the directors and chairs of the seven regional accrediting commissions. Before assuming the position of president in 1996, Elman was the associate director of the Commission on Institutions of Higher Education of the New England Association of Schools and Colleges. Before joining regional accreditation, Elman held a variety of administrative and faculty positions at the John McCormack Institute of Public Affairs at the University of Massachusetts; the University of Maryland, and the University of California at Berkeley. She has published extensively in the fields of public policy and higher education and is coauthor of *New Priorities for the University: Educating Competent Individuals for Applied Knowledge and Societal Needs.*

Elman has lectured nationally and internationally on issues related to quality assurance; institutional finance and governance; and the roles of government and business/industry. She is an adjunct faculty member at Oregon State University. Elman serves as an evaluator for international quality-assurance agencies, including the Center for Accreditation and Quality Assurance of Swiss Universities. She is a past chair of the Board of Trustees of Unity College in Unity, Maine, which is an environmentally focused liberal arts institution. Her academic areas of interest include accreditation; quality assurance in the United States and Europe; governance of public and private higher education institutions; and conflict resolution and international peace. Elman received her B.A. degree in history and political science from Hunter College in New York and her M.A. and Ph.D. degrees in policy, planning, and administration from the University of California at Berkeley. She is a 2005 graduate of the Department of Defense National Security Seminar, U.S. Army War College.

MICHAEL HOYLE is the former president of McIntosh College in Dover, New Hampshire. He received a bachelor of science in accountancy from Bentley College in Waltham, Massachusetts, a master's in public administration from the University of Massachusetts at Amherst, and a Ph.D. in higher education administration from New York University. Hoyle was appointed to the Board of Trustees of Roxbury Community College in Boston, Massachusetts, in 2001. He also serves as a member of the Board of Directors of Seacoast Outright.

Before joining McIntosh College, Hoyle was the director of finance for the three campuses of the University of Phoenix in Massachusetts. Before that, he was the associate director of the doctoral programs at the Harvard Business School. Hoyle served in a number of state agencies in Massachusetts in the administrations of Governors William Weld and Paul Cellucci, including the Office of Business Development, Mass-Jobs Council, and the Department of Employment and Training.

W. STEPHEN JEFFREY has been the vice president for development and external relations at the American University of Beirut (AUB) in Beirut, Lebanon, since January 2002. He was vice president of development at the University of Hartford (1996–2001) and worked at Mount Holyoke College (1981–1996), where he was director of development and external relations and secretary of the board of trustees.

Before his career in higher education, Jeffrey spent twelve years as a fund-raiser for several voluntary health organizations and an arts group. He is a graduate of Waynesburg College in Pennsylvania.

D. BRUCE JOHNSTONE is Distinguished Service Professor of Higher and Comparative Education Emeritus at the State University of New

York at Buffalo. His principal scholarship is in international comparative higher education, higher education finance, governance, and policy formation. He directs the International Comparative Higher Education Finance and Accessibility Project, an eight-year examination of the worldwide shift of higher education costs from governments and taxpayers to parents and students. The project has been the principal single source of descriptive and theoretical work, as well as ongoing research, on tuition, financial assistance, and student loan policies worldwide. During a twenty-five-year administrative career before assuming his professorship at Buffalo, Johnstone held the posts of vice president for administration at the University of Pennsylvania, president of the State University College of Buffalo, and chancellor of the State University of New York system, the latter from 1988 through 1994.

Johnstone is also the distinguished scholar leader through 2008 of the Fulbright New Century Scholars Program, a group of twelve American and thirty-two international scholars who are examining higher education access through international perspectives. In the 2006–2007 academic year he was a part-time Erasmus Mundus lecturer in higher education administration at the Universities of Oslo and Tampere. He has written or edited more than 115 books, monographs, articles, book chapters, and book reviews and is best known for his works on the financial condition of higher education, the concept of learning productivity, student financial assistance policy, system governance, and international comparative higher education finance. His newest book is *Financing Higher Education: Cost-Sharing in International Perspective* (2006). Other books include *New Patterns for College Lending: Income Contingent Loans* (1972); *Sharing the Costs of Higher Education: Student Financial Assistance in the United Kingdom, the Federal Republic of Germany, France, Sweden and the United States* (1986); *In Defense of American Higher Education* (co-edited with Philip Altbach and Patti Gumport, 2001); and *Financing Higher Education: Problems and Solutions* (2004; translated into Chinese by Professor Shen Hong).

Johnstone holds bachelor's (in economics) and master's (in teaching) degrees from Harvard, a 1969 Ph.D. in education from the University of Minnesota, and honorary doctorates from D'Youville College, Towson State College, and California State University at San Diego. His personal website is www.gse.buffalo.edu/faculty/viewfaculty.asp?id=30. The website for the International Comparative Higher Education Finance and Accessibility Project is www.gse.buffalo.edu/org/IntHigherEdFinance.

YVETTE JONES is chief operating officer and senior vice president for external affairs at Tulane University. As the university's senior administrative officer, she is responsible for all nonacademic functions and externally related activities at the university. She oversees Tulane's $700 million fund-raising campaign and all related development and alumni activities, as well as government relations, public relations, and university communications. In addition to her role as Tulane's chief external officer, Jones leads the university's technology transfer and business development, strategic planning, and campus development efforts and has responsibility for human resources and information technology and services. She has served Tulane University in a variety of administrative roles since 1979.

Jones is also a facilitator for the Association of Governing Boards and has served as an evaluator of the Commission of Colleges of the Southern Association of Colleges and Schools. She is active in the New Orleans community as a member of the boards of Idea Village, the Greater New Orleans Biosciences District, and the New Orleans Regional Medical Consortium. Jones holds bachelor of arts and master of business administration degrees from Tulane University.

STEVEN LANASA is associate dean of the School of Education at the University of Missouri–Kansas City (UMKC). He has experience working in administrative and academic roles at several institutions, including George Mason University and Pennsylvania State University. Most recently LaNasa served as assistant vice provost for academic planning at UMKC, where he was responsible for outcomes assessment, institutional research, planning, and program evaluation. LaNasa holds a Ph. D. in higher education from Pennsylvania State University and a master's in public administration from George Mason University. He teaches in the higher education program at UMKC, and his research interests focus on college-going decisions and student persistence and engagement.

DANIEL J. LEVIN is currently the director of publications for The Education Trust in Washington, DC. Prior to this, Levin joined the staff of the Association of Governing Boards of Universities and Colleges in January 1988. He was vice president for publications and editor of *Trusteeship*, the organization's bimonthly magazine for presidents, board members, and senior executives, until 2008. He also led the development of the association's books, monographs, and special reports. Levin has led the repositioning and redesign process for magazines on four occasions, including twice for *Trusteeship*. When *Trusteeship* was first published in 1993, the magazine won first-place awards in two national competitions. Levin led similar efforts in 1986 as editor of *Campaigns and Elections*, an independent magazine for political candidates and professionals, and in 1984 for *TechTrends*, a magazine published by the Association for Educational Communications and Technology.

From 1978 to 1984 Levin was associate editor of the *American School Board Journal* and the *Executive Educator*, published by the National School Boards Association. His feature articles about education policy won five national reporting awards. Levin graduated from Boston University in 1975 with a B.S. in journalism.

PATRICIA LONG became the twenty-eighth president of Baker University in July 2006. Her thirty-two-year career in education includes service as acting executive vice chancellor at the University of Missouri–Kansas City and dean of student services at Johnson County Community College. She holds a doctorate in educational policy and leadership in higher education from the University of Kansas, a master's in adult education from Central Missouri State University, and an undergraduate degree in mathematics from Southwest Baptist University.

Long has served with numerous professional and civic organizations and chaired various committees for the National Association of Student Personnel Administrators (NASPA). Her achievements in student affairs administration have been recognized by several honors, including the IBM Best Practice in Student Services Partner, the David Pierce Team Award from the National Initiative for Leadership and Institutional Effectiveness, the James J. Rhatigan Outstanding Dean Award from NASPA, and a life service award from Southwest Baptist University.

CHARLES R. MIDDLETON has served as the fifth president of Roosevelt University since July 2002. As president, Middleton heads the most diverse private university in the Midwest. Roosevelt's seventy-four hundred students take courses in the liberal arts and sciences, business administration, education, and performing arts at comprehensive campuses in downtown Chicago and northwest suburban Schaumburg. The university also owns the Auditorium Theatre, a historic Chicago landmark, which it operates through a separate contract.

Building on Roosevelt's historic commitment to social justice, Middleton has emphasized service learning across the curriculum. He also has instituted a number of programs for students, including a new flat-rate tuition structure that reduces tuition for many undergraduate students, an innovative registration process that is responsive to student needs, and a new orientation program for freshmen. Before joining Roosevelt, he was dean of the College of Arts and Sciences at the University of Colorado at Boulder, provost and vice president of academic affairs at Bowling Green State University, and vice chancellor for academic affairs at the University System of Maryland. Middleton is also a fellow of Great Britain's Royal Historical Society and author of *The Administration of British Foreign Policy, 1782–1846*.

Middleton is a member of the American Council on Education, the National Association of Independent Colleges and Universities, and the Illinois Federation of Independent Colleges and Universities, of which he is vice chair. In November 2006 Middleton was elected to the Chicago Gay and Lesbian Hall of Fame and was inducted alongside Mayor Richard M. Daley. Middleton was also appointed by Daley to serve on Chicago's 2016 Olympic bid and planning committee. Middleton earned an A.B. degree with honors in history from Florida State University and both an M.A. and Ph.D. in history from Duke University.

LORI REESOR received her bachelor's in business administration from the University of Wisconsin–Whitewater, her master's degree in higher education from Iowa State University, and her doctorate from the University of Kansas. She spent ten years working at the University of Kansas in residence life, orientation, and admissions. She then served as the Dean of Students at Wichita State University. After WSU, she served as an Associate Dean in the School of Education and as Assistant Professor in Higher Education at the University of Missouri–Kansas City.

Reesor returned to KU as an Associate Vice Provost for Student Success, and she oversees the offices of Admissions and Scholarships, Counseling and Psychological Services, Department of Student Housing, Multicultural Affairs, and the Student Involvement and Leadership Center. She is an active leader in the National Association of Student Personnel Administrators (NASPA), teaches in the higher education program, and conducts research related to new professionals in student affairs, women in higher education, and academic leadership.

JOHN ROSS is the lead author of *Public Relations and the Presidency: Strategies and Tactics for Effective Communication* (2001) and principal of RossWrites, an affiliated consulting team that provides strategic communications, editorial services, and media relations to higher education and related organizations. Ross served as a senior media relations and public relations officer at Tusculum College, Plymouth State University, Dickinson College, the University of Miami, and the University of Cincinnati. He entered consulting as vice president and senior consultant at College Connections/Halstead Communications, and he successfully launched RossWrites in early 2004. He is the recipient of a gold medal for news and information from the Council for Advancement and Support of Higher Education, a former vice president of the National Education Writers Association, and a frequent speaker at professional conferences. Ross's articles have appeared in *Trusteeship*, *CASE Currents*, and the *Chronicle of Higher Education*.

JOHN F. RYAN is assistant provost and associate director of institutional research and planning at Ohio State University. He coordinates program review for over one hundred academic departments across the university's eighteen colleges and supports a variety of institutional effectiveness projects and initiatives. His areas of expertise include higher education policy and administration, academic program review, learning-outcomes assessment, student persistence, and quantitative research methods.

Ryan is a member of the Publications Committee of the Association for Institutional Research. He worked in student affairs before serving as a policy analyst for the Ohio Legislative Budget Office and as the assessment officer at Franciscan University. He earned his master's degree in political science from Ohio State University and his Ph.D. in higher education administration from the University of Nebraska–Lincoln.

KEVIN W. SAYERS is vice president for planning and strategy and assistant to the president at Capital University in Columbus, Ohio. He holds a Ph.D. in higher education from Boston College, an M.Ed. in education leadership from Pennsylvania State University, and a B.Mus. from the Dana School of Music, Youngstown State University.

Sayers's professional expertise and research interests are in institutional research, assessment and planning, and technology issues in higher education. Sayers has held posts in these areas at Brown University, Boston College, and Berklee College of Music and has consulted on various planning and assessment topics nationally. Sayers regularly publishes and presents his research at various professional conferences and has most recently served as president of the Ohio Association for Institutional Research and Planning. He is currently researching the use of key performance measures in an institutional change context.

MICHAEL TOWNSLEY is the dean of the Business Division and professor of business at Becker College in Worcester, Massachusetts. He was previously the president of the Pennsylvania Institute of Technology, where he implemented a strategic redesign of the curriculum to respond to major changes in the institute's student market. The plan also incorporated new marketing plans that applied new tactics to reach out to new student markets.

Before Townsley went to the institute, he was senior vice president for finance and administration at Wilmington College. He was the chief financial officer with additional responsibility for marketing, information systems, and off-campus sites. As senior vice president, he helped craft and implement a turnaround strategy that put a college with a declining enrollment of seven hundred students and a decade of deficits on a path where the college enrolled seventy-eight hundred students and did not report another deficit during his tenure. He has authored *The Small College Guide to Financial Health: Beating the Odds* (2002), recognized as a leading book on strategically managing private colleges, as well as *The Financial Toolbox for Colleges and Universities* (2004). Townsley holds a Ph.D. from the University of Pennsylvania. His dissertation analyzed the impact of market share on pricing policies.

WILLIAM A. WEARY, president of Fieldstone Consulting, works on strategy with colleges, universities, schools, associations, governmental bodies, churches, and other nonprofit groups around the country and the world. Fieldstone Consulting's services include facilitation, assessment, planning, governance, and transition management. Over 250 institutions have been served since 1994 and Fieldstone Consulting's founding. Weary has been a full-time consultant for twenty-two years. A Phi Beta Kappa graduate of Amherst College, he holds both master's and doctoral degrees in history from Yale University. He taught European history at Amherst and Bowdoin colleges, did research on early modern France as a graduate fellow at the University of Wisconsin's Institute for Research in the Humanities, and headed the upper schools of Abington Friends School in Philadelphia and the Dalton School in New York City. After leaving Dalton, he worked for some years at Independent School Management in Delaware.

In addition to his ongoing consulting work in higher education, Weary has led the workshop on presidential and board assessment at the National Conference on Trusteeship of the Association of Governing Boards of Universities and Colleges (AGB) each year since 1995. As a consultant to AGB, Weary has developed its presidential search workshop, designed and coordinated its presidential and board assessment service, and written its Essentials of Presidential Search and Guidelines on Selecting a Presidential Search Consultant. In 2000, he co-developed AGB's *Presidential and Board Assessment in Higher Education: Purposes, Policies and Strategies*. In 2005–2006 he assisted AGB's incoming president in the preparation of the association's new strategic plan.

Index